Almanach
De douze Sports
Par William Nicholson

WILLIAM NICHOLSON

WILLIAM NICHOLSON.

WILLIAM NICHOLSON

by

MARGUERITE· STEEN

COLLINS
48 PALL MALL LONDON
1943

THIS BOOK IS SET IN FONTANA, A NEW TYPE FACE DESIGNED
FOR THE EXCLUSIVE USE OF THE HOUSE OF COLLINS, AND
PRINTED BY THEM IN GREAT BRITAIN

CONTENTS

ILLUSTRATIONS

Colour

Black and White

DEDICATORY

I

THIS is the story of a painter's life.

To make phrases about William Nicholson's work is to insult it and to offend him. Painting which requires a vocabulary to explain it, in his own words, fails of its purpose. There will inevitably be those who seek such a vocabulary in a book about a painter, and they will inevitably be disappointed: since this is a book about a very simple person whose language is his brush. No commentator can improve on this language, nor does it require analysis to make it legible to any person of intelligence; yet there is a certain class of writer who, posing as art critic, takes it upon himself to translate it into an idiom of his own, thereby satisfying his own vanity but contributing no iota to our love and knowledge of the painter or of his work. More pretentious and windy nonsense is written about painting than about any other art, and it may be laid down as a general principle that the painter who is dependent upon these camp-followers of the artistic "movements" is the ephemeral, and that real painting needs no literary bolstering to implant itself in the history of the race.

It is the opinion of certain people who are qualified to judge, that William Nicholson is the greatest master of Still Life of his own or any other age. Surely such a person should not be required to analyse his own genius, or to bestow more than a smile of tolerance upon those who attempt to do so?

The history of a painter's life is the history of his work and of the conditions under which he does his work; after that let the work speak for itself. William Nicholson will not want for witness, for the volume of his output is not equalled, for quality or variety, by any artist of his day.

2

Perhaps someone—why not Max Beerbohm?—will some day write an essay on the evocatory power of the Name. Names of places, names of people : names that cling in the memory like burrs and invoke an image, clear-cut or blurred, according to the imagination that conjures it. Tamurlaine, Granada, Campaspe ("Cupid and my Campaspe played"), Famagusta, Sally (in our Alley) and Marcus Aurelius. We need no photograph or drawing of the originals to prompt us: they are there, the very colours of life, on the canvas of the mind.

To play the name-game properly, you must choose such remote and fantastical names as cannot possibly enter into the orbit of your personal experience. There is nothing remote about the name William Nicholson, and no law of association that I know of, which can account for my picturing him (when I pictured him at all) as a Big Man With a Beard.

The Big Man With a Beard came into existence when, having saved up my weekly pocket-money to buy Ellen Terry's Autobiography, I came for the first time on the names of the Beggarstaff Brothers (*sic*). (*W.N.* "We never called ourselves the Beggarstaff Brothers; the posters were signed J. & W. Beggarstaff." *M.S.* "Well, I've put ' *sic* '; and everybody wrote and spoke of you as the Beggarstaff Brothers." *W.N.* "Well, say that." *M.S.* "Well, I've said it—' *sic* ': see?")

There was no reason for underlining the name William Nicholson, and apparently ignoring the more obviously picturesque James Pryde. Beggarstaff Brothers meant William Nicholson to me, as, presently, woodcuts meant William Nicholson, and none of his contemporary imitators and copyists. "The man who puts a thick black line round everything": I was not the inventor of the description, but by the time I was fifteen years old I knew all about the thick black line . . . was there, perhaps, some indistinct connection between the "roaring romanticism" of the name Beggarstaff, the thick black line and the Beard?

The Beard must have grown considerably by the time I read my first "grown-up" novel, Lucas Malet's *Far Horizon*—and discovered that Poppy St. John's sitting-room was hung with William "Nicolson's" woodcuts; an eclectic choice, surely, for the Lady of the Windswept Dust?—But perhaps Alaric Barking gave them to her. Another pencilmark went under the misspelt "Nicolson." That must have been about 1910; when we turned over the yellowed pages (it was a cheap, paper-backed edition) some time in 1935, we found the faint, wobbly line. . . .

3

The cactuses, with their flat, pear-shaped leaves and prickly fruit the country people call *chombos*, were throwing their shadows down the shaley path, and a bit of the Mediterranean that showed in the gap at the end of the valley had faded to dark blue, because it was late afternoon. Down at the Caleta Palace the tourists were ordering cocktails, and up the *arroyos* the peasants sat in the doorways of their white cottages, basking in the last glow of the setting sun.

William came up the steep path with his hands in his pockets. He came walking slowly, with the light, weaving movement of a little cat, neat and delicate: with a holiday air of serenity and of mild interest in the strangers towards whom he was advancing. "A new adventure"—his own expression for any new experience— was written all over him, as he picked his way leisurely across the runnels, the olive green coat and white ducks so merging into the background of cactus and sun-faded earth as to make him seem almost as transparent as one of his own shadows. Thin as a lath and lithe as a whiplash—and an ivory-coloured, inquiring little face, with a hat cocked at a knowing angle. . . . These were the things which registered an immediate impression: to be followed by an embarrassing realisation of the fact that I must have gone wrong in my calculation of time.

To me, William Nicholson was a contemporary of Ellen Terry; had we not often talked together about him? That Ellen was "in her thirties" when William was at his public school, had not, of course, entered into my consideration; it is easy to slip a decade or two in the lives of one's elders. And now that idea was blown to pieces—along with the Big Man With a Beard! The fact that I had been thinking of William in terms of "And did you once see Shelley plain?" would have upset his gravity as much as it—nearly—upset mine, when this apparent contemporary of my own came strolling up from the Villa; and it is a fact that I have never since been able to remember the trifle of twenty-two years that separate us.

"I wish you'd ask me to meet Nicholson," I had said, some time during the previous winter, to the friend who was having his portrait painted. But Nicholson, I was given to understand, was the least accessible of beings; when not engrossed in his portraits, he was involved in a social whirl whose brilliance was only equalled by its continuity. I felt rather depressed; I hadn't, somehow, seen Nicholson hung in the social galaxy.

"I'd like to meet this woman who wrote *Matador*, some time," observed William (only, being William, I feel sure he employed the nice, old-fashioned term "lady") to the same informant, who looked dubious, and said that on my rare visits to town it was quite unthinkable to get hold of me without pre-arrangement—so hemmed about was I with the supposed paraphernalia of a literary career!

If Sir Peter Chalmers Mitchell drew on the resources of a prolific imagination in representing William and me to one another in these unrecognisable colours—for indeed, in both cases, they could hardly have been farther from the truth—he made noble amends in the invitation to Malaga.

When darkness fell, when we all collected under the loggia, where the geckos, like miniature dragons, raced behind and hung over the picture frames : with old María's good coffee and our host's excellent liqueurs—the conversation seemed very good. Or is that part of the illusion which hangs over an occasion which, in retrospect, seems very like the conclusion to a pleasant story? That it was only the beginning of a new one was in nobody's mind—least of all in William's.

4

In an attempted word picture of William Nicholson which appeared a few years ago in an Art magazine, someone used the word "elfin." This word, discredited for its use by writers of the whimsy school, was often in my mind during those early days at Malaga.

A dash of Puck and more than a flavour of Ariel; if a great deal too absent-minded to "put a girdle round the earth in forty minutes" (he would inevitably forget what he was supposed to be doing, and turn up several hours late, with a collection of small feathers and very tiny odds and ends of vegetable matter, picked up within a stone's throw of his own door), he would take the greatest pleasure in burning his way along some giddy spar for the benefit of shipwrecked mariners. Levitation, flying, exquisite tricks of legerdemain and acrobacy haunt that world from which he is separated only by the slender bridge of sleep :

with the result that he has often an unconscionable air of trailing clouds of glory, which find their way on to his canvases.

It struck me once or twice that it was really a lighthearted affair—this business of being a genius: all mixed up with spotted silk dressing-gowns and spotless white ducks and a fancy for chrome yellow; with the manipulation of a bilboquet and the flinging of a boomerang. To some people the addition of a four-pound bilboquet and a sheaf of boomerangs to one's luggage for a month abroad might give pause; to William (as I was to discover in the course of the next few years) it was as inevitable as packing his white lead—which nearly disqualified us for our reservations in the plane to Venice, in 1937.

William up to his knees in the garden pool, fishing for gold-fish with one of my sleeping nets ingeniously arranged over a little loop of wire, was a pretty sight : as was William solemnly dancing in the dusk to a pleasantly blasphemous little song of his own invention. William making cork mice for the kitten was a lesson in concentration—the only one, I may add, apart from his own work, that I ever learned from him.

One day, out on the hillside, where William had been throwing his boomerang, the rain came down in drops like five-*peseta* pieces. The others ran for the house, but we, realising we should get drenched in any case, linked arms and strolled up through the downpour, which patched William, in nothing but his white ducks, into a very presentable resemblance to Nijinski in *L'Après Midi d'un Faune*. When we reached the first of the terraces, with my sunhat plastered round my neck and shoulders, and William transparent and pink as a lobster with the lashing of the rain, he paused, faced me, and inquired with the utmost solemnity, "And what do you *really* think of Keats ? "

If we were to try to convey that exact variation of sunshine and moonlight on a blue jacaranda-tree, the patterns thrown on red earth by cactus coloured like milky jade, the strange, Aztec beauty of Armillita, blind Manuel singing in the Albaicin, and a certain day when you, William, painted a little Spanish farm, moulded lovingly to the shoulder of a hill, while I wrote the short story, *The Witch*, farther up the same hillside, to a ceaseless tinkle of goatbells and flickering of large butterflies over the dark Spanish lavender—would any one but you or I think much of it? Or of our foolish jokes, our irresponsible bursts of laughter that made us so annoying, because they were so incommunicable to any one but ourselves?

Let's cut the jokes and the jacaranda-tree, and, as much as possible, me; because this is the book of you, and my only share in it is that of being your partner, for the last ten years, in the best times, and, sometimes, the worst.

CHAPTER ONE

Newark Background

I

THE WALLPAPER had quite an ordinary pattern, nothing subtle or mysterious about it: the sort of cheerful, nondescript affair one hung in a night nursery or a servant's bedroom. Nobody knew its secret: that if you looked at it steadily, the small, reddish clumps of leaves and berries that composed it made themselves into hundreds of little faces, which only needed a dot or two with a pencil to bring them to life.

Nobody knew, either, about the magic. That happened when one was tucked up for one's afternoon rest. It was a magic made up of the soft, enclosed silence, hardly disturbed by the humming of a mower across the lawn, or May (too old to be put to bed in the afternoon) thumping downstairs and being shrilly hushed by Nurse: "Sh-h-h! Master Willy's having his nap." Such sounds seemed very far away, on the edge of the magic that was taking place on the ceiling overhead. Light refraction—camera oscura—such words meant nothing to the occupant of the cot. There, on the ceiling, minutely reflected, was the gardener, bending over the flower-beds, were the ladies coming to call on Mother with card-cases in their gloved hands, was the errand boy, swinging his basket and whistling on his way from the kitchens; there, on certain precious afternoons, was the old woman with the one-legged hurdy-gurdy, which had an explosion of red satin in the middle of its front panel.

There was no sleep for Master Willy—already beginning to lead that excited "life of the eyes," which was to mean so much more to him than anything heard, felt, tasted, smelt. I honestly believe you might strip William of four of his five senses, but leave him his sight, and he would be perfectly happy.

"How strange," said the great oculist, in whose waiting-room he chanced to find himself one day, "how strange—that you should have eyes exactly like any one else." An odd, perceptive thing to say: for it does seem strange that any one gifted with William's vision should have just the same ocular equipment as you or I.

The camera oscura is gone; but at the foot of his bed in the little yellow-walled, blue-ceilinged room in Apple Tree hangs—no, *hung*: for Apple Tree is gone, and with it a part of our lives—the empty canvas, primed in green or red, on which, with the earliest morning light, he was painting with his eyes. There were other pictures as well: the Cock o' the North which Penny, who now likes to be called Liza, drew when she was little, and a needlework ship she gave him for his birthday; my *Divina Pastora*, which came from a tavern in the Albaicin, and which William appropriated because he said there was never in the world anything so innocent as those lambs up-ended with daisies in their mouths against a background of salmon pink and olive trees; and a little nineteenth-century print of Newark which he kept because it was his father's. But there, in the direct range of his eyes, must always be the empty canvas, on which took shape all the work on which he was engaged during those last crowded years before the war.

What shall replace Apple Tree? In this year of grace nobody knows; but whether it is the little Georgian manor of which we are always dreaming, or just another London house, there will have to be the yellow and blue bedroom, and an empty canvas at the foot of the chintz-covered bed.

2

"William," rebuked his father, "I thought you had been told that if you must draw on Sunday, it must be Sunday things."

"It is Sunday things, Father," objected William. "It's the brush and comb I do my hair with before I go to church."

There were always pencils, or crayons, or a box of coloured chalks lying around. When William's nurse, whom he adored, was dying of typhoid, and the children were sent to Woodstock to be out of the way, his grandmother gave him a little box of water-colours, with which he proceeded to execute his first landscape, Blenheim Bridge by Sunset.

He was still at his dame school, which he enjoyed, until an incident occurred which (temporarily) blighted his life. The baby at home, the object of his nurse's constant and adoring attention, he had not yet mastered the relationship between buttons and buttonholes. His return to the classroom with pieces of shirt bulging inefficiently from his breeches brought sniggers from the scholars and the hot blush of humiliation to William's cheeks. It was a very sensitive and self-conscious little boy, and the effect of this early social *gaffe* was to make him miserable for a very long time.

3

In the General Elections of 1880, the town of Newark-on-Trent in Nottinghamshire sent four candidates to the poll. They were Mr. Bristowe and Mr. Earp, Liberal; the Honourable M. E. G. Finch-Hatton (later Lord Winchilsea) and Mr. Nicholson, Conservative. Those were the palmy days of bribery and corruption, when you knew by a look how much a man's vote was worth, and the support of the simple-minded went to the candidate who made the bravest show. The little town fluttered from end to end with Conservative scarlet, for which Mr. Nicholson, of course, footed the bill—no one knew for how much.

William Newzam Nicholson had already three grown-up sons, Philip, Arthur and Edward, and a daughter, when he fell in love with Miss Ann Elizabeth Prior, the daughter of Mr. and Mrs. Prior of Chaucer's House, Woodstock, whose sweet and charming sympathy had helped to console his widowerhood, and who, as Mrs. Nicholson, had already, at the time of which we are speaking, given him three children, James, Mabel Prior and William Newzam Prior—whose three resounding names must have seemed to the mother, as she held him at the font, somewhat cumbersome for so tiny an infant.

Of this adorable lady more will be written; for the moment Mr. Nicholson monopolises the limelight, galloping from husting to husting in his carriage drawn by the two fine greys (a recent indulgence), drawing the attention of his agent with an irascible finger to some alley or row of cottages where an unseemly show of blue eclipses the scarlet, addressing meetings in the Corn Exchange—he was, let's admit it, a poor speaker, and the principal animation of his addresses was furnished by the Liberals, who, on at least one memorable occasion, stormed the hall while Mr. Nicholson was speaking, and brightened the scene in more senses than one by flinging in lighted torches.

The Trent Ironworks, on which the family fortune depended, were a notable feature of the Newark landscape. Specialising in agricultural machinery, the name NICHOLSON, embossed on

B

the bright red driving-seats of the Trent ploughshares, impressed itself on the fustian and corduroy of every farming district in the British Isles. (To this day, in our country expeditions, we never see a reaper but William must satisfy himself that it comes from "the works," before passing on.)

"The works" were accountable for a solid, handsome house—number 12, London Road : its dignity only a very little impaired by its being semi-detached. In the adjoining portion lived Edward, with "Auntie Sap": Edward, whose marriage to the younger Miss Prior had made him brother-in-law to his own father, and wrought chaos with the genealogy of the rising generation. To "the works" the two Mrs. Nicholsons owed their pretty gowns, and the boys their scholastic careers; they provided for continental holidays—with true British conservatism, the destination of these never varied; each year, on their parents' return from Lake Como, the toy chests of the little Nicholsons were enriched with boxes inlaid with designs of Swiss peasant costumes, carved chamois and cuckoo clocks. It was "the works," and all they stood for, that constituted Mr. Nicholson's claim, as a man of property and substance, to represent his native town in the House of Commons.

A dutiful wife, Mrs. Nicholson canvassed for her husband; in the afternoon, when he was not using it, the carriage was ordered to the door, and passers-by admired the pretty vision of a young Victorian lady in her best calling attire, accompanied by her son, young Master Nicholson—a little thin boy with grey eyes too big for his face, alert as a rabbit, restless as a bit of mercury, plunging from side to side to see "Father's colours," as the delicate hooves of Babille and Bijou tittup from the drive on to the broad highway.

"Billie, Billie, mind my gown!"

She was not so much more than a girl herself, though Victorian convention and a middle-aged husband imposed on her a sobriety that was only skin deep. The sweet, melancholy face, the heavy-lidded wistful eyes suggest that she had already learned her *métier*, as a kind of fragile buffer between the moods of father and son—and that they were moody, the pair of them, heaven only knew! Perhaps some of her tenderness towards the younger William was rooted in her perception of the essential difficulties of adjustment between an elderly, conventional man and a high-spirited little boy with a prematurely developed sense of humour. ("Hush, Billie—Father's tired—don't disturb Father.")

W. E. Henley.

W. E. HENLEY.

She spoiled him, of course, outrageously. ("Put that great boy off your knee, my dear.—William, don't pester your mother!") When he did his graceless imitations of the local ladies who called on her At Home days, instead of reproving him, she rocked with laughter; her "Don't, Billie!" was so perfunctory, an infant would have seen through it—let alone any one so astute as Master William Newzam Prior, who merely grinned and resumed his Famous Impersonation of the vicar's wife, or whoever happened at the moment to be engaging his histrionic talent. She had to laugh, helpless in her sense of guilt; what would Father have said? (She had another guilty secret besides: something about a hole in the drawing-room carpet, over which plants and little tables had constantly to be arranged; her anxious glance went to it sidelong, whenever her husband was present, for she was so young at the time of her marriage that housekeeping responsibilities which would naturally have fallen on more experienced shoulders were assumed by Mr. Nicholson as a matter of course. It was Mr. Nicholson who drove to the butcher's shop to make personal selection of the joint, who summoned the cook to the dining-room when the sauce was not to his liking, who called down anathema upon the household when the door to the domestic quarters was left ajar and a smell of cooking was allowed to pervade the hall.)

There was not so very much laughter in the house in the London Road, apart from that provided by Billie, who, for some perverse reason, had elected to be born under a dancing star. The elder William was grave, often, and absent; Jim was a typical, self-contained schoolboy and May a matter-of-fact buzzfly, bursting with energy and nothing in particular coming of it.

It was left to the younger William to infuse the star-dust sparkle into a somewhat sober, and typically Victorian, scene by the exercise of an imagination which varied between the mischievous and the romantic: the mainspring of romance, for the moment, being Sherwood Forest, with its haunted glades and companies in green, its tuckettings and chivalries whose echoes, faint in adult ears, were clear as bird-song to a fanciful little boy. Sherwood Forest, in a sense, was brought into the London Road, by the happy chance of Edward's being a pillar of the famous company of volunteers, and one of William's pleasantest memories is of being taken to a review of the Foresters, and seeing among the lines of scarlet one inexplicably black figure. When Mrs. Nicholson inquired the reason for the black, the officer escorting the party gravely explained that the black figure was a tallow chandler in private life, and could never appear in uniform without the flies swarming on to him in such numbers as to completely obliterate the scarlet.

Another joy of the period was visiting Chaucer's House, Woodstock, where Mrs. Prior dosed her youngest grandson from the deep cupboard where the condiments were kept, and afterwards consoled him with comfits, "to take the taste away"; and so was the privilege of watching Father shave in the mornings, and looking from his dressing-room window across the lush Nottinghamshire meadows. For all his occasional asperity, Mr. Nicholson was an affectionate father; it was he who got up in the night to get Billie the "drinks of water" which are a childish euphemism for a feeling of loneliness, or a longing for a little extra attention. It was rather a delicate little boy, given to attacks of croup, given to appearing, strangulating, in his nightshirt, at the parents' bedside, to be snatched up in his father's arms, while all the nursery apparatus for dealing with that nightmare of childhood was got under weigh. . . . It was just too bad that his father could not laugh with him. . . .

("Mother, Mother!"—Billie's shrieks rend the air; she is visiting him to say Good-morning. "Mother, you're ill-treating me—don't beat me so, Mother! Oo-oo, Mother, don't strike me again—Mother, Moth-ER!" "Billie, Billie, for goodness' sake be quiet—you're disturbing Father—*and what will the servants think?*"—But young William, abandoned to his latest and most exquisite jest, continues to raise the welkin, while she flees from the uproar created by this adorable, diabolical, youngest son of hers.)

And one more picture: A certain green velvet arm-chair (known as "Father's chair"), Mr. Nicholson, with his handsome silver head and neat imperial, slowly turning the pages of the book he is reading—the reading interrupted from time to time by furtive operations with a handkerchief, and muttered asides about "catching a cold." What has given Mr. Nicholson his "cold"? *Little Lord Fauntleroy.*

4

She and he, Babille and Bijou, the coachman and Benjamin the groom (William's later insistance on calling his firstborn Benjamin, and lightly fobbing off the inquiries of a puzzled family by declaring he couldn't think of any other name, was taken as distressing proof of the incorrigible levity of his character; nobody seemed to remember that there was already a Benjamin Nicholson—the great-grandfather—in the family tree) were all decked out with favours, because they were going canvassing— an aspect of election week which William deplored. It was a sort of aggravation of district visiting, of which he had plenty, his mother being very grave and remindful of her duty to her poorer neighbours, a duty impressed upon every lady of her day; and well instilled into her daughter, one may be sure, by Mrs. Prior of Woodstock.

He knew his part in the performance: to stand by with a fixed, polite smile while his mother was gracious to a lot of dirty people, kissed a lot of even dirtier babies, and was more than ever linger- ingly sympathetic to old women who insisted on showing her and Master Willy their sore legs. Master Willy managed not to vomit, but privately considered it a hard price to pay for getting Father into Parliament.

But there were brighter moments. There was, for instance, the great day when Mr. Finch-Hatton honoured the house in London Road by lunching with his fellow candidate. That an aristocrat should thus condescend to a manufacturer meant something, in the heyday of Victorian patronage. (It did not mean so very much to Mrs. Nicholson, née Prior, whose ancestors had hobnobbed with kings.)

The drawing-room (violently ornate, with painted cupids on the gilded ceiling: young Jim, May and William had the pleasure of having united whooping cough in the drawing-room, where they whooped at the cupids, thus adding appreciably to their enjoyment) and the dining-room (gilt frames like monstrances enshrining prize-ring cattle, with purple mountains in the background, bore witness to Mr. Nicholson's by no means negligible interest in art) were burnished for the visitor's recep- tion, and Mrs. Nicholson spent half the morning in the billiard- room, arranging the flowers on the billiard-table, which was protected for the occasion by its mackintosh cover. This billiard- table, on which William made his first break, was one of the wooden bed period, and the noise of a game of billiards was audible from top to bottom of the house. The skeeball players on Brighton pier always remind him of the sound.

Of the imposing occasion itself, only one incident impressed itself on his mind: during luncheon, Mr. Finch-Hatton rose and helped himself from the sideboard. This struck William as the acme of lordly ease and *savoir faire*.

The Election Day (which happened also to be All Fools) was enlivened by the Conservatives dressing up a woman in scarlet, raddling her face with red ochre, filling her up with Warwick ale and sending her to yell "Vote for Finch-Hatton and Nicholson" throughout the town. The Liberals, not to be outdone, blue-bagged a man from head to foot and sent him after her. In the early stages of its polling day inebriation, Newark laughed itself hoarse at this simple jest.

The scene on the morning when the poll was declared was Hogarthian. William (who had not yet made acquaintance of Hogarth) had taken advantage of the favouritism which, admitted by neither, was tacitly assumed by both, to accompany his mother to hear the results of the poll from the balcony of the Clifton Arms.

The brawling round the doors of taverns whose supplies of beer and spirits were running low, the bandsmen whose slack lips failed to produce from their instruments more than an occasional disjointed crow, the fights that went on among the crowds in the market place registered a thousand impressions on the mind of an attentive little boy. In his excitement he actually did not hear the announcement of his father's triumph, but he saw, with mingled terror and delight, the victor being hoisted, at peril of his life, on the shoulders of his tipsy supporters, and trying hard to look as if he enjoyed it.

The next thing William knew was that he was being bundled into the carriage, while Uncle Fred Prior, who had snatched up the whip and reins, laid about him on the heads and shoulders of the mob, and drove the Conquering Hero back, hell for leather, up the London Road.

From the numbers polled (Earp, 1,073, Nicholson, 993, Finch-Hatton, 985, Bristowe, 982) it is clear that, even for those days, it was a bumper election!

But the final thrill was yet to come. Hardly was dinner over, or the popping of champagne corks abated, when an uproar outside and the crashing of panes of glass announced the arrival of the Liberal mob, rum-valiant, and out to avenge the defeat of one of their candidates.

Someone rushed into the little bedroom where William lay, far too excited to go to sleep: turned out the light and snatched him out of bed—just in time, for a brick crashed through the window and landed within an inch of the pillow on which his head had been laid. And while Mr. Nicholson, snatching a Turkish cutlass from the wall, defied the mob in true heroic fashion on the doorstep, Uncle Fred Prior was out and away, across flower-beds and walls, to summon the defensive army which, apprehending some such reprisal as this, he had warned to lie in readiness. These stalwarts came up, taking the Liberals— who had brought a brass band with them—in the rear . . . and William spent the next few weeks in digging bits of trombone out of the lawn.

5

When the excitement of the poll was over, and the time came for Mr. Nicholson to take his seat in the House, the family moved to town. It was William's first visit to London. Round-eyed, he drove in a fourwheeler the colour of a meerschaum pipe, with straw laid down under foot, via Seven Dials—which Father pointed out as "rather a shady neighbourhood"—to the flat in Queen Anne's Mansions, Westminster, which the new member for Newark had rented; and while Mr. Nicholson attended to his Parliamentary duties, or drove his smart equipage up and down that strip of Pall Mall behind Carlton House Terrace which was then known as the Member's Mile, Mrs. Nicholson introduced her son to some of the milder pleasures of London.

Small and young as he was (he had not long passed his eighth birthday), she encouraged him, with fortitude rare in so devoted a mother, to adventure a little for himself. She gave him some money and made him promise to take a cab back to Queen Anne's Mansions if he got lost; but beyond discovering the Aquarium, where his admiration was divided between two men who did an ape turn inside a cage, and a lady who dived from the roof into what he afterwards described as a sort of little footbath, he does not appear to have made much use of his liberty.

These simple ventures were varied by expeditions with his mother, who, on one occasion, blameless lady, took him to what she had heard described as a "nice little wine bar" in Sackville Street, off Piccadilly. There were small tables where one sat to eat oysters, for which she had an innocent *gourmandise*. Everything seemed very discreet.

That William enjoyed his glass of champagne and his first oysters is not to be questioned; but the real thrill for him was the forcible ejection of an over-gladsome patron from the inner bar, who, in his passing, went further than to turn down an empty glass. William had the exquisite pleasure of watching this son of Omar snatch at the tablecloths and sweep them and their contents with him on his progress between door and door. Mrs. Nicholson took it very calmly. She finished her oysters, tipped the waiter and walked out. No one who saw the pair of them walking sedately along Piccadilly would have guessed that Mrs. Nicholson and her son had been Seeing Life.

It was the briefest glimpse. The holidays come to an end. William has to go back to Newark. Back to the school he loathes.

CHAPTER TWO

School—Learning to Draw

I

"IF YOU lick your brush, Master Willy," his nurse told him, "you'll die of poisoning."

One night in bed the urge came to create a little something, so Master Willy got his paintbox, took out his brush, primed it nicely with Chinese white—and, absent-mindedly, licked it.

. . . Five minutes later, he was creeping in his little white nightshirt to look his last on Mother.

There was a dinner party that night; from his eyric on the landing, clutching the banister rails, he saw her come out of the drawing-room on the parson's arm. The rustle of her silk gown and the echo of her laughing voice came up the stairs to William—calm and aloof as the angel he expected within the next quarter of an hour to be. There was something very noble and inspiring about not disturbing Mother's dinner party: just dying quietly, up there on the landing, by oneself. It was a pity, really, that the heroism fell a little flat: that the chill of the landing air eventually sent one back to one's bed, very cold, but indubitably alive.

But this unintentional attempt at suicide was followed soon after by another, less innocent.

It was Uncle Fred Prior who, pointing to the water tank by the greenhouse wall, observed, with his comfortable, adult chuckle, "I'd be sorry for anybody who took a drink out of that—*he* wouldn't last long!"—an unfortunate remark to make in the hearing of a sensitive little boy, already green and sick in the stomach at the nearing prospect of returning to school.

On the last day of the holidays, William took a glass, dibbled up enough of the dirty, stagnant water to fill it, and drank. In case the first glass should not prove enough, he took a second. Once again, and this time with more necessity, Providence intervened. He was not even sick.

2

It is evident that all the boys at Magnus did not hate it. We dined one night at Leoni's with two of them: Sebastian (Jack) Smith, of the older generation, Donald Wolfit of the younger. These two were openly amused by William's surly dislike of its very memory. To them the lack of privacy, the routine existence, the hard life, the compulsory games were ordinary, to-be-taken-for-granted aspects of school life, for which other things compensated. The party—arranged, if I remember rightly, by Donald—was not a success; it was obvious from the start that William hated being reminded; and, having already heard something from him of those years, his attitude seemed to me more reasonable than the complacence of the others, although things had certainly altered in Donald's day.

In a more genial moment he admitted that he liked the Headmaster, the Reverend Herbert Plater, who was, according to William, "a Head not to be trifled with." Lame, eccentric, kindly, he had a neat hand with the cane. "We had," says William, "to choose our own cane from a sheaf, when necessary, and its applications often drew blood: I can answer for that, though I don't recall the sin I had committed." At a guess—the sin of idleness; he hated lessons because he had the smallest possible power of concentration, and loathed coercion. "Greek before breakfast on an empty stomach—after breaking the ice in the washbowl—prevented me from ever wishing to visit Greece."

He suffered, moreover, from the patronage of an elder brother. Jim also was at Magnus; he was a clever boy, and ashamed of the shortcomings of his junior; they saw as little as possible of each other.

It sounds as if the Reverend Plater had High Church leanings, for one of the horrors that stand out in William's memory is that of Good Friday, when they were herded to church before breakfast, and again for matins, returning to lunch off watery cod whose watery eyes appalled him: a meal eaten in silence, behind drawn blinds, and followed by a third visit to church.

Cod apart, the food must have been shocking; they never tasted fresh butter from the beginning to the end of term, during all the years William was at Magnus. Instead, they were given Irish tub butter, a vile concoction of grease and train-oil, which the boys surreptitiously scraped off the chunks of bread on which it was served, and daubed through the holes in the iron gratings which covered the primitive heating apparatus under the floor of the schoolroom. Most people have recollections of the sour ink-and-blotting-paper smell of their schooldays, but the stench William remembers was something even more revolting. The butter attracted the rats, which arrived in scores under the gratings; the gratings themselves were never cleaned from year end to year end, and in the winter, when the furnace was lighted, gave up their hideous reek of rancid butter and rat droppings, which nearly asphyxiated the boys who sat nearest to them.

Playtime was hardly more endurable than lessons. Unsupervised, unorganised games for small boys always develop into the same thing: lots of fun for the bigger, stronger fellows, and something approaching martyrdom for the smaller, weaker ones. In cricket the strongest fellow took the bat, the next strongest the ball, and if you happened to be a little one, you were put in long field for the afternoon. If you muffed a catch you were in for a beating from the bowler, with one of the stumps. It was hardly the way to make an active, athletic, little boy enjoy cricket, and William was too small to put up much of a defence for himself. One could only endure, and dream of the big chestnut-tree at home, and of a nice green bank in which, one was by this time old enough to realise, Father did *not* keep his money.

An ingenious system invented by the staff for evading its responsibilities consisted in "extra drill," and the hours William put in, marching up and down the school yard (all round and about the school was paddock, but for some imponderable reason the pupils were forced to take all their exercise on stone) sickened him for life of enforced exercise. The drill-sergeant was not a bad fellow, and they managed to play at least one good trick on him. On wet days the school drilled in the dining-room, and some bright spirit thoughtfully removed the breadcutter from the side table to a position just inside the door. When the sergeant, who had not seen such an implement before, asked what it was for, he was told it was to scrape his boots on: which he did with a thoroughness that led to later investigation. Who had been playing tricks with the breadcutter? Not me, sir. Not me, sir. "Please, sir," pipes up one hopeful, "I saw the sergeant scraping his boots on it. . . ."

It is positive that Mr. Nicholson never realised the cruelty of sending William as boarder to a school whose daily promenades allowed him to gaze with longing at the flower-beds and green lawns of his own home. Nicholsons had always gone to Magnus, so William went to Magnus; and as a boarder, because boarding was part of the tradition.

There was one advantage, and one only: that, when the end of term came, and other boarders had to go long journeys by train—wasting even so much as a whole precious day of the holidays, before being united with their families—William had only to rush out of the school gates and home to the hot bath his mother always had waiting for him. Oh, poignant luxury, after the weekly dip in the corrugated-iron bathhouse, and Plater's operations with the ice-cold hosepipe which it was a point of honour to endure as long as one could, but which effectually dispelled any sensations of pleasure and well-being one might be enjoying after one's brief, lukewarm immersion! To be alone, to take one's time, to steep one's small, battered limbs in warmth that one could renew at one's pleasure—this was rapture, in which all but the joy of the present was blotted out: to be followed by a kind of dimness.

Emancipated from routine, but not yet attuned to freedom, there seemed, for a while, nothing to do but wander from room to room, taking in all the remembered gentleness and sweetness of home. It was in one such mood that he found the poems of Keats, and lay on the sofa for hours, reading and re-reading *St. Agnes' Eve.*

Half of the holidays had seeped away before this dimness wore off, and then there was only a week or two before the shades of the prisonhouse again descended. With his book and his pencil he managed to hold them at bay: Dumas and Scott provided him with enough images to blot out (if only temporarily), the grim recollections and grimmer apprehensions that drew nearer with every sunset. Those fat little brown volumes of Dumas were a treasure. It may here be noted that William had great difficulty in learning to read, until he came across pictures whose captions he wanted to understand. But he was excellent at his copybook; he could reproduce a line of script that his gratified teacher could hardly distinguish from the copy, holding his pen, as he does now, very much as if it were a paintbrush and laying, rather than scratching, the letters on to the paper.

They realised at last how miserable he was, and, to his delight, William was allowed to become a "day cad." No longer need to dream nostalgically of the Chantrey meadows, with the dappled deer moving gently under the trees—a dream which had tormented one often, behind the high, playground wall that shut out all beauty—as though to look on beauty were vice—from the eyes of the Magnus scholars. One went freely, like a bird, between home and school, filling one's eyes and one's head with pictures which were of a great deal more importance and value than the algebraic symbols which seemed so nonsensical when the mathematics master chalked them up on the board.

3

The only prizes William ever gained were for Scripture and Drawing, and the runner-up was always a boy called Cree. "Old" Cubley, the drawing master, offered one of his own paintings as first prize—the subject was always the same: a little water colour of the English Lakes. The second prize was a book, and, having as many sketches of the Lake District as they wanted, William and Cree competed for the second prize.

It was "old" Cubley (one wonders really how old he was) who won William's lasting devotion by suggesting to Mr. Nicholson that William should be allowed to go to his house for private lessons once a week. After thinking it over, Mr. Nicholson, whose limited but sincere appreciation of art was reflected in his own collection, interviewed the Headmaster, who agreed that William was probably as well employed in this way as in drawing caricatures of the staff when he was supposed to be doing algebra. (His formula for Bussell, the Latin master, had gone through Magnus like an epidemic; it was so beautifully simple, any one could copy it, and it flourished on walls and wainscotings like the victory V. It may fairly be counted as the first of the Blokes which Faber and Faber were to publish nearly half a century later.)

So William, by now about twelve years old, had his first serious lessons in art. The first discovery he made—and it was not entirely a pleasant one—was that Cubley considered painting secondary to draughtsmanship, and insisted on teaching him to draw. When it came to painting, it was in the Reynolds tradition, for "old" Cubley was a pupil of Sir William Beechey, who was a pupil of Reynolds, and his methods were those of the Master.

Reynolds painted, so William discovered, principally in Indian red, white and black; when the original study was finished, it was brought to life with the transparent glazes which were afterwards applied. A sound but dangerous method: the danger being that when the varnish was removed the glaze automatically clung to the varnish, rather than to the canvas. A sample of this is to be seen in Reynolds's *Three Graces*, in the National Gallery, efforts to restore which have reduced it to the condition prior to its final painting; the removal of the glazes has, in fact, taken it out of the category of Reynolds's completed works. (According to William, he himself was too impatient a character to follow out the tradition, and the direct statement was more in tune with his ideals.)

In the holidays Cubley took his favourite pupil sketching to his beloved Lake District, where he was a familiar figure to the locals during "the painting season." There was always the same little procession: "old" Cubley in front, his white beard blowing in the breeze, followed by his little wife, carrying his paints and easel, and the pupil straggling behind.

The beauties of Seatoller and Watendlath were thus known to William at a very early age, but they never took hold of him. It is a district overpictured, a little too conscious of its beauties, to appeal to the painter of the southern downlands and meadows; as he says, "the picture is there without painting it." At thirteen the painter of "Blenheim Bridge at Sunset" was shying off the picturesque. It was at about this age that he painted for his mother the little scene of the tennis party which is remarkable for its manipulation of greens, a colour always difficult for the student. The lawn splashed with sunlight under the trees, and the charming, vague figures in sun-dappled white, moving languidly as between sets, have a charm and spontaneity which suggest contemporary French art, of which, at that time, William had certainly seen nothing.

During one of these holidays, he accompanied his parents to Berne. Some of the party went in for mountaineering, and an expedition was planned to see the sun rise from one of the Alpine peaks. William begged to be allowed to join it. No, no, he was told; he was too young, he could not stand up to the long climb, he would be a nuisance. Nuisance or not, he persisted, and triumphantly vindicated his character as a climber by reaching the *châlet* at which they stopped overnight well ahead of the rest of the party.

But the real importance of this holiday was that it taught him what he is pleased to call "all he ever knew" about architectural perspective. Wearing a Glengarry cap to cover his small, earnest halo of the neophyte, he took out his paintbox and sketching-block and set himself problems among the steep streets and sharply pitched roofs of the little Swiss town. It was hard work, and it marked an important step in his progress towards mastery of his art.

In these days William is often asked by fond parents whether the works of their offspring do not show "a genuine talent for an artistic career." Almost all children's drawings, before they have been corrupted by adult instruction, show some sort of talent; drawing, after all, is the natural expression of the primitive mind. But unless the will to labour is there—to labour unprompted by anything save the desire to excel—he is inclined to discourage these fond and foolish parental aspirations.

It was now that he got his first commission—well, not exactly his first: it was during the elections that Mr. Nicholson had an idea for a political cartoon based on Millais's painting, *St. Bartholomew's Eve*. William was to execute it, and William did, and it was published in "the newspaper": but what newspaper, or the date of publication, or any means of tracing it have been defeated by William's stubborn disinclination to disinter this and other "early works."

But he was commissioned by the vicar to make a picture of the font, and did quite a good little architectural drawing, for which he received the sum of one guinea. William had always wanted to draw in church; during the sermon he used to draw with his foot in the dust under the pew. He was delighted at the authorisation of this (so far) surreptitious occupation. In Newark church there are two little panels of Chaucer's time, depicting the Dance of Death; he loved them, and often tried to copy them; his love for the Chaucerian period runs like a motif through the history of his life.

School no longer troubled him; it was merely a tiresome background to the realities of his painting life. To Cubley, for whom he had a great affection, he owed another stroke of fortune, for it was Cubley who now put it to Mr. Nicholson that there was very little point in William's hanging about in a school to which, by his scholarship, he was highly unlikely ever to do credit, and who pointed out that at sixteen one was old enough to begin the serious study of art.

This indeed was a grave matter. No Nicholson had ever been an artist. But perhaps his father felt a little guilty about Edward. With all his persuasion that a business career was the only safe and suitable one, Mr. Nicholson could never have persuaded himself that William would be a success in "the works." Nor did he show the slightest interest in anything except painting.

It is easy to picture the age-old struggle between paternal doubt and maternal confidence in a son's ability going on above William's young head. It was the mother's belief that won the day, and that gave William himself the confidence to choose his future profession; and it was Mrs. Nicholson who, thanks to a fortuitous meeting with a Miss Brewer, an art student at Herkomer's school, obtained all the particulars needful for launching William into the world of art.

He had to do a charcoal study for his entrance, and chose the head of an old Newark woman; when it was finished he showed it to Cubley, who said it was very good.

WILLIAM NICHOLSON.
From a photograph by Malcolm Arbuthnot.

CHAPTER THREE

The Herkomer School—The Prydes, James and Mabel—
The Adenoid Family—Prydeian Background—End of the
Herkomer Phase

I

IT WAS an intoxicating experience, at sixteen, to be plunged into the independence of lodgings of one's own, with no one—as he expresses it—to tell him to take his feet off the mantelpiece. It was all too new and thrilling for him to have any of those pangs of homesickness which his mother had foreseen when she gave him, at parting, a gift which he treasured, but which his new-found manhood prompted him to hide away: one of her Shetland shawls, whose smell and texture of thistledown was woven into all the years of childhood. She gave it to him as she would have given him, if she could, the embrace of her arms, to comfort and encourage him through the empty moments which she foresaw, though he, in his excitement, did not.

His landlady was an elderly spinster who (presently) objected to his adorning his walls with studies from the nude. She invariably took them down while he was out, until he had the bright notion of cutting out little paper bathing-drawers, which he pinned on in the appropriate places—evidently satisfying her notions of propriety, for after this she left his works of art alone.

He was actually so young that he was kept for a year out of the Life class, although he had passed his entrance. Resentful of the injustice, he left the school and returned to Newark and "old" Cubley, until his time of probation had expired.

One may note here that William's first reaction to the nude was one of acute disillusionment. He had only once previously seen a naked woman, which was when he happened to wake up when the nursemaid who slept in his room when he was a baby was taking her bath; there did not seem much in that to make a fuss about. But the sight of the model, an elderly Jewess, so hirsute that she seemed to be wrapped up in a thin black fur rug, was not calculated to arouse any emotion beyond a faint repugnance. It was probably a deliberate choice on the part of Herkomer, whose Life classes were all very pure and proper

C

(the male students segregated from the female), and the atmosphere on the whole heavily reverential—though this sometimes broke down, as in the case of the over-conscientious student who prided himself on detail, and who drew five fingers on the hand of the current model. During his absence from the room, his fellow-students drew footsteps in charcoal from the door to the offender's easel, with a printed inscription: FOLLOW THESE.

As far as a sixteen-year-old student could judge, and a painter of seventy-one remember, the standard of work was a fair average. The *tour de force* of the studio was The Oil Dog, painted with more zeal than technique by a well-to-do student, who used such plenitude of oil that he found it necessary to reverse his pet's portrait on the first day of every month. This was given the place of honour on the mantelpiece.

The women students were earnest young women in chintz smocks, wedded to art—which, according to William, showed no enthusiasm for the nuptials. Among them was a strapping hoyden, with no reverence for art whatever, more talent than all the rest put together, and incorrigible laziness. She engaged the attention of young William—her junior by twelve months— by driving a flock of geese she found grazing on the common, into the Life class. She also was the youngest student—on the women's side; and this formed a natural bond between them. In conversation with Mabel Pryde—her friends called her "Prydie"—William heard a great deal about a brother Jimmy, who was endowed with heroic proportions by an obviously infatuated sister; he was also favoured with a highly-coloured version of his new acquaintance's escape from her home in Edinburgh, to come to England and study art.

What with one thing and another, these two bright spirits do not appear to have allowed themselves to be unduly weighed down by art. Mabel Pryde, who had no sense of humour whatever, but a strong sense of the ridiculous, and William, whose sense of humour (according to his family) was already over developed, found plenty of material on which to exercise their wit.

Herkomer's own monument to his advancing prosperity was the house itself, a large, vulgar affair of Bavarian stone, each block imported from Germany, displaying the worst features of the Teutonic pittoresque. As a side show, he kept his old Bavarian father, a nice, simple old man, who worked with much conscience and application on small tasks deputed to him by his son, and had never managed to acquire more than an impractical modicum of the language of the country of his adoption. Visitors were always taken to see old Herr Herkomer at work in his little atélier; it was part of Herkomer's pose, not to be ashamed of his humble beginnings.

On the occasion of the birth of a grandchild to the old gentleman, Herkomer gave a tea party, to which students were invited: the *pièce de résistance* being a pencil drawing mounted on an easel and bearing the caption: "I declare this to be an accurate portrait of my son—age 2 hours 5 minutes." Perhaps even Herkomer meant it for a joke . . .?

2

Shortly after the acquaintance with " Prydie" was cemented by the affair of the geese, William made another contact which, ripening into friendship, was to have a strong influence on his future career.

The god so frequently invoked descended on Bushey: James Pryde saw fit from his Olympian heights to visit his sister at her art school. (Perhaps that Olympus was not very high, but Prydes had a habit of regarding themselves as Olympians. What was more important, they had a singular power of impressing themselves as such on other people—not all as naïve and naturally admiring as the little boy from Newark.)

Jimmy Pryde was very big, very handsome, very impressive indeed in the somewhat colourless surroundings to which fraternal sentiment had induced him to submit himself. Against another background he might conceivably have dwindled; at Herkomer's he evoked, inevitably, the superlative. Very talented, vain, lazy: with complete persuasion (which was to strengthen with the passage of years) that it was not only the privilege but the duty of all with whom he came in contact to contribute to the upkeep of Jimmy Pryde. Most people agreed with him; there was something irresistible about Jimmy, and, at least so far as artistic ability went, no pretension whatever. If not precisely what is perilously called a genius, he came very close to it.

It was Edward Gordon Craig who said of Jimmy that he had every qualification of the actor, without being able to act. He would spend time in front of a mirror, arranging his expression and the set of his brows, before entering a room. (After one of

Irving's visits to Edinburgh, he went to the Lyceum and offered his services to the great actor manager, who, however, returned Jimmy to his father with a note of thanks.)

Among Jimmy's idiosyncrasies was that of "nesting"; in other words, once get Jimmy under your roof, and his departure was dictated only by some question of personal policy. Mabel was living in some squalid little lodgings at Merry Hill, kept by a Mrs. Mutton—aptly rechristened Mrs. Smutton, and here Jimmy settled in: in a sitting-room hung with brown paper and unfurnished except for a broken-down chair or two, a ricketty secretaire on which meals were laid for want of a table, and the ministrations of the Adenoid Family—of whom more hereafter.

Mrs. Smutton was an adoring slut who fell for the *beaux yeux* of Jimmy, and used to send her son (called Rupert the Villein) out to steal chickens or rob orchards when Jimmy had not the price of a meal—a matter of frequent occurrence. She washed up once a week only, kept the ham on the sewing-machine and her old black bonnet in the fender, and spent most of her Sundays lying on an unsafe horsehair sofa, reading Dickens.

Jimmy was, in those days, very amusing company: a great wit and a great *poseur*. That he was flattered by the attentions of his new admirer goes without saying; they lost no time in striking up a friendship which was unfortunate, to say the least of it, so far as William's attendances at the Herkomer school went. Or was it?

It had not taken Jimmy to point out to William that one did not gain much from Herkomer's instructions. Herkomer had a vast conceit of himself as a famous portraitist, little interest in his students, and little power of expressing his views—such as they were—on the art of painting. His ideas were purely conventional, and all came back to the same point: that a student was a good student who could turn out a copy of Herkomer, and a bad student if he showed any signs of originality in his work.

One learned something—obviously: as one was bound to learn by the mere experience of handling brushes and paint; but it did not take William long to realise that one could learn just as much in that way outside the studio as in it. The company of Jimmy Pryde, moreover, was a great deal more enlightening. than that of his fellow-students—Jimmy, who had already succeeded in making himself something of a "cult" in Bushey, and was very *mal vu* by Herkomer, for the supposed bad influence he had on the school. "School" was the way Herkomer liked to regard it; he wrote plays, and had them acted in his theatre by the students, for the benefit of week-ending celebrities. It was unfortunate that one such eclectic evening's entertainment should coincide with a soirée of Jimmy's at the nearby "local," where Jimmy, who played the piano, as he did everything else, with no knowledge whatever, but immense *brio*, was accompanying himself in Albert Chevalier's songs. Every now and then Jimmy declared that certain notes would not strike, when some member of the audience would ring the bell and order a bottle of Bass, which was solemnly poured into the interior of the piano—to the instant revival of the notes. The piano must have been doing quite nicely—as well as some of the guests—when somebody made the discovery that a steady stream of beer was trickling from its interior, across the floor and down the stairs. There was a good deal of trouble about that. . . .

No doubt it was all very good for art. The last thing they ever discussed was painting, but William was receiving his *éducation mondaine* from one whose worldly experience, although perhaps not so very extensive as both of them imagined, was presented with a dazzling assurance that could not fail to carry conviction to a simple mind.

Meanwhile, the friendship with Mabel prospered. There was nothing sentimental about it; one can hardly imagine so robustious a figure as "Prydie's" capturing the chivalresque imagination of William, who had already a slight romantic attachment to a charming young cousin who, through the death of both her parents, had come to live in the house in London Road, and whose portrait he was painting. Dorothy was reading *The Talisman* to William during the sittings; delicate and feminine, she was not at all the sort of young person to drive geese into a Life class. Mabel, moreover, was conducting an affair of her own, *sub rosa*, and William was made confidant when this came, in due course, to a sad end.

Jimmy, of course, was also well away on his *vie amoureuse*. Wearing his pale, Scots tweeds and his impossibly heroic air, he was for ever treking between Merry Hill and the mansion of his inamorata, whose father kept up a handsome establishment in Bushey High Street; and all might have gone well but for the trifling discovery on Jimmy's part that he was not in love with that one at all, but with her little sister Dolly.

3

Jimmy was doing some of his best work at Bushey, including the pastel of an ugly little girl, the *Little Girl in Black*, recently lent by William for exhibition in the National Gallery. (William also had a "little girl" on hand, and, largely to impress her, had done a small pastel of Cawsand Bay.) They both decided to send work up to the old Grosvenor Gallery, and, in due course, Jimmy received his first Press notices. About the *Little Girl in Black*, *Punch* elected to be facetious: "Mr. Pryde has put in all the black and left out the little girl." This was, however, more than balanced by a letter from one of the critics, who wrote to Jimmy: "What a swagger you have cut with your chalks!"

The Little Girl in Black is the only known portrait of a member of the Adenoid Family; this is Our Lill-I, the daughter of Mrs. Smutton, whose offspring furnished William and Jimmy with some of their brightest passages. William's impersonations of the Adenoid Family (they all seem to have had permanent colds in the head) are a classic in our circle, and it is to be feared that phonetics hardly do justice to them without the vocal effects that accompany the performance.

" Muvver. MUV-ver. Mr. Pryde's mockin' may."

"Buvver. BUV-ver. BUV*VER*. One of by doses won'd blow."

And from the horrid little patch of garden at the back, cluttered with tin cans and dreary little plants, where the mangy retriever was tied up to the mangle:

"Muvver. MUVVER. Muvver-muvver-Muv-VER. Ken Oi ev a bit of luv-loys-bleedun?"

Lill-I, author of this final gem, can little have dreamed that her portrait would one day hang in the National Gallery.

4

Mrs. Pryde (according to William) was "an old lady of great determination, charm and character. She had odd, definite and changeable views of life. She studied chess and French when well into her eighties, and played a very good game."

His further description of Mrs. Pryde as, if not a creature of sweetness and light, a delightfully sentimental old lady who always sent her parcels by Carter Paterson, "because it was so nice to think of their travelling by an old-fashioned carter," does not seem to fit in with that of the woman who, in the presence of her young family, slapped a plate of cold porridge on the top of her husband's bald head, as a conclusion to some argument. It would seem to take more than Dr. Pryde's laughter to clear the air after that.

Dr. David Pryde had risen from very humble beginnings to the position of headmaster of a girls' college. A great old gentleman, a profound scholar and an excellent raconteur (especially of Scottish stories; his lecture on Scottish humour would pack the biggest lecture hall in Edinburgh)—his figure stands up like a rocky background to the antics of his wife and offspring. She was, before her marriage, a Miss Lauder—one of the Lauders of the Bass, a family which contributed something to the history of its times, and which included two painter brothers, Scott and Eckford Lauder, Mrs. Pryde's uncles.

There is a pleasant story of Scott and Eckford, glowering over their pipes on a winter's night, not uttering a syllable until Scott takes his pipe out of his mouth to say:

"Eckford."

"Ay," says Eckford.

"A straight line's a ter-rrible thing," says Scott.

Eckford considers the point, decides there is no harm in committing himself, and nods.

"Ay, mon. It's an emblem of eter-rr-nity."

Another long silence. It is Eckford's turn to break it.

"Scott."

"Ay," says Scott.

"I've been thinking. It's an awfu' deeficult thing—to paint."

"Mon," says Scott . . . "It's *impossible*."

The trouble with the former Miss Lauder—now Mrs. Pryde—was that she was a feminist in advance of her time. Whereas the average mother would have made a favourite of her only son, she set her small, good-natured-looking face utterly against the prevalent idea that girls should be sacrificed to their brothers. Of her five daughters, there was not one who could not claim her mother's support and sympathy in precedence of Jimmy; yet it was typical of her muddled thinking on this (and many other) subjects that the daughters must be prepared at any moment to sacrifice their own personal wishes and convenience to her service. She would never write a letter or send a telegram, but kept the girls running with trivial messages all day long. Mabel refused, and Jimmy escaped these impositions; she probably knew she had met her match in these two. All the same, a queer, ironic affection obtained between them, based on mutual appreciation of each others' parts.

"Jimmy," said his mother one day, "do you know you've never written me a letter in your life?"

"As a matter of fact, Mother," replied Jimmy, "I did write you a picture postcard—once. But I tore it up. I thought you might think it fulsome."

It is to Mrs. Pryde's credit that she had quite enough sense of of humour to appreciate this admirable Roland for her Oliver, which is on a par with Jimmy's wire to his wife at High Wycombe after a night out: "Did not come home last night." Jimmy was the only one of the children who inherited his father's wit.

Not content with being a follower of cults, her habit was to force them on the circle of her acquaintance. When she abandoned them (she was a woman of violent opinions but no convictions) her family and friends must abandon them as well, or run the gauntlet of her satire; not only would she revoke all her former creeds—she would flatly deny ever having held them. Totally lacking in intellectual stability, there was one tenet to which she was faithful: which was that her children existed simply and solely for her personal convenience. Oddly enough, people of this type, who never cease to make exorbitant demands on those around them, generally succeed in commanding a quality of affection which is denied to the more unselfish.

Dabbling now with spiritualism, now with the cold water cure, it will readily be seen that Mrs. Pryde had little time to spare for the cares of a household or the upbringing of a family. She read a great deal, knitted sometimes—and saw the girls were kept on the run. They would have had little opportunity to make lives for themselves, had not their own slyness and determination got the better, sometimes, even of filial duty. They had, at least, only one task mistress; the woman who slapped a plate of porridge on her husband's head was not likely to reprove her youngest daughter for refusing to carry her father's dinner up to his room. Plumping it down at the foot of the stairs, Mabel shouted that he could fetch it for himself—which, with perfect good humour, he proceeded to do: it was no part of a daughter's duty to wait on a father!

William's explanation of Mrs. Pryde's resentment of the idea of any of her daughters marrying is that the idea of marriage, even in the abstract, was so distasteful to her that she instinctively rejected it on behalf of her girls. It seems improbable, even taking into account her affection for Dr. Pryde, that she ever wanted any of her six children, and if any of the girls happened to attract the fleeting attentions of a young man, Mrs. Pryde's chilly comment, "You must have been behaving in a very odd manner!" was quite enough to nip romance in the bud.

Bella was the eldest, and much the most lovable, of the five girls; she had a heart of gold, good brains, dabbled in astrology—and lived in the porch to be out of the way of the rest of the family.

The fact that they were always "at outs" was Fanny's doing. She was the mischief-maker; she was also her mother's favourite, and used her influence to make constant trouble between Mrs. Pryde and the other children. Her violently jealous disposition made her a dangerous partisan, but her devotion to Mabel lasted to the grave—and perhaps beyond; but that is another story.

Netty was a clever girl, and, later, a very good teacher, although never popular with her pupils.

The fourth daughter, Dora, was the only one besides Mabel who found the courage to defy her mother's strictures on marriage. She trained as a nurse, and, through William's influence, went out to South Africa to nurse during the Boer War.

The youngest, Mabel, had the advantage of the others in being gifted with a very positive talent, which lent her a little of the ballast which seemed lacking in their badly orientated lives. She had never had a lesson in drawing—which did not prevent her teaching it; with the little money thus earned she managed to make her break-away from an atmosphere which must have been stifling to them all.

The only subjects which united this odd, assertive, violently individualistic family were, first, a hint of external criticism, which banded them together immediately in ferocious self-defence, and, second, the theatre, for which they had that provincial enthusiasm which put gold in the pockets of the old actor managers. It does not seem that any of them had any intellectual appreciation of the drama; their attitude to the theatre was one of unbalanced, uncritical sentimentality. Any play featuring their favourite actors and actresses (of whom

Irving and Terry were the stars) was perforce perfect; and as
Irving had a great respect for Dr. Pryde, with whom he had
become acquainted on visits to Edinburgh, there was something
proprietorial in their attitude to the (London) Lyceum, the names
of whose productions and performers were apt to buzz with
somewhat wearisome reiteration across the table at Fettes
Row.

What with Bella in the porch and Mabel in the kitchen (she
would spend days there, in preference to mingling with her
family), it must have seemed a very odd household to William,
after the gentle, well-bred, well-mannered atmosphere of his own.
Unaccustomed to argument, to the violent expression of violent
views, he found it enormously stimulating.

He and Mabel hobnobbed in the cellar—where Mrs. Pryde's
latest craze had caused to be installed a vapour bath: one of the
old-fashioned kind wherein the subject sits, to be guillotined by
the lid, while hot steam is distilled from some sort of lamp in
the interior. This bath was an exhibition piece for all Mrs.
Pryde's visitors. There were not many; the Prydes were too poor
to entertain often, but when visitors were expected, preparation
took place on a scale that thunderstruck William, unaccustomed
to Scottish hospitality, and brought up in a house that took
entertainment very much for granted.

While the two young people chattered among the coalsacks,
steps were heard on the stairs: Mrs. Pryde descending with a
convoy of guests, whose duty was to admire the new purchase.
Not wishing to be caught in what would undoubtedly be regarded
as a compromising situation, William leapt into the vapour bath
and held down the lid. It was surprising, and a great disappointment to Mrs. Pryde, when her most strenuous efforts failed to
raise the lid and display the interior of her new toy. Mabel's
relief may be taken for granted; her mother would certainly have
thought she was behaving "in a very odd manner" if she had
been discovered entertaining Jimmy's friend from Bushey in the
cellar.

5

It was during his second year at Bushey that William received
his first portrait commission. Dean Hole of Rochester, a charming
man and a great amateur of rose-growing, was a friend of Mr.

Nicholson, who suggested he should get William to paint him; to which the Dean amiably agreed, stipulating—good man!—for a full-length life size, which, as he stood between 6 ft. 3 and 6 ft. 4 in his socks, was no light undertaking: at least, so it appeared to William, as he earnestly stretched an eight-foot canvas. It was the first time he had attempted any work on this scale, and before he was through with it he had made the important discovery that a so-called life-size should not be painted the size of life to get the desired effect. The result (he says to-day) was "terrible," and the *magnum opus* (in the literal sense of the term) was never finished.

The holidays in Newark were not unpleasant, by way of a change, but there was something exhilarating in getting back to Bushey—Bushey, of course, being synonymous with Jimmy, who, in the course of a walk across the snowbound country, paused beside a manure heap to execute a flourishing "H.H." with his walking-stick in the snow: "H.H." standing, of course, for Hubert Herkomer, and delicately expressing, with its background, Jimmy's opinion of that gentleman and all his works.

William, by now, was well inoculated with the virus of Pryde-ian opinion, and his attendance at classes had become more and more perfunctory, his flaunting of the Herkomer tradition had reached lengths when it had ceased to amuse even himself. Thanks in no small degree to his association with Jimmy, he had become a revolutionary, and revolution was a quantity not appreciated in the Herkomer school.

By the time he reached the status of senior student, he was at odds with the whole system, and would have left, but for the uncertainty of his future prospects.

One of the duties of the senior student was that of arranging the model, and when for some reason she failed to turn up, the study of the nude was suspended for that of some man or woman whom the senior student had managed to pick up and persuaded to sit, in the professional model's place.

This duty falling to William, he got hold of a village woman and posed her with a big black umbrella open behind her head: a lively and original subject which naturally appealed to the future master of black and white.

He sat down at his easel, made his *croquis*, and, as there were no signs of Herkomer's appearance, wandered out. When he returned there was trouble in the air. The rest of the students were working with an unwonted concentration, and before

William's easel sat Herkomer, in a towering rage. As William sauntered up to him, he roared out:

"This is a piece of Whistlerian impudence!"

William, as white with fury as Herkomer was red, remarked, "Thank you," turned on his heel and sauntered out again.

He went back to his lodgings, wrote out his resignation and sent it to Herkomer by hand. The messenger crossed with Herkomer's—bringing William his dismissal for "bad attendance and bad work."

CHAPTER FOUR

*Making decision—Paris—Experiments with a Wood Block—
Marriage*

I

WHEN William left Bushey, the question arose of what to do with his future. His father was very much concerned, and all the doubts and fears which had surrounded his leaving Magnus revived. Mr. Nicholson wanted William to paint at home, so had a studio built in the garden for him: but the atmosphere of his home and Newark in general was lethal to his work, and the work he hoped to do.

It is difficult to see how any one ever visualised the adult William fitting into the Newark scene. It was, after all, only the utmost of parental love and indulgence (not to mention the idolatry of Nurse) which had adapted the moral and mental temperature of number 12 London Road to a fantastical little boy, who might have been a changeling in his cradle for all his resemblance to his sister and brothers. He got on with them in an off-hand sort of fashion, but there was no actual warmth between them; no question of mourning at separations, no particular enthusiasm in reunions. He adored his mother and was very much attached to his father; but as for subscribing to the ways of thought and action which governed them and their circle—it was not within the bounds of his capacity.

The William who came home from Bushey was in that uncomfortable "standing water between boy and man": nervous, erratic, aloof—with disconcerting bursts of the old confidence and demonstrativeness of affection; very thin and delicate-looking—the delicacy only one of those forms of deception that annoy hearty elder brothers and sisters—and absorbed in one thing only: painting. His tongue had acquired a tang, too—possibly from Jimmy—that gave him an advantage; wit—of Jimmy's sort—was at a discount in Newark society.

The struggle of William's psyche against the typical upper-bourgeois home into which he had been born must have been grievously complicated by his warm heart and his loyalty to those whom he loves; but, fortunately for posterity, there has

45

always been one loyalty in his life which overrides all others. In the end, it is to his work that William is loyal, and with those whose limitations will not allow them to understand and accept this higher loyalty, any lasting relationship must always be an impossibility.

He could not have explained to his mother and father, for fear of hurting them, the sense of strangulation his home surroundings gave him, after the freer life to which he had been introduced by Jimmy; he could not have expressed, in any terms which would not have been wounding to them, his deepening conviction that his only way of salvation lay in escape from an environment which could contribute nothing to his advance in love and knowledge of his work. He had in some way to get his personal life in tune with his working life, and the problem of how this was to be done had been occupying him for some time before he made his actual break with Bushey.

Small as can have been her intellectual appreciation of her son's ideals, his mother was in sympathy with him; her love made her see his point of view in everything that concerned his work, and he had already taken her into his confidence over his desire to go to Paris.

It was she who eventually broke the truth to her husband: that Billie wanted to go away, to go to France and study under the French masters, and she who, at last, by her quiet persistence, broke down Mr. Nicholson's objections to what, from his point of view—considering the trouble and expense he had already been to, to meet the unfortunate vagaries of Billie's temperament—was a most unreasonable proposition.

Before William's departure a painful incident took place. He had started the beautiful small portrait of his mother which was the best, so far, of anything he had attempted. It has darkened very much with age—he did not know much, in those days, about varnish—but the delicate carriage of the head, the sweet, heavy-lidded eyes and fine-drawn profile are very true and sincere; there is no suggestion of arrangement or pose, just a Victorian gentlewoman in a dark dress and bonnet, such as she probably wore every day of her life when there was no occasion for fine attire.

When it was finished, shy of his father's criticism, William gave him the key of the studio and asked him to go and look at it by himself. Whatever he may have apprehended, it was not his father's return, livid with rage, inarticulate with resentment.

"What *is* it?—But what *is* it?" he kept on repeating, as though he had no words to express his shock and bewilderment.

Knowing the uselessness of trying to explain to his father an art which rested on truth and not on flattery (one can imagine the sort of portrait Mr. Nicholson would have liked of his wife), William could only say, "I'm sorry you don't like it."

His mother understood; her understanding took, as usual, the bitterness out of the situation.

2

The Hotel de l'Univers et du Portugal, in the rue Croix des Petits Champs, was, for all its resounding name, a small, incredibly dirty and shady little place that stank of bad drainage and unaired rooms. It was an elderly student from Bushey, named Deacon, who had turned from the study of medicine to that of art, who took William there; it was Deacon who also took William to Julian's—then crammed with English and American students—and introduced him to the life of a Paris atélier: a very different proposition, as the pair of them were to find out, from l'atélier Herkomer.

It was a miracle if one learned anything at Julian's. The atélier was frightfully overcrowded; you drew lots for a place. If you were lucky enough to get in the front row, you were so thrust upon by neighbouring easels that you could hardly lift an arm. Behind you the crowd milled for occasional glimpses of the model. These were the circumstances in which you studied the nude—the most difficult subject in the world.

The stench was dreadful—human bodies, the palette scrapings that made a frieze up to the height of one's stretched-out arm, gave up their ancient reek of oil in the heat of the stove, caporal cigarettes—everybody smoked, either cigarette or pipe, and there were times when one could hardly see for the water running out of one's eyes.

But it was an experience, as going to the 'varsity is said to be an experience, and the levity of Julian's provided a nice counterbalance to the solemnity of Herkomer's. Not that the atmosphere of Julian's was entirely frivolous: there was one student who had been there for fifteen years. William drew him—a little, fat figure, curled up earnestly on top of a very high stool.

When not working, William was absorbing Paris in his usual

fashion—through his eyes. He learned a love of Paris which has never left him to the present day: not only of her grace, her architectural beauty, the formidable beauty of the long vistas of her boulevards, the magic of her fountains and the exquisite shadows of her Bois—but of the *little* life of Paris: the things and people he observed in small streets where the scent of coffee and hot-baked bread was part of the freshness of morning, where the *blanchisseries* with their lime-blue façades brightened the long channels of smoky-grey, where all the little shopkeepers seemed to be good-natured and friendly and all the young working girls pretty and neat: and this love colours for ever his outlook on France, and accounts, I think, for the peculiar sensitiveness he brings to the rendering of the French scene. It is an outlook wholly romantic, wholly untouched by realism: the outlook of one whose ignorance of a language has preserved his ideals, as the closeness of his observation has quickened his sympathies. Paris is, among all foreign cities, his first and last love—but for him it is still the Paris of Murger, of Balzac and de Maupassant, of *Auprès de ma blonde* and *Le temps des cérisés*, of Barbizon when it belonged to painters and of the Left Bank before the American invasion. *Où sont les neiges d'antan?*—For William they are always there, like the eternal snows that crown the Himalayas.

For some reason or other, he was given a very small allowance on which to keep himself in Paris. Perhaps Mr. Nicholson had been advised by Cubley; perhaps he had heard that poverty was an essential condition of the artist's life. More likely he had already received intimations of difficulties at "the works," which were to come to a head at a very inconvenient moment of William's future. It was only by exercising a very strict (and unnatural) economy that William managed to make ends meet; but since everybody was in the same boat, there was no hardship in that. There were always a few extra francs to be picked up at cork pool—when he had reason to bless the old wooden billiard-table at home, which had made him into an expert player: enough to pay for an outing to Fontainebleau or Barbizon.

Deacon was sometimes in request as a cicerone. Together they visited the Moulin Rouge, where William saw the Can-can, and La Goulue dancing with her grisly partner. The medical student in Deacon suffered recrudescence, as he gazed with ghoulish satisfaction upon the pair.

"*He* can't last long!"

"Why not?" asks William innocently.

FIRST COMMUNION.
In the possession of J. W. Bacon.

"Eaten up with syphilis."

The magic is stripped from the scene; horror stalks across the shining floor, and when a young woman comes to sit on William's knee he is petrified, and doesn't know what to do about it. He has already been so scared by Deacon's warnings that he dares not put his lips to a spoon or glass without surreptitiously cleaning them with his napkin. This strange Paris, with its exquisite and glittering shell, its hidden fearsomeness!

He went to the church of St. Germain des Prés, and found it empty, save for an old negress, lighting a candle in front of one of the shrines. He painted flamingos in the Jardin d'Acclimatation, and copied the Velásquez of an Infanta in the Louvre—a copy which, to-day, looks much older than the original, which has been cleaned. And all the time he was feeling that expansion of the spirit that comes with one's first sojourn abroad. Newark and the life of the English provinces retreated, and the future became very clear and definite—reflected sometimes in a *bassin* of the Tuileries, sometimes in a mirror of one of the cafés which even the poorest of students manages to frequent.

He was down to the last gold coin in his pocket when he bought his first bilboquet in the rue de Rivoli. There was a Spanish student at Julian's who was a virtuoso of the bilboquet and William set out to rival him, and succeeded. This, his first, is much the biggest of his collection; it is made of boxwood, the ball is the size of a bowl and weighs three pounds, and its manipulation requires muscle as well as expertise.

He made no particular friend, certainly sustained no "influence" in his painting, from this first visit to Paris. That habit of "living through the eye" was well established; he was less interested to make personal contacts than to maintain his role of observer. One gets the impression of a lonely and self-contained little figure, moving largely in a dream. Going home to his lodgings, strange figures accompany him: the ladies of the night, *Les Passades* of Beardsley, cluster like moths, swirl, pause, pose momentarily under the high oil lamps—and dissolve in their own uncertainty.

Although much alone, he was never lonely. He was writing regularly to Mabel Pryde, and, when the time came to return, bought her a red Persian kitten, Frou-Frou, in the Place Vendôme.

3

He arrived in Newark with Frou-Frou, a number of canvasses, and a more settled frame of mind than before his departure, sold a still life—a red handkerchief, a violin and a prismatic shell—and settled down to work in his studio. It could not last, but he owed this much at least to his father's kindness. It is easy to picture William in Paris at that time; less easy to visualise him in Newark, where he must have looked about as much at home as an antelope in Regent Street.

The vivid life of Paris had left him ardent for experiment, and there was no possibility of art that he was not eager to explore. Among other things he now evolved the system of reproduction of which an early example is the little portrait of his grandmother, Mrs. Prior of Woodstock, drawn in 1894; the method was later used in the illustrations to Siegfried Sassoon's *Memoirs of a Foxhunting Man*. His first experiment in the medium was a little picture of Newark Fair, a night piece very Whistlerian in effect, and his latest is the magnificent head of a negress which he did as a jacket for my novel, *The Sun is My Undoing*.

It was now that he also became interested in the woodcut. In Ridge's bookshop in Newark he came across woodcuts for the first time. Ridge's had published some of the early work of Byron, and had a unique collection of old woodblocks which William always regrets not having acquired. When he got home he looked for a suitable piece of wood, planed it down, and knocked a pattern into it with nails and penknife. From this he printed his first woodcut; something might be done with that—some day.

4

When William and Mabel announced their intention of getting married, people took it as a joke. They were each the youngest of their respective families, and William, at twenty-one, would have passed for seventeen or eighteen. At Bushey they called him "The Kid," an appelative which lingered, it may be said, long after it ceased to be appropriate, and which, when its use came to be usurped by unauthorised persons, William grew to dislike. When the grandchildren took to addressing him as "Kid" he felt it was time to put his foot down, and the only person to-day who is authorised to use this *petit nom* is the enchanting Dolly Mann, William's partner of dancing class days, and constant and valued friend. He painted Dolly some time in 1905, and called the picture *The Brown Veil*; acquired by the Birmingham Corporation, this lovely picture of a lovely person is now labelled *Portrait of Mrs. Harrington Mann*; it was exhibited in the Goupil Gallery in 1911 under its original title. It was not the only time Dolly sat for him; he also painted her on glass, wearing a blue gown—a picture which, at the time of writing, is still in William's possession.

Mabel Pryde was twelve months older than her future husband and, as girls are said to grow up more quickly than boys, her sex may be said to have given her advantage. They decided to get married and tell their families afterwards.

After buying the wedding ring, William had one pound in cash and a commission of sorts. His father thought that Lord Radnor might buy a copy of the Velásquez which William had copied in the Louvre, and which his lordship had been pleased to admire. (The project did not mature; William painted the copy, but his lordship's admiration did not extend to purchase.)

The Prydes had moved to London on Dr. Pryde's retirement from the headmastership of his school. His theatre-mad clutch of women dragged him from his beloved Edinburgh (which they professed to despise, having the Northerner's naïve persuasion that London is the hub of the universe) and established him in town: where he was peacefully writing novels that were very bad imitations of Scott, and paying for their publication under a pseudonym.

The house they had taken in Bloomsbury was infested with mice, and whenever a mouse was trapped, Mrs. Pryde rang for their Scotch maid, Margaret, and gave her her bus fare to Victoria, with instructions to let the mouse out at the station. They left this house eventually because Mrs. Pryde, who spent most of her time knitting by the window, declared she could not bear to watch the people going by, in case they might be going to the British Museum Reading-Room: an experience she had once sampled, and which seemed to have left an unfortunate impression.

Mabel, who had the servant under her thumb, packed a small box and had it smuggled out of the house and taken to the Euston Hotel. Next day she and William took the train to Pinner, and walked to Ruislip, where William, having "established domicile" at a charming cottage called Primrose Hill Farm, had put up the banns. The news got out that a runaway couple were being married and when they arrived at the church they found a crowd assembled.

William and Mabel, grasping the situation, joined the crowd, and put up a very good pantomime of gazing up and down the road for the expected pair before slipping quietly into the church and getting married. When they emerged, the crowd was still patiently waiting, and took no notice of them when they strolled casually away. They walked back to Pinner, had a wedding breakfast of tea and plum cake, returned to town, and William left Mabel walking up and down the street in a high state of agitation while he went in to break the news to Dr. and Mrs. Pryde. The reactions of the latter were, to begin with, exactly what might be expected of a Victorian parent whose daughter has just eloped with a penniless young man; but it is to be presumed that William succeeded in "bewitching" her, as she eventually calmed down and sent Margaret out to fetch Mabel in to receive the parental blessing, in the midst of which scene William tactfully departed for Newark to take the second of his fences.

He found his father asleep in the green arm-chair in front of the fire, and, for the second time, made his confession.

His own family was charming about it. It is impossible that Mrs. Nicholson was not a little wounded at not having been present at her son's marriage, but she was angelic to him. She had been angelic to the girl, from their first meeting. One of her letters turns up in the black box which holds so many of our records. (She used to fold them in little triangles; when she wrote to William there would be a sovereign hidden under the wax with which they were sealed.)

"My dearest Mabel," she wrote, in her fine, pointed, gentle-woman's hand.

"Some of our friends cannot come, so now I am delighted to write and say we have room for you. I have written to your Mother this evening, asking her to spare you to us on the 23rd, I do hope she will let you come." (Dear Mrs. Nicholson! In her world young ladies still asked their mothers' permission before visiting friends.) "I am so pleased to hear you are better, and I do hope you will have a merry time with my dear ones and feel quite at home with us all, my husband included. I know you hear every little bit of news from Billie, he is so bright and well, and always hard at work. Dorothy is in bed with a bad cold, I must go and look after her.

"Yours with much love,

"ANNIE NICHOLSON."

Few young women can have received an equally reassuring letter from their prospective mothers-in-law, and few a more tender welcome than Mabel Nicholson, when her husband took her to Newark after the wedding.

William's father promised him an allowance of £150, which, in addition to his anticipated earnings, seemed affluence to the young pair. When he came to realise that, in taking on Mabel, he had taken on her family, he was young enough to be proud, rather than appalled; he liked being the strong man on whom this strange, exotic, exciting family depended. They spent their honeymoon at Primrose Hill Farm, of which William made a little woodcut, and he went to town twice a week to copy the Velásquez. They had been married on April 25th, 1893. He was a family man. And he had settled down. Metaphorically speaking. He had yet to discover that he had married a woman whose mania was for moving house. Within ten years they were to move eight times . . . but this prospect was mercifully hidden from William, who, in an even greater degree than the average man, hates domestic upheavals. One of his oldest friends said to me recently, "I always felt Nicholson loves houses more than people."

Honeymoons, however, do not go on for ever, and, seeking a permanent home, they heard that a little public house, the Eight Bells, at Denham, was to let.

CHAPTER FIVE

The Eight Bells—" J. & W. Beggarstaff"—The Woodcut—
" Queen Victoria"

I

A FEW DAYS after they settled into the Eight Bells, Jimmy Pryde arrived on a two days' visit and stayed two years. It was however an embarrassment that paid for itself, for during this period the Beggarstaff Brothers came into being. Not that they ever called themselves the Beggarstaff Brothers; the famous posters are signed J. & W. Beggarstaff—a name which Jimmy had found on an old sack, and which struck both of them as a good one for their partnership.

Life at the Eight Bells was very pleasant. They had as their neighbours a Mr. and Mrs. Butterfield—she had been in service at Buckingham Palace, fell in love with a groom and married him: and the pair of them kissing at the gate when he went to his work every morning was the prettiest sight in the world. She was a fine housekeeper and a splendid cook—her dinners, when they could afford dinners, were the envy of all the young Nicholsons' visitors. Now and then Mrs. Butterfield had a child as casually as she made a batch of her excellent loaves—and very nearly as quickly; she was back again, active, smiling, ready with good counsel for Mabel, almost before they had time to notice her absence. The only service apart from her occasional ministrations that they enjoyed was that of a village youth whom Mabel insisted on putting into page-boy's livery. He was as lazy as sin, would not get up in the mornings, and pulled the buttons off his livery to pay his losses in the games of marbles the Denham boys played in the lanes.

Now and again customers came—not knowing that the Eight Bells no longer had a licence—and were gravely served by their amateur hosts; their embarrassment when payment was refused added to the enjoyment of the game. Once the local squiress called, and Mabel, somewhat tousled with housework, opened the door. Eyeing her coldly, the visitor asked whether her mistress was in. Mabel lost her head, said she would find out, and fled to William to ask what she was to do. Eventually she changed her gown and descended to make stiff conversation with the caller, who, evidently deciding the household was crazy, did not call again.

In consideration of his friendship with Dr. Pryde, Irving always sent first night seats, with a little personal note, to the young married couple. William and Mabel, who were incapable of saving a penny for practical purposes, kept two boxes, one labelled FOR BOOTS, which was always empty, and the other THE IRVING FUND, to be used on Lyceum first nights. A "command" to the Lyceum (they regarded it as no less) meant a tramp along country lanes (no question of affording a carriage), Mabel's gown held up out of the mud, William guarding the immaculacy of his solitary dress-shirt, specially laundered for the occasion.

(It was the day of solitaire studs; a sad instance is on record of a night when the stud refused, in spite of all persuasion, to stay in its hole, and the nervous fidgetings of its owner surrounded it with a little dark halo, which blackened, not only the shirt, but his enjoyment of the evening, particularly as they were always invited to go behind for the first-night party. "It was *then*," says William, "I hated my damned stud most!")

It meant returning to Uxbridge on a midnight train and tramping out again to the Eight Bells. On one such night it snowed, and they read in the morning papers that some of the bus-drivers had been frozen to death on their boxes. Devotion to the theatre could go no farther; William's might not have gone so far, but from the day of their arrival in London, Mabel and her sisters had been using every cent they could beg, borrow or save to get into some pit or gallery where they fed their young souls on the highly-coloured fare of the Victorian theatre. For the glory and honour of being Irving's guest she would have walked barefoot across cinders. It was the merest chance that Ben Nicholson was not born in the theatre, as she insisted on seeing Mrs. Patrick Campbell in *The Second Mrs. Tanqueray* within a day or two of her accouchement.

Ellen Terry also showed them hospitality; she asked them to lunch at Barkston Gardens, where they met the late Lord Oxford, then Mr. Asquith; after luncheon (one uses the full word in deference to Ellen, who hated abbreviations) they played spillikins, at which, says William, Irving cheated. One may be sure he did it in the grand manner.

2

In spite of such diversions, life went on earnestly at the Eight Bells. The posters were coming to life, hours were spent in discussion and design, in simplification and resimplification, in cutting out and placing shapes and lettering. "So long," says William, "as we could make the bus horses shy, we knew we were on the right lines. You can't do that in oils."

The floor was littered with scraps of brown paper, black paper, red paper, William and Jimmy argued for hours about spacing—for which Jimmy had a great eye. Oddly enough, he was impatient and clumsy-handed when it came to execution. It was so in his painting; he had so unlikely a manner of holding the brush that he was almost painful to watch, and the results would hardly have been foretold by the most optimistic spectator. With the scissors he was completely outclassed by William—who used a knife on glass, and on whom fell most of the execution of the schemes they planned together. It was William, too, who used to go up to town in search of commissions, in the course of which came about his first meeting with Cochran (C.B.), who was then running a little theatrical agency in the Strand.

Thirty years later he was in Manchester, watching from the stalls one of those night-long dress rehearsals of a Cochran show to which he had contributed designs for one of the ballets—"The Rake," in *On With the Dance*. Mrs. Cochran, who was sitting next to him, turned suddenly to say:

"You've known Cocky for a very long time, haven't you?"

"Yes. I remember walking in the Strand with him when neither of us had a penny in our pockets.—And that, by the way, is exactly our position to-day!"

From all accounts, William did the lion's share of the Beggar-staff work, so it is amusing to find in a published interview of the period Jimmy taking the lead, "telling the tale," with only an occasional, rather lordly, reference to his partner.

"'I suppose,' I suggested" (it is the interviewer who speaks), "'that your views on art coincided greatly to commence with?'

"'I don't know,' said Pryde with some hesitation. 'It is very hard to relate, or even to trace the steps by which we grew together into our personal style; as a matter of fact, our opinions on artistic matters differed widely when we first became acquainted. Is that so, kid?' he added, looking towards Nicholson, the younger of the two, but the married man and father. Pryde always addresses Nicholson affectionately as 'Kid.'

"'Indeed it is,' said his friend, adding frankly and amiably, 'I am afraid I had very much to learn at that time.'"

If we concede that Jimmy had magnificent publicity value (a quality William has never cultivated, but which has come to him in its own subtle degree), it is not to belittle his share in the Beggarstaff conceptions. It was an excellent partnership, and each would, at that time, have been lost without the other. They were described (by the same interviewer, in *The Strand Magazine*) as "Pryde, tall, good-natured, stoical; Nicholson, nervous, anxious and intensely sensitive." He had plenty, at this time, to make him anxious.

Into this scene of peace and industry now bumbles the figure of Edward Gordon Craig, accompanied by his first wife, May; they wrote to say they were just coming back from tour, and could the Nicholsons put them up until their own place in Uxbridge was ready for occupation?

The Eight Bells was tiny. William would have refused, but Mabel . . . What! Refuse the son of Ellen Terry, to whom they were indebted for so many favours?—It ended in Teddy's sharing a bed with Jimmy, while May was tucked into the single small spare room. It was a marvel the walls contained them: Jimmy, as we have already said, always a little larger than life-size, with spacious attitudes and redundant gestures, Teddy, short-sighted, flapping his arms, swinging his "disguise cloak," incredibly clumsy—because of his short-sightedness—to such an extent that whatever he brushed against was sure to be knocked over, whatever he touched, broken.

From the moment of their entrance, they—characteristically—made the place their own. William opened the door one day to find a grand piano being delivered on the step.

"What's this about?"

"This is the Eight Bells, ain't it?"

"Well, what about it?"

"Well, this 'ere pianer was ordered yesterday by two gents."

"This is my house, and I wasn't one of them."

"We corn't 'elp that, guv'ner; this 'ere pianer was ordered and we was told to deliver it."

"I don't give a damn who told you to deliver it; take it away."

Jimmy and Teddy, much crestfallen, consoled themselves by

starting to tune the spinet, a beautiful little instrument which was William's particular delight, though he could not play a note. Mabel, who had a deep, pretty singing voice, used to sing Scotch songs, and sometimes to accompany herself on it. They tore the guts out of the spinet, sprinkled them round the carpet, and then, with those fine, those Irvingesque gestures which Jimmy could imitate, if anything, better than Teddy, abandoned it to its fate.

Even Mabel began to have enough of it. She was pregnant and the housework was too much for her. It likewise dawned on William that he might be better occupied than in pumping water, carrying coals and acting as man-of-all-work to his uninvited guests. Jimmy must stay—the posters had got to be worked out; but the Craigs must go, even if it meant a breach of the sacred laws of hospitality. Mabel would hardly have agreed, but that her time was imminent. It took, however, some lengthy series of hints, ever more and more pointed, before Teddy and his belongings were dislodged.

Ben Nicholson was born on April 10th, 1894. (A month and two days later a small girl was born in Liverpool, who, by the time she reached her fifteenth birthday, was underlining the name of William Nicholson whenever she came across it in print.) Fired by the dauntless example of Mrs. Butterfield, Mabel was up and walking into Uxbridge within a week of Ben's birth. For this indiscretion (she was warned by every one who knew her of the danger of her action) she was to pay in indifferent health for the rest of her life.

Meanwhile, the Beggarstaff posters went on. There was the grand Cinderella poster for Augustus Harris: red, black and yellow statement on white ground. There was the distinguished and beautiful Don Quixote commissioned by Henry Irving, which might, had it ever been used, have revolutionised the theatrical poster, so different was it from the gaudy vulgarities which then monopolised the hoardings. There was the fifteen-foot-high poster for Rowntree's Cocoa—all these were done at Denham, before the Beggarstaffs rented the Cromwell Road studio where, later, they carried on their work. There was also the beautiful *Girl on a Sofa*, acclaimed by *The Studio* as the Beggarstaffs' masterpiece, and turned down by Macmillan (who commissioned it) as "representative of a morbid French type." This is typical of the witless criticism against which the two young revolutionaries had to struggle; any one familiar with the psychology of their work would recognise that it is as English in inspiration and conception as a piece of Dover chalk.

Between August, 1894, and December, 1895, the Beggarstaffs produced ten designs, the almost illegible records of which afford ample evidence of the ups and downs of the artist's life. In some sporadic effort to be businesslike, William has drawn out five columns, headed respectively : 1, Design, 2, "For," 3, Price, 4, Date of Payment, 5, Notes. From these it appears that all they stood to earn for all those hours of labour which lasted often "until dawn came across the frosted fields" (again we quote the *Strand* interview) was the sum of £205. Actually, they made much less, for in the Notes column you may read:

"*The Hour*" (a paper which had commissioned a design) "failed, never got other £5" (on account of ten); while for *The Girl on the Sofa* there is a whole saga of effort and frustration:

"Macmillan didn't like the first design of Girl Reading (20 x 30) so exchanged it for Girl on Sofa on condition that size should not be altered. (*May.*) Altered size of Girl on Sofa so designed other of Girl Reading. (*July.*) Didn't like Girl Reading so got back all designs. (*September, 1895.*)" Dead loss, not only of the £20 commission, but of precious months of labour.

Patience. Hard work. Disappointment. They had plenty of all three. Now and again there was some encouragement, as when Henry Irving doubled the modest £50 the young artists were asking for the Don Quixote poster; yet, knowing them, it does not seem that this act of generosity would make up for the fact that the poster was never reproduced, "on score of expenses and short run." (The same tragic fate overtook *Robespierre*: this Play also was one of the Lyceum failures, and the superb Beggarstaff poster never saw the light.) They split their earnings fifty-fifty; sixty or seventy pounds did not come amiss to the bachelor Jimmy, but it was a seriously little sum to William, burdened with a family, and faced with an unpleasant shock regarding his private means. Mr. Nicholson wrote that, owing to temporary difficulty at "the works," he was unable to continue William's annuity.

3

No sooner was Mabel well (or as well as she was likely to be) than she insisted on another move: this time to a little house in Bedford Park—the attraction being the Craigs, who were living there at the time. She must get once more cheek by jowl with the adored Craigs, who perhaps had not been quite well treated over the Denham affair.

William made no demur; his finances were in such a bad way that the added expense of a removal was neither here nor there. The only thing to do was, by some means or other, to make more money. The posters had brought him and his partner some *succès d'estime*, but you cannot support a family on esteem.

It was now that his mind was turned seriously towards the woodcut, which in modern times was degenerated into a means of reproduction, the two forms of magazine illustration most in vogue being the line drawing and the woodcut, which got its effects of light and darkness by cross-hatchings and variation in depth and thickness of line. The illustrators themselves did not make their own cuts, which were done by skilled craftsmen from the original drawings.

Up in Northumberland, old Crawhall, father of Joseph Crawhall, was producing some woodcuts which William had seen and admired, and which fulfilled his conception of the woodcut as a direct means of expression; and presently the scissors and pastepot were laid aside for the woodblock and chisel, as William started to evolve his own "rule of the woodcut," which was as revolutionary in its turn as the Beggarstaff posters had been in theirs.

He never had a lesson in the woodcut, never saw one made, in his life; contrary to Edward Gordon Craig's claim to have "learned all he knew of the woodcut from William Nicholson," he never gave a lesson in it. But this was perhaps no more than one of Teddy's graceful ways of acknowledging a source of inspiration.

The idea was simplicity in itself. The posters had been an excellent training in the balance of masses and economy of means. The woodcut, as William saw it, was an extension of this method— black no longer limited to line, but equal in weight and value to white. "The nail hole that didn't register," previously referred to, was the whole germ of the new idea, which was pure statement in equally balanced masses of black and white, as solid as moonlight and shadow, and as decorative in effect as the posters themselves.

With the memory behind him of the little old blocks he had seen at Ridge's, and of Bewick's cuts which adorned the broadsheets of their day, William set to work to evolve the style which, even more than the Beggarstaff posters, was to "put him on the map" as an artist and innovator of existing art forms.

4

The Prince of Wales's horse, Persimmon, had just won the Derby, and William, who knew little about horses or equine anatomy, and had never drawn a horse in his life, got hold of every available pictorial record of Persimmon and produced his first serious woodcut, which he took, at Phil May's suggestion, to Brown (father of the present Oliver Brown of the Leicester Gallery) who was running the Fine Arts Society in Bond Street.

Brown showed no enthusiasm, held out no hopes of a sale, but promised to show it, and to advertise it, if William could supply him with a certain number of prints. William possessed no printing press at the time, and did his printing in the most primitive fashion; in fact, he described his work, correctly, as "Printed by foot and coloured by hand."

Persimmon, advertised, sold only one copy, which was later returned with the following letter—more explicit than flattering in its contents:

"*18 High Street, Doncaster.*   *September 4th, 1896.*

"Dr Sir,—I return you the Persemmon (*sic*) you sent—I really cannot show it—to me it's a nightmare—can't describe it in any other way.

"Yrs v. truly,

"John Fogg."

In spite of which crushing dismissal, it gained him an important admirer. Whistler, who was going through the gallery to arrange for the hanging of some of his etchings, saw *Persimmon* and inquired the name of the artist. Brown told him, and suggested that Whistler should recommend William to Heinemann, with whom, at that time, Whistler was staying.

Artists are proverbially generous to each other. Whistler remembered, and the outcome was a letter, inviting William to call at the Heinemann offices.

He had hardly the price of a square meal, but felt it was incumbent on the dignity of the occasion to arrive in a cab—

a wasted gesture, as the offices turned out to be upstairs, and there was no witness of this opulent arrival. Heinemann received him cordially; it was not every day he received young artists bearing such credentials as an introduction from James McNeil Whistler. He wanted, he said, *ideas*; and William, who, on this occasion at least, showed some of the paternal shrewdness, suggested an Alphabet, at a fiver a letter. Having commissioned A, it was bound to go on to Z, which would secure the rent for twenty-eight weeks at any rate!

The Nicholsons had moved again—this time to a dingy little basement flat in Avonmore Gardens, where Mabel was sickly most of the time, and William powdered Ben with one hand and did woodcuts with the other. There was hardly any light in their cramped sitting-room—and Jimmy was again with them. A hammering came on the door one night when they had gone to bed, and Jimmy rushed in gasping—"Put out the light—and, if anybody comes say no one's here!"—with which he went to earth, and, sure as fate, footsteps descended to the basement door and the hammering started again.

William insisted that no one had been, and when the tumult and the shouting died, Jimmy, emerging, admitted to having, as sequel to a night's carousal, knocked over a coffee stall on top of its owner and patrons, who had sent the police after him. As a consequence of this escapade, he continued to nest with his brother-in-law for some weeks.

Heinemann's next suggestion, when the Alphabet was finished, was a calendar. He showed William a luridly-executed almanack of heraldic German designs, and asked him if he could do something of that sort. William said No, he was afraid not, but suggested the Almanack of British Sports, which he intimated was more likely to go down with the public than heraldry. This, and the series of portraits in woodcut he started for Henley, then editor of *The New Review*, may be said fairly to have launched him, and he reached fame for the first time with the great Jubilee woodcut of Queen Victoria.

The Queen Empress had invariably been presented with every device of pomp and panoply that could conceal from the notoriously truth-disliking public eye the fact that Victoria of Great Britain and India was a dumpy little old woman whose dignity (which none who saw her would deny) derived from her own perfect conviction of her own omnipotence.

It was William who first had the temerity to present this

unheroic old figure just as it was: an animated tea-cosy, walking an Aberdeen in the gardens of Kensington Palace. He did it lightly, unmaliciously, and in terms that would startle, yet, on second thoughts, appeal to the British public. Plastered with jewels, the Garter ribbon bulging over her improbable bust, Victoria was all very well; but here was a nice old lady who would offer them tea and inquire after their rheumatism if they happened to drop in when passing the palace! In place of their old illusion William gave them a new illusion; it was bound to be a success . . . but Heinemann did not see it in that light at all. The sensitive Teutonic nose smelt *lèse majesté*; he did not want to publish it.

His partner, however, Sidney Pawling, at once recognised its merits, and showed it to W. E. Henley, who, fired with enthusiasm, asked William if he minded its being "doubled in half," in which way it could be published on a double page in *The New Review*. William agreed, and it caused an instant furore. Heinemann regretted his misjudgment—and William was launched on a new venture: for Henley commissioned a series of portraits, suggesting, among others, Whistler and Rudyard Kipling as subjects.

Kipling was just coming into the limelight; Henley had received *Hanging Danny Deever* on the back of a postcard, and could talk of nothing else. Conrad was another of the subjects he suggested, for *The Nigger of the Narcissus* was running as a serial through *The New Review*.

The New Review, with Henley's personality behind it, was a beacon to the literary genius of the day, and to all who came in contact with him, William included, Henley was a source of mighty inspiration. It may not be generally known that Stevenson's conception of Long John Silver derived from Henley: the bellow from the head of the stairs, the crutch hurled down, the heavy, helpless body crashing after it, clutching by the banisters, were all Henley, coming down to join his guests for lunch: as the "face like a ham" was Henley—a description that so obsessed William, when he started on the portrait, that he could hardly get on, until one day he happened to notice Henley's hat, the big, broad-rimmed, crumpled, generous hat that seemed to have absorbed its owner's personality. The Ham in the Hat!

Henley was delighted with the portrait, and William deeply touched when, after the hero's death, the widow sent him the hat, which, she wrote, Henley had wanted him to have.

CHAPTER SIX

*Whistler and Walter Greaves—Rudyard Kipling—Working
for Heinemann—The Roaring 'Nineties*

I

ON WHISTLER'S suggestion, William was asked down to Heinemann's house at Thames Ditton for the week-end: a great occasion, for it marked his first meeting with Whistler.

It was getting on for lunch-time when William arrived, and Whistler had not put in an appearance. Heinemann, a great stickler for the social proprieties, was fussing and fuming, and finally insisted on going out in search of him: and there, in the village street, was the Master, clad, as usual, in spotless white, peacefully doing a little pochade of a woman in a red dress, leaning against a shop window—quite undisturbed by sections of the proletariat which, leaning on his shoulder and blowing down his ear, admonished him at intervals to "go an' get 'is 'air cut"—a terrible act of irreverence, from William's point of view.

Whistler, however, was taking it in the best of good parts; he closed his box and accompanied his host and fellow-guest back to lunch, after which they strolled off to Hampton Court, where William made the gratifying discovery that all his favourite pictures were also Whistler's.

The Victorian laurels were still wreathed about his young brow, but no compliments brought him such delight as the Master's:

"A wonderful portrait, Mr. Nicholson."

William modestly replied that it was "a wonderful subject," to which Whistler, with his usual happiness in turning a neat phrase, replied:

"You know, Her Majesty might say the same of you."

The sitting for the portrait began shortly after this meeting. For the purposes of the woodcut, Whistler changed out of his usual white suit into a dark one. When the preliminary drawing was half-finished, he said suddenly, "Oh—excuse me: I've forgotten something"—went into his dressing-room and reappeared with the little crimson thread of the Légion d'Honneur

64

WALTER GREAVES.
By courtesy of the City Art Gallery, Manchester.

in his buttonhole: a decoration of which he was very proud, less for its intrinsic value than as a fleer at the British Government, which had not seen fit to make any recognition of his genius.

The name of Whistler must be for ever linked with that of Walter Greaves.

The Greaveses were a family of watermen on the Thames, who used to row Whistler about when he did his paintings. The father had been boatman to Turner, and Walter became studio man and general factotum to Whistler.

He knew a great deal about painting, and was very good indeed, even before he came under the Master's influence. He said he had "picked it up" in painting his boats. The Tate has an excellent specimen of Walter's work, and William has a little snow scene on the Embankment which was given to him by our friend Ada Pringle, who picked it up at Christie's. Walter had something of the same primitive outlook as the Douanier Rousseau, with much more accomplishment; he knew Chelsea by heart, and could paint the Embankment brick for brick; the Redfern Gallery recently exhibited a little scene of Cremorne which was typical of Walter at his best.

Whistler had a tender passion for Walter's sister Tinny, and painted her; Walter did a beautiful full-length of Tinny, which was bought by the Johannesburg Gallery on William's recommendation. He now regrets it went so far away.

He had an amazing street make-up, to which William does justice in his *Portrait of Walter Greaves*: the angular figure of Walter, striking an attitude against a white piano (who else would have thought of painting Walter against a piano?), is clothed in a tail-coat, topper and bright yellow necktie. The latter was almost always grimy, as he used to dye his hair and moustache with a kind of charcoal mixture, which, towards midday, started to fall off on his ears and collar. There were terrible heartburnings when, later in life, Walter became a pensioner of Charterhouse, and, as such, was required to take hot baths. "Wocher want to wash yer 'ands for?" he used to say bitterly. "Wash 'em all away, won'cher?"

Walter, hard up, took a bundle of his canvasses to a dealer in Holborn, who sold them to Marchant of the Goupil, who arranged an exhibition. *The Times* came out with a spanking notice, and Marchant sent a message to William: "I wish you'd come down and look after Walter Greaves for me; I've got the

E

place full of Pressmen, and poor Walter doesn't know what to do with them."

William and Augustus John went up, secured Walter, pinned him down on a settee, and primed him in the gentle art of dealing with the Press, and, in the middle of it all, in came Tinny, looking like Queen Elizabeth in a red window curtain. "Well, Walter, we're going it, aren't we? One day we'll be able to 'ave a motor-car wiv a footman sitting up be'ind, 'n'ev'rything!"—a bright prospect which, unfortunately, was never realised; all the drawings had passed out of Walter's possession, and he was not actually due for a penny, though Marchant was generous and gave him a good present.

Among other offices, he was a kind of watchdog for Whistler. When Whistler was painting Sarasate, he could not get enough sittings, and was in despair. At last he sent Walter for the famous Italian model, Antonio, known to all contemporary painters of the nude. When he had got, as it were, the framework, it would be easy enough to graft Sarasate's clothes on to Antonio.

Mrs. Whistler, dropping in one day when her son was out, inquired how the portrait was getting on. Walter said it was getting on fine. Mrs. Whistler said she would like to see it; Walter replied that he didn't think Jimmy would like her to see it —yet. Perhaps resenting Walter's assumption of authority, the old lady insisted, turned the canvas round from the wall against which it was leaning, and got the shock of her life, when she saw a fine nude, crowned by Sarasate's head.

Like most painters, Whistler was always being plagued by his creditors, whom it was Walter's business to keep at bay. On one occasion, however, a Jew got in, and Walter was obliged to admit he couldn't get rid of him. Whistler bounded into the room, eyes flashing and head like a white flame, to confront his unwelcome visitor.

"Are you the chap who killed our Lord?—Come on, Walter: open the window and out with him!"

The terrified Jew went like a stag.

In more recent times—it was shortly before the war of 1914—William thought he would take Walter to see an exhibition of the moderns: Cézanne, Picasso, Van Gogh and so forth. Making a party of it, he picked Walter up in a taxi, which he stopped at Dash and Bellamy's, bought a basket of plovers' eggs, rushed into another shop for some red pepper, and told the man to drive on—Walter solemnly munching plovers' eggs (for the first time in his life), with an expression that suggested he regarded them as a much overrated delicacy. The paintings made no more impression on him than his *hors d'œuvres*; his only comment was : "Expensive, them bright colours ; you don't want to use a lot o' bright colours like that."

William was painting Smuts in a studio lent to him by Harrington Mann while the latter was in America. Walter would often drop in from his home nearby in Chelsea, and arrived one day when Smuts was there. William introduced him to the General as "a famous painter."

"Well, Mr. Greaves," said Smuts. "So you're another of these London painters. Why don't you people come out to South Africa?—You'd see some light and colour there."

"I don't know so much about that," said Walter sturdily. "Jimmy says——"

"Jimmy?"

"Jimmy Whistler; everybody knows Jimmy. Jimmy always said, in London there's atmosphere. You don't want all them bright colours, do you? A bit of Antwerp blue, an' white, an' black's all you want: *and paint thin.*"

His parting shot from the door when he took his departure was: "Don't you forget, General: you don't want a lot o' colour. You *paint thin.*"

One thing brought a little grist to the mill during this lean period: William obtained a post as visiting master at one of the art schools in Kensington. He enjoyed it to begin with; teaching has at least one virtue—it obliges one to crystallise one's knowledge. Never of an analytic nature, it is probable that he had never before troubled to examine the steps of his own artistic progress; his new task obliged him to do so, and to formulate a theory which he had previously taken very much for granted.

But when one set of students had been taken through their course, another was waiting to be started. The weary, cyclical grind of teaching was the last thing to appeal to William, who could do a thing once brilliantly, but to whom repetition spelt the end of inspiration. He was stale and bored before the second set was through his hands, and was glad, even though it meant loss of emoluments, to escape from an occupation which meant *talking*, not *doing*.

2

In pursuit of Henley's commission for a woodcut of Kipling, William took lodgings down at Rottingdean. On his arrival he had occasion to go into the local chemist's, in whose shop was the as yet not very common public call-box. Waiting for his order, William was entertained by the loud, resentful trumpetings of a male voice. The speaker was evidently trying to hire a carriage—he specified a carriage with rubber tyres—from Brighton: with no effect, for he presently burst out of the box exclaiming, "My God! One might be asking for a nickel-plated dragon!" The fiercely tufted eyebrows, deep-set eyes and choleric cleft chin of Kipling were instantly recognisable; it presently appeared that he was trying to get a carriage to take his pregnant wife for a drive in the country.

The portrait was started in Burne-Jones's house, which had been lent to the Kiplings, and in the evenings, Kipling, who had taken a fancy to Mabel, used to come round, sit on a black box in their little, flea-infested lodgings and tell stories. He and William took to walking the downs, exercising William's son and Kipling's daughter. On such a day they sat watching a downland shepherd folding his sheep. As each sheep popped into the pen, the old man counted it in a strange formula which sounded to William like "Eena, meena, mina, mo." Kipling said, "Do you know what he's doing? He's counting them in Saxon numerals."

William had brought down with him his *Almanac of British Sports*, on which he was then working, and Kipling became very interested, and started to write verses for them. William told Heinemann, who at once suggested a collaboration. The proof of *Coaching* in William's possession bears an unpublished verse in Kipling's writing:

"Youth on the box and Liquor in the boot,
My Lord drives out with My Lord's prostitute."

During this visit to Rottingdean, William had his first and only glimpse of Burne-Jones, wheeling his grandchildren in a perambulator. It had started to rain, and Burne-Jones was running up the village street for shelter. In the approved manner of the interviewer, I asked William if he got any sort of impression of the great pre-Raphaelite.

"Well . . ." said William, after serious thought. "I thought he ran well for his age."

3

Heinemann, who had so disliked the *Queen Victoria*, was only too glad to republish it after the failure of *The New Review*.

William was now well "in" with the firm; he had followed up his *Alphabet* and *Almanac* with *London Types*, for which Henley wrote the verses, and his *Characters of Romance* and *Portraits* (both published in 1900) were coming along. From the black box comes, haphazard, a charming letter from Walter de la Mare, which, written in 1936, shows that the fascination of the *Characters* was not a thing of the moment.

"DEAR NICHOLSON,—This letter has only the very frailest excuse, but I thought it might amuse you a little. It is only to say that when I am ill I shift my quarters to another bedroom where hang six of your 'Characters of Romance.' About eight years ago I spent weeks in bed there when I was very ill, and recently spent another four, more or less ill. You know what queer prejudices may spring up in illness, and how weary one may get of even the familiar and the delighted in. Well, I have surveyed these six pictures in those circumstances—the other six are not yet framed—thousands of times, and never once without interest and delight. And why the hell *not*, you may reply. But I am sure you will understand and excuse this infantile confession. I felt impelled to make it.

"With all best wishes,
"Yours sincerely,
"WALTER DE LA MARE."

The admiration was reciprocal; William, whose love for poetry—in particular the lyric form—has filled a box with the manuscript poems of his many friends among the contemporary poets, cherishes this tribute from one of the loveliest of them all.

At this time he designed as a present for Heinemann the well-known windmill which is the colophon of the firm. Years later,

E. V. Lucas made an appeal for the preservation of the windmills of England, which was given much publicity by Heinemann. Asked to subscribe, William replied, With pleasure, so long as the good work started with the restoration of the Heinemann mill— the care taken in the original design of which had entirely vanished in the reproduction. The delicate hint was taken, and the mill of to-day is true to William's original.

Among some book-jackets which he designed was that for Magda Heinemann's brilliant translation of D'Annunzio's *Il Fuoco*. Magda was Heinemann's handsome and dazzling wife, who kept Heinemann on the tips of his toes until he divorced her. At one of his dinners, at which Whistler was present, the hostess failed to put in appearance until half-way through the meal, when she entered in furs, hat and veil, with complete nonchalance. Heinemann, fussily mortified, instantly assailed her with questions.

"Why are you late? What have you been doing? Where have you been?"

For a while she ignored them, but, as he persisted, put a stop to them with the blistering answer:

"Willy, dear, if you ask me that again, *I shall tell you*!"

One can imagine the success such a retort—so completely after his own heart—would have with The Butterfly.

With the idea, no doubt, of providing a suitable frame for this syren, Heinemann bought her a sumptuous bed, belonging to an eighteenth-century French courtesan. William, who admired it very much, bought it in the sale after the divorce, and it became a kind of gorgeous white elephant, spending much of its after-life in storage, until we were refurnishing the front bedroom at Apple Tree.

4

Those were the last great days of Bohemia, the roaring 'nineties, when the Victorian octopus was beginning to lose its stranglehold on the art of the nation, when barmaids, flower-girls and cab-drivers contributed their racy aroma to the London bouquet, when painters, poets and actors had not found it necessary to look like stockbrokers and the anæmia of Mayfair had not broken into the world of art. There was no mingling of the *beau monde* with Bohemia—to the disadvantage of both; the terms artist and gentleman had not become confused, and each would have been offended had the description which properly belonged to one been applied to the other.

While the stage-door johnnies were buying diamond garters for their mistresses in the chorus, while prosperous City men rented little houses for their lady friends down at Twickenham, Bohemia had its own aristocracy: almost its own livery. Whistler was the first to strike a blow at the popular conception of the artist as a seedy, velvet-coated, long-haired Bohemian; it was William who dealt it the *coup de grace.*

The first present he bought himself with the lifting of the financial cloud was the spotted silk dressing-gown which was later to figure in Orpen's picture of *A Bloomsbury Family.* (On the left, William, a neat Georgian skeleton, draped in folds of black and white silk; the children in a somewhat self-conscious group round the table, with Kit, long-skirted, staring out of the portrait with boot-button eyes, on the right; and Mabel, most inappropriately shadowy in the background. Painted, for some reason, in a hat, she has more the air of a casual visitor than of the rightful mistress of the *mise-en-scène.*)

The yellow waistcoats—delight of William's caricaturists—had also come into being, and the spotted shirts, which, having now almost an air of "period," were then all the rage; they were, however, worn with plain white collars, until William carried dandyism to the extent of having shirt and collar made in one, and of the same material—an extravagance which the mutability of collars and the expense of laundry bills has since modified. Collars were worn high; William's were a little higher than any one else's—he admits it himself, in the self-caricature, "seeking glory even in the cannon's mouth"; and Max's immortal drawing published in *The Owl* shows a minute, hypochondriacal segment of face wedged in between a six-inch collar and the brim of a pork-pie-shaped fedora.

Nor did fancy stop at this. When Jimmy Pryde burst into a "Gentleman Joe" of café-au-lait with buttons the size of Abernethy biscuits, William came back with a covert cloth riding-coat with more cut and waist to it than any horseman ever dreamt of. With this creation he sported, sometimes a brown bowler, sometimes a topper of hatter's plush. He and Jimmy had each invested in one in Seven Dials, where the cabbies got the hats that gave them such a knowing air. They were told by the hatter that the way to keep these sleek and in order was with applications of stout: which was all very well in chilly weather, but converted them into positive fly-traps in summer. The object of the green veils worn by the dandies in Frith's *Derby Day* became apparent. There is, however, no record of William and Jimmy taking to green veils.

What with Augustus John's ear-rings and apostolic beard ("How old is Gus?" someone asked Jimmy one night at the National Sporting Club. Jimmy looked across the ring. "I don't know; but it must be getting dam' nearly time for his cruci-fixion"), Orpen's muffler and cape, Sickert's hobnailed boots, peg-top trousers and choker, there must have been a pleasant air of *bal masqué* about the Café Royal, then, and up to the time of the last war, the resort of all Bohemia. They trailed with them an odd-looking set of young women, who roused the sometimes irreverent attention of the occasional actress or lady of joy whose escort brought her to the café, with their trailing versions of the dead-as-mutton pre-Raphaelite styles. John was already putting his women into early Italian gowns. It may be imagined that the scanty bodices and clumsily-gathered skirts roused much mirth in the beruffled and corsetted followers of contemporary fashion. Mabel was among the few who did not subscribe to the accepted vogue for painters' ladies; she had a fancy for the fashionable herself.

Among that coloratura assembly stands out a figure whose long lachrymose face, plastered about the brow with its black cowlick, and loose-hung limbs clad in the invariable horsey check and riding-breeches, is almost as familiar to us to-day through contemporary sketches as it was to those who knew it in the flesh. Out of the black box comes a flat, architect's pencil, labelled in William's writing, "This is Phil May's pencil"—Phil May, gentlest of beings, beloved by all who knew him; seldom sober, always penniless—having given away all the money that he had not "liquidated" in the bars where, not only on account of his custom, he was the most welcome and respected patron. Phil would give away his gold watch to a tramp, and the stories of his generosities are legion.

He was married to a sweet-natured, easy-going creature called Lil, who told him one morning that she must have some fish for Sunday's dinner. Phil said he had no money, but there was always a box in the studio into which he threw the sketches from which he worked; he put a roll of these into his pocket and set out to cash them at the Fine Arts Society, which would always

buy Phil's drawings. Unfortunately, the way to Bond Street—
for Phil—lay via the Savage Club.

. . . At about one o'clock on the following morning, he
thought it was time to be getting home—and suddenly remembered the fish. The cabby, who, like all the London cabbies, knew
Phil, was told to stop at a fish shop near Toole's theatre in the
Strand, where Phil was well known. When they arrived there, the
shop was, of course, closed up, but Phil, nothing daunted, climbed
on the box, borrowed the whip and hammered on the upper
windows. When the fishmonger appeared, blinking with sleep,
Phil explained that he had promised to take his wife home some
fish, and dared not appear without it.

Willing as the fishmonger was to oblige Phil, whom, like
everybody else, he adored, he had to tell him that, as it was
Saturday night, he was sold out; there was not so much as a
whitebait in the shop—only a lot of cracked ice. Phil insisted upon
looking for himself, so down came the fishmonger in his nightshirt, opened the door, lit the gas, and Phil poked about among
the unsavoury relics of the day's trade until he found a big conger
eel lying in a corner. He declared that would do, wrapped it up
himself, and set out for home and beauty.

Experience had taught Phil that he could get away with
murder if he made Lil laugh; so he woke her up, showed her the
conger eel, told her the story, and she laughed herself sick—until
the conger turned out to be wrapped up in the drawings which
Phil had set out to sell.

Those were the days! Yet the giants were not all of Phil's
generation. William has a charming story of old Dr. Pryde, who,
having thrown off the restrictions of a dominie's life, was
rapidly "reverting to the briar." It will be remembered that he
came of humble origins—his brother was a cab-driver in
Edinburgh: a fact which rankled in the memory of the ex-
Miss Lauder of the Bass, whose attitude to her husband was
always tinged with tolerance, if not superiority. Transplanted
from his native soil, Dr. Pryde's accents became more sturdily
Caledonian than ever, and he and his old friend Dr. Wallace, some
time minister of the Church of Scotland, some time editor of the
Scots Observer, some time law student—he actually passed his
articles, and practised as junior to his son in London—and briefly
Member of Parliament, when his oratory filled the benches, got
together to glorify the flowing bowl.

Mrs. Pryde, for her own inscrutable reasons, elected to make a hero of Dr. Wallace; it was she who invented the astonishing and quite unfounded story of a double, for whose indiscretions poor Dr. Wallace invariably got the blame. Dr. Wallace's daughter, who knew better, tried to curb the old gentleman's propensity for convivial society by hiding his hat: a quite useless manœuvre, as Dr. Wallace, with perfect equanimity, appropriated one of his daughter's hats, and beamed upon his favourite company in total indifference to the knots of ribbon that dangled upon his shoulders.

So when Tom McNee gave a birthday party at the Roebuck, William was delighted to act as escort to the two old roisterers, who, from the moment of their introduction, had the whole party in their hands. Tom was the son of Sir Daniel McNee who was President of the Royal Scottish Academy; he had been a student at Julian's before William went there, and the legend still lingered of "*le grand écossais*" who might well have been the original of du Maurier's Laïrd of Cockpen. He stood well over six feet in his socks, had played International Rugger for Scotland, and married a barmaid before settling down as mine host of the Roebuck at Richmond.

Dr. Wallace drained the punch bowl at a draught, before "obliging" with "Wullie brew'd a peck o' maut" to an enraptured audience. Phil May also sang and danced on the table; when in his cups, Phil used to sing "I am but a poor blind boy" with such pathos that the listeners were reduced to tears.

Lil must have waited long on the night of Tom McNee's birthday party, of which William's clearest recollections are of his struggles to get the two old gentlemen home to Bloomsbury when it was over.

CHAPTER SEVEN

Woodstock : Happy Days

I

ELM LODGE, MITCHAM, was quite a nice little house: the nicest they had had since they were married. Not only Mabel, but, this time, William as well, was anxious to move as soon as possible from the squalid little flat in Avonmore Gardens. But this time William, overburdened with work, told Mabel she must shift for herself, and gave her *carte blanche* to find a new domicile. He was turning out hand-coloured copies of the woodcuts as fast as he could for Heinemann: printing them in Chiswick and finishing off thirty or forty a day. The whole floor was covered with sheets of white cardboard, and all the slow, tedious work of mounting was left in his hands.

Mabel, enjoying herself immensely, found the house, and one day brought him the lease, which he signed for five years. He was hardly conscious that the furniture was being carted out under his nose, that he had only a chair and a table to work upon, when she informed him that the new house was ready, and that William was to catch an afternoon train, which she would meet, and take him to the new home.

He missed the train, got involved in other matters, and ended by catching the last train, which got in at midnight of a black night, pouring with rain. His only companion in the railway carriage was a cheerful drunk, who declared he knew every inch of the common, and would show William the way; but after they had been stumbling about in the dark for something like an hour, and were soaked to the skin, William's confidence in his escort died.

He and Mabel had had a signal whistle at Bushey, and at last, worn out with wandering, with the rain beating into his face and running down the back of his neck, he stood still and sent the thin little summons ringing into the darkness. At last came a faint reply, and, William whistling and Mabel answering, at some black hour of the morning he stumbled into his new home.

There were trees, and some garden, and the common to wheel

75

the perambulator on: but in spite of the five years' lease, they were out of it within a few months of Tony's birth, on April 23rd, 1897. Chaucer's House, Woodstock, came into the market: the house which, for its associations and its intrinsic charm, was most truly *home* to William of any he has ever occupied. Even Sutton Veny, with its high hall, its green lawns flowing up to the walls and the room in which his bed was level with the windowsill across which he looked at his beloved downs, never compensated William for the deep cupboards from which Mrs. Prior had dosed her little grandson, and the door from which he sallied forth to paint Blenheim Bridge by Sunset.

From that same door Miss Ann Prior had passed, all white satin and orange blossoms, to her wedding with Mr. Nicholson of Newark-on-Trent; William has a charming record of his parents' wedding taken under the original Blenheim Orange-tree in the garden; and "Auntie Sap's" name was scratched with the diamond of her engagement-ring on a pane of glass in one of the windows. All the planning and arrangement of the in- and out-of-doors was the work of his mother's family. No wonder that, in coming to Chaucer's House, William felt he was coming home.

Among some papers belonging to Mrs. Edward Nicholson was found the following:

"The family of Prior, formerly settled in the counties of Essex, Oxford, Lancaster and Cambridge, and since the year 1636 in Ireland, derives from John Priorur, who held a charter from Henry III., and did homage for the same in the year 1218.

"Thomas Priorur, who died possessed of considerable property in lands both in Oxfordshire and Essex, and was living at Woodstock, was sent for by the Officers of the Queen's Household at the time Queen Philippa was in Woodstock, on the occasion of the birth of her eldest son, and he was admitted to the Queen's bedchamber to see the Royal Infant, and to be a witness of the birth, and was then immediately despatched to inform the King, Edward III., of the event."

The house itself, of grey Oxfordshire stone, flush with the pavement and immediately opposite the great gates of Blenheim Palace, is built into the old wall of Woodstock Park, one of the country estates of Queen Elizabeth, the manor itself having been pulled down when Vanbrugh built the palace. It takes its name from Chaucer's chapel, part of which was incorporated into the building.

There were all sorts of charming things about Chaucer's

House—including the walled garden which lay behind. The rooms were small, with beautiful panelling, which William painted white; from the back of the house one looked down the garden and across the wall into a wide dip of valley, through which ran the Banbury Road. Beyond the garden lay a yard and two cottages—one of them occupied by the gardener and the other let, which should have been a minor source of revenue; its rent was supposed to pay for the studio which William was obliged to take, as there was no suitable room for painting, but in point of fact, like most cottage property, it was a continual drain on its owner's resources.

There is always something peculiarly restful in returning to the scene of a happy childhood; young May and little William had played under the Blenheim Orange-tree; now there were young Ben, Tony in his perambulator, and, presently (the Nicholsons seemed to have had a way of celebrating new domiciles by producing a new child there) Nancy, who a few years later was toddling about the grass, solemn in plaits and a checked frock, with a pet dove on her head.

The old walls, the familiar scene struck William with a sense of permanence—that permanence which, since his marriage, seemed to have been mislaid. They were worth working for, they held the pattern of a future which, up to that moment, was but dimly planned. William is a liver in the present; he is neither shadowed by the past nor befairied by the future—which, indeed, is the essence of content. Of his kind, to whom every new day is an adventure, it must have been written, "They shall not grow old . . ."

But one could not see Chaucer's House without looking back and looking forward: back to the grandparents whose graves were hard by in Woodstock churchyard, and forward to the time when Ben and Tony, and perhaps others as well, should be tall enough to pluck the fruit from the Blenheim Orange-tree. Not, let it be said, that William is a naturally paternal person; one has only to see him with the grandchildren to realise that he is a child among children. He has none of the desire to control, to command, which is the adult attitude to the young. It was perhaps Mabel's failure to recognise that which robbed their relationship of an element which would have strengthened and made it happier: an odd oversight, on the part of so maternal a being. As each child appeared she idolised it more than the last; to be separated from them, if only for a day, made her miserable.

Even their little possessions were invested, for her, with maternal sentiment.

In some vague attempt at clearing up Apple Tree, hundreds of letters from the children to Mabel were discovered, tied up in bundles, as she left them at her death; she must have kept every line that Ben, Tony, Nancy and Kit ever wrote to her from the moment they could hold a pencil—and not only all their own letters, but all the letters relating to them: trite notes from nurses, saying that Tony was just cutting a tooth, and Nancy was growing out of her dancing slippers and wanted some new underclothes.

Somehow the money was found, and Chaucer's House was William's. How pleased his mother was! For her too it was a homecoming, when she paid her first visit to her son under his own roof, and Mr. Nicholson, walking in the garden with Ben's hard little fist clasped in his hand, shared her pleasure. He was tremendously proud of William in these days; *William's name had been in the papers*—that was enough, according to simple Newark standards, to justify paternal pride. There was nothing of the shoddy Bohemian life, from which his imagination shrank, about this dignified little house which had come, very properly, into the possession of a Nicholson. (There was one thing which desperately shocked the old gentleman. William, for some inexplicable reason, took it into his head to work a cross-stitch kettleholder. When he exhibited it with pride—a speaking likeness of the fox terrier, *with a loose tail that wags*—Mr. Nicholson's comment was coagulated with Victorian ice, on the unseemliness of such an occupation for a married man of twenty-two!)

On New year's morning they awoke to the tinkle of bells and the rhythmic clumping of hobnailed boots: the Morris dancers from Witney, with their smocks and their top hats wreathed with flowers and ribbons. No more of London!—William breathed in the crisp morning air and felt himself a countryman, which he is at heart. And in another two years' time Tony was up on his sturdy legs, big enough to wear the little smock made for him by Mabel, to have a red and white spotted bandanna knotted round his neck and to ride the ass with garlanded neck and beribboned tail which accompanied the Morris dancers. It was Tony, with his round, smiling face, who took round the hat for their collections, and who, at some moment in the dance, was lifted high in the air, up above their heads.

William painted the charming scene; he did at least two more paintings of the Morris dancers—entering on one of the most productive phases of his career. Financial pressure had lessened— or perhaps one was less aware of it, within those friendly walls.

The one drawback to Chaucer's House was that it had only one door, through which, not only visitors, but household goods, had to be admitted. On a frosty day, when William and a friend had been riding in the park, and were relaxing in dressing-gowns before the drawing-room fire, the door bell rang. Mabel entered in a fluster.

"Get out of here quickly! That's the duchess—the milk and the bread have been!"

Jimmy came down at Christmas, full of a murder story he was by way of writing, and wanted William to illustrate. After listening to Jimmy's recital, William came to the conclusion that the best illustration would be a record of the house in which the murder took place, and suggested an old inn called Sturgess Castle, a few miles along the Banbury Road.

Jimmy said he would like to see it, so they took their bicycles, the house met with Jimmy's approval, and William made the drawing. A few weeks after Jimmy's departure, William saw a placard leaning against the wall outside the Post Office: MURDER AT STURGESS CASTLE. He got a copy of the poster and sent it to Jimmy—then living at High Wycombe—who wrote in reply that he had just witnessed the arrest of the murderer, who had disguised himself as a labourer and was actually working with a stonebreaking gang opposite the house in which Jimmy was living, when he was taken by the police. It was one of the occasions when literature has nothing to add to bald fact. The murder story was never finished, but William kept the drawing of Sturgess Castle as a souvenir of the curious incident.

2

Up in a studio in Victoria Street a successful young actress was sitting for her portrait to a successful young artist. Many people know that portrait—full of mischief and *espiéglerie*: the snub-nosed, full-breasted young woman sitting opposite the snub-nosed, full-chested little dog, each competing with the other as a study in impudence.

Marie Tempest had misgivings about the dog.

"I hope you aren't like Sargent, Mr. Nicholson; because they say whenever he paints a dog it dies."

William did his best to reassure her, but when, after a few days' sitting, she turned up without Koko, he inquired—having forgotten all about the previous conversation—for the missing sitter.

"My dear, don't speak of it. He's dead."

William borrowed one of the Duchess of Marlborough's Blenheim spaniels to finish the portrait of Koko, whose death must have been a coincidence, as he proved, by his portrait of Lena Ramsden's Napoleon, that he is not lethal to dogs. (Nap was an enchanting sitter, who sprawled on the black and white chequer of Apple Tree in his own peculiar attitude of an exhausted seal for just as long as his portraitist pleased. He was one of our best dog friends, and the sidelong glance of that dark *rusé* eye from the wall of his mistress's studio still warms our hearts, now Nap has descended to the shades.)

William insists that Marie Tempest—who suggested the portrait herself, though she was not yet in a position to commission it—did him a favour by sitting to him at this time, when her status as an actress was assured, and his as a portraitist yet to be made. But it will be remembered that the artist of *Queen Victoria*, who was known to a vast public through his woodcut portraits, and whose *Alphabet*, *Almanac of British Sports*, *Characters of Romance* and *London Types* were selling all over the country and had commanded the most glowing reviews from the Press, was very far from being the nonentity which William in his modesty would have us believe.

Of the *Almanac*, *The St. James's Gazette* had written:

"You must turn to the best specimens of Japanese colour printing to get anything better than these boldly-constructed blacks and reds. And what the Eastern work will gain in its delicacy of outline or of tint, it will lose by comparison with the truth of modelling in face and figure, which is the characteristic of this modern work."

And of the *Alphabet*, *The Art Journal* wrote:

"Since his famous portrait of the Queen in *The New Review*, Mr. Nicholson's success has been assured. With some of the grandeur of Velásquez, combined with much of the decorative ability of Caldecott, Mr. Nicholson has found a path for himself, and he reigns there without rival."

Such extracts as these suggest that Miss Tempest was at least

CHAIRING THE DANCER.
By courtesy of the Beaux Arts Gallery.

as shrewd as she was generous. The portrait was exhibited, gained *réclame* for both artist and sitter, and was sold. It was not until the death of the purchaser, W. Claude Johnson, Esq., some thirty years later, that it came back into the sale room, and was eventually acquired by its subject.

There was no end to the work which was going on, down at Woodstock. As always, when he finds himself in happy surroundings, the creative spirit was flaming; he was working on a dozen things at once, of which his memory, heartbreakingly undependable, provides us with little data, but we are indebted to the catalogue of the so-called "Retrospective Exhibition" of his work which was given at Nottingham Castle Museum and Art Gallery in March and April of 1933 for many details which had slipped into the back of his mind.

William was "all against" that exhibition. It was proposed at a moment when he was planning one of his own in London, and it was feared the two might overlap. He happened to be in Spain at the time, and the telegraph wires hummed with inquiries from people who had been approached to lend their Nicholsons for the Nottingham show, and frenzied replies from William, forbidding them to contribute to the scheme: in spite of which, a remarkable collection was assembled, and William, in due course, was invited to open the exhibition, an invitation which, like the rest of its kind, he refused. No private view of his own works (and very few of other people's) had ever been graced by William, who goes out of his way to put as much distance as possible between himself and any gallery on opening day. Private views in general give him "a cold grue"; their social aspect is as distasteful to him as it is embarrassing, for only an incurable naïveté could contend that art is a serious consideration with the regular patrons of private views. This state of affairs is much improved since the beginning of the war: at most private views now the "fashionable" element is conspicuous by its absence, and an earnest and appreciative company concentrates on the pictures, rather than each other's clothes.

The title chosen by the Nottingham committee was another sore spot; "Retrospective Exhibition" sounded, considered William, as if he were dead. (As a matter of fact, it came to his knowledge that the compiler of the biographical foreword to the catalogue had spent some time seeking for the date of his death.) Taking all in all, he had always had a grudge against that Nottingham show, until it was pointed out to him that no other

F

collection of his works was so admirably catalogued; it has proved invaluable in the compilation of the present record of his career. •

From the Nottingham catalogue we learn that the Woodstock period produced, among many other works, the well-known *Landlord*, acquired by the Manchester Corporation—a portrait of Jordan of the George Inn at Dorchester; *The Brown Veil*; *Marie Tempest*, and the delightful painting of little Rosy Craig, recently exhibited at the National Gallery. During this period appears for the first time the name of T. W. Bacon, Esq., of Billericay, who, in the course of the next three decades, became William's principal patron, and lent no fewer than forty-one paintings, drawings and woodcuts to the "Retrospective Exhibition," among them the portrait of his son Anthony, which was done at Woodstock, and, of others belonging to this period, *Hawking* and *The Jewelled Bandalore*.

The drawings of the Oxford Colleges, afterwards lithographed by a Dutch firm, were another aspect of William's activity; he used to bicycle into Oxford and hunt about for bits that he wanted to draw; while in the evenings he began a task which awaits completion to-day—the pack of playing cards whose Kings, Queens and Knaves are drawn from historical characters of England. Three more court cards, and this labour of love is ended—after forty years.

He was also doing inn signs, a form of decoration to which his style lent itself with peculiar aptitude: one for the Bear at Woodstock: one in collaboration with Jimmy Pryde for the Goat at Kensington, which was later sold ; and, up to the time of the blitz on London, two more of William's signs were on view—one over Roberson's in the Ritz Arcade, and the other over the doorway of Swayne and Adeney's, the Jermyn Street outfitters. For the occasional refreshing of this sign Messrs. Swayne and Adeney always made graceful recognition with a beautiful pair of chamois gloves. It survives the holocaust with only a circular hole, which might be shrapnel or a machine-gun bullet, through the coachman's left eye.

It is a pleasant phase to look back upon—that of Woodstock; the world was "so full of a number of things," ideas came so abundantly and were translated so gaily into whatever medium they seemed to call for; the days seemed so long and time so endless, and one was not driven at every hour of the day with the carking necessity of the commission. The family was increasing, but so were one's means, and living at Woodstock was simple and unextravagant.

Above all, there was the joy of *doing* at every hour of the day. His independence of intimate personal contacts preserved William —as it has done ever since—from the cliquism that is the ruin of many artists. He subscribes to no côteries; the notion of inspiring one would fill him with horror. "Movements" meant —and mean—nothing to him, long, abstract discussions, involving obscure co-ordinations of art, politics, psychology and so forth, less than nothing: you can see him fidgeting, his brow agonised with the desire to get away from all the talk, to get down to *doing*. The painter's form of expression, his brushes and his canvasses, have always been enough for him—which in itself explains the enormous range of his output.

About this time he designed some special paintbrushes, with very long black stems and rather short bristles bound with twine, instead of being set into the usual metal grip, which is apt to cut the bristles when they are washed, and got Roberson to make them for him. He was surprised one day, on going by the shop, to find a jar-full of them on sale, labelled "The Nicholson Brush." Protesting against the unauthorised use of his name, the salesman cut short his complaints by cheerfully remarking:

"It's all right, sir—we haven't sold any!"

3

One dark shadow came to cloud the idyllic existence at Woodstock. Mr. Nicholson died, after one of those short, desperate illnesses that drain the life as well from those who can do little but watch its progress. William went home for the funeral: by a grim coincidence he travelled in the next coach to a bride and bridegroom; the confetti blown from the hands of their attendants fluttered through the window and bespattered his funeral garments. He found his mother worn out with her weeks of nursing.

"Would you like to see Father, or would you rather not?"

He realised suddenly that he had never seen death before, and felt a little sick.

"Of course I want to see him."

She lifted her sweet, heavy-lidded eyes to his, and the shaft of understanding that was always there sped between them.

"You can always console yourself, Billie dear, with the thought that you added ten years to your father's life."

It was hard for William to realise that the Press notices of which he thought so little had been a real factor in the old gentleman's life. He got through the funeral somehow, his mind less on the tragic present than on the future. The little cottage in the garden at Woodstock: he would make it lovely for Mother; for her, as for him, it would be a homecoming. . . .

Mabel had not been well, and his father's death had taken it out of William; they decided to go down to Brighton for a few days, and have the benefit of that tonic air. Shortly after their arrival, the news came from Newark that Mrs. Nicholson was very ill. William left at once . . . but he was too late to see his mother.

CHAPTER EIGHT

*Mabel Nicholson—Max Beerbohm—First visit to New York
—Good-bye to Woodstock*

I

AMONG other introductions that came to William through Heinemann's was one to the Baroness von Hutten, who had just published *Pam*, and who wanted her portrait painted. She suggested that William should bring his wife out to Portofino, to stay with her while the sittings were going on.

Mabel was unenthusiastic about the project; she hated foreign places, and she hated being among strangers; she knew she was never at her best in company. She could form violent attachments, and become voluble in the company of an intimate, but even in her own house, when strangers, or mere acquaintances were present, she would lapse into silence the more complete when it was contrasted with the ceaseless, rattling conversation that had gone on in Fettes Row. Mrs. Patrick Campbell, who was "intrigued" by "Prydie," boomed at her suddenly: "What are you thinking about, you strange, silent woman?"

The truth was that, like many people who have shown a premature brilliance, she had exhausted her own fire. The balance of her health had never adjusted itself after the birth of Ben.

The most interesting light which query throws on the character of Mabel Nicholson is the violence of opinion she aroused in all who knew her. She was one of those who evoked no half measures: her admirers admit no shadow of adverse criticism, her critics have no good word to say of her. This in itself indicates a powerful character, and powerful, in her own small orbit of the home, she would appear to have been. She was worshipped by her children, and held in high esteem by the few who knew, or thought they knew, her. Her son-in-law wrote of her as a "beautiful wayward Scotch-melancholy person," and this, for her friends, must summarise her memory. Her ideas, her interests, her eccentricities show her to have been her mother's daughter. Spurred on by opposition, she would flash momentarily into violent partisanship—usually for someone to whom she felt society was not giving a square deal. She made a heroine

85

of a village girl who was having an illegitimate baby, and saw no unreason in demanding of William that he should assume the maintenance of the child and mother on a scale equal with that of his own family.

Now and again she picked up her indolent brush and painted something: it might be one of the children, or the cat, or a family group, with an ease and certainty hair-raising to William, to whom success never came easily. She could have sold her work, but it never occurred to her to do so, and William had enough to do, marketing his own wares, without acting as impresario for his wife.

There is a fine sobriety and sincerity about Mabel Nicholson's work; she painted honestly what she saw, and the fact that she was not, like Jimmy, a visionary, does not detract from its value. Hard, literal, and described by one critic as "lacking in the milk of human kindness," there is both quality and accomplishment in her painting, into which, oddly enough, her theatrical obsession, no less acute than Jimmy's, does not obtrude. Looking at a Mabel Nicholson, one has no sort of feeling that its proper place is inside a proscenium arch. Her love of her home, her love of her children, and her desire to record them for her own satisfaction speak almost defiantly through these portraits of Ben, of Tony, of Kit and Nancy. There is no invention, the scattered accessories of a bit of harlequin stuff or a drum bring no levity into the atmosphere—as, handled by William, they inevitably do: there is no delicacy of fancy, but a hard, uncompromising truth which is redeemed through its honesty. She might idolise her children to herself; she never, as a less sincere artist might have done, idealised them on canvas. A scowling Nancy, a perky and self-sufficient Ben are real children, observed with a coldness that differentiates the painter's from the mother's eye. There is, perhaps, an occasional hint of old-fashioned "Christmas supplement" in the colouring, and the brush does not always follow the intention which inspires it: that it could have done so, had she applied herself to the mastery of her art, cannot be doubted by those who study her work. These Nicholson children are flesh-and-blood people, self-willed, self-assertive, even on canvas; allowing themselves reluctantly to be painted, resenting having to keep still while their mother worked.

William has often spoken of having an exhibition of Mabel Nicholson's pictures; apart from Mabel's never wanting to exhibit, there are, unfortunately, not enough of them to make an exhibition—although what a family show could be arranged: starting with the Lauder uncles, Scott and Eckford, continuing with Jimmy and Mabel, and ending with their descendant, Ben. I am afraid that the problems of hanging such an exhibition would daunt the majority; it might well baffle the genius of Lilian Browse, to whom the National Gallery owes so much for her excellent arrangement of many of the war-time exhibitions.

It is, perhaps, that "Scotch-melancholy" recorded by Robert Graves that accounts for her description, by several people who had long acquaintance with her, as a pathetic figure: a pathos, one feels, deriving from her inner self, rather than from the circumstances of her life.

What had she expected, what had she wanted from life, that eluded her to the very end? It cannot have been the fulfilment of personal ambition, for she would seem to have had none. She could have been a painter of distinction. It is impossible to reconcile the report of her social ambition with her recorded actions; long before the time came when she ceased to be included in her husband's invitations, William was practised in excuses for her non-appearance—Mabel, having dressed, refusing at the last moment to accompany him to the dinner party, dance or reception to which they were both invited. This kind of "moodiness" is less explicable to a man than it is to a woman. Almost any woman would understand, and take it for granted. William did not understand—how should he?—and Mabel, being Mabel, did not explain.

The happy tomboy who drove geese into the Life class had vanished. Perhaps she was too tired to share William's zest for the adventure of living. With the birth of the children, her whole horizon had narrowed to the domestic scene; she took no pleasure in new environments (save those of the home), had no sympathy to spare for those who had. It would seem that she, too, was a sufferer from the *Weltschmerz*, which, hanging over the Prydes, cheated Jimmy, as it cheated Mabel, of the pleasures their talents should have brought them.

Despite her objections, however, the Nicholsons went to Portofino, where William, who has never been interested in painting professional beauties, found the Baroness unpaintable, but began a portrait of her little son. The main diversion of Portofino was contributed by the presence of Max Beerbohm, with whom William had been friendly for some years.

2

Jimmy had made acquaintance of Max when the Beggarstaffs were working in the Cromwell Road studio, and invited him to a party which was memorable for being the first occasion when paper confetti was seen in England. Up to then "confetti" had been used only in its native significance, and its function in adding to the self-consciousness of bridegrooms and the responsibility of flustered bridesmaids had not been exploited.

A French manufacturer, to whom William had sold his *Square Book of Animals*, presented him in return with an enormous sack of confetti, which was hoisted up to the ceiling. At a given signal, a string was pulled, the sack burst open, and the studio was snowed under in pink and green and lavender patches. These created an immense sensation, and the party worked up to such a riot that the people on the floor below sent out for a policeman, who came up to see what was going on. Pelted with confetti by the whole company, he took it with the utmost good humour, anxious only to know how he was going to get it all off before facing his superintendent. While some of the party volunteered to brush him down, others clamoured for a song, and the policeman, who by now had entered thoroughly into the spirit of the occasion, took off his helmet and "obliged"—unconscious that, as half a dozen assiduous members of his audience got to work on him with clothes brushes, others, no less assiduous, were filling the helmet with confetti. . . .

This typical studio jest was much appreciated by Max, who was then living with his family at 48 Upper Berkeley Street, where he had a little top room, practically an attic, where he lived, slept and worked at a table several feet deep in correspondence. Max never threw a letter away and has never been known to answer one; after reading them, he tossed them on the table, which was covered with the accumulation of years.

No one who saw the dapper little figure on its progress about fashionable London was likely to suspect the stark simplicity of its background. The model of elegant sophistication, Max valetted himself, ironed his own silk hats and contrived to look beautifully turned out, although, says William, "there were sometimes little rifts in the gingerbread"—a button off somewhere, or a split in the seam of an immaculate white glove. Max entertained William to breakfast on the last Sunday in each month.

One Sunday, William, arriving in Upper Berkeley Street, found the front door open and a stream of firemen issuing from the upper regions. Mounting to Max's eyrie, he found the last of the firemen in the act of descending through the skylight on top of Max's correspondence. A chimney had caught fire and the Fire Brigade had been summoned to put it out.

Max drew William aside.

"Do you think I ought to offer him a tip?"

Uncertain of the etiquette of Fire Brigades, William thought a tip would be quite in order, so Max, turning in his slightly fussy, *empressé* manner to the fireman, thanked him *so* much for being so efficient, and so on, and pressed half a crown into his hand. The fireman thanked him, but said they were not allowed to accept gratuities: whereon Max, losing his head completely, brushed the man's hand aside with the superb rejoinder—"Oh, please, treat it as a loan!"

Calling another morning, when Max happened to be out, William was entertained by old Mrs. Beerbohm, who, somewhat to his surprise, said how delighted she was that he and Max were getting on so well together and making a success of their new venture. It was not until after a period of hedging and cautious inquiries that William discovered that it had pleased Max's fancy to regale his mother with an elaborate account of a mythical antique shop, over which he and William had entered into partnership. It is easy to imagine the pleasure the pair of them would get out of improvising on so promising a theme.

When the children were small there were holidays at Dieppe; the same visitors turned up year after year at the little Hotel Robinson—the Nicholsons, Max Beerbohm and Reggie Turner. There was quite a glut of notabilities—Sickert, reducing with immense application the robust light and colour of Dieppe to fine grey ash, Pamela von Hutten, Marie Tempest and her second husband, Cosmo Gordon Lennox, and Violet Hunt, heavily veiled, qualifying for her latter-day rôle of pre-Raphaelite ghost. Max's dictum on Dieppe deserved to be recorded: "There's practically nobody here save the unfrocked, the drummed-out and the struck-off-the-rolls!"

Dieppe was always, for William, as it has been for many painters, a source of fruitful inspiration. Of the many Dieppe pictures he painted, *Première Communion* is, perhaps, the most exquisite in atmosphere and suggestion.

Jacques-Emil Blanche lived just outside Dieppe, and invited

them to visit him; his greeting to his guests was peculiar. "Have you made *quite* sure of the time of your train home?" Among the permanent residents in Dieppe was also a Miss Clementine Hosier, who later became the wife of Winston Churchill. Miss Hosier had a schoolgirl passion for Sickert, to whom, out of a full heart, she offered a box of chocolates—and lost the chocolates and her illusions at one fell swoop, as, taking for granted the box was for him, Sickert wolfed the lot.

"I'm going to take some lessons in this new game Bridge," observed Marie Tempest one day. "Would you care to join me?"

The lessons took place in her *cabine* on the beach, but progress was slow, William having the least possible card sense and Miss Tempest showing little more talent. At the end of a week, she remarked pensively:

"Do you understand anything at all about this game?"

"No; do you?" promptly replied William.

"No," admitted Marie; which was the end, so far as they were concerned, of the lessons in Bridge.

Their chief form of diversion was writing sonnets, of the kind that the euphemism of booksellers' advertisements classifies as "curious." At this game William, Max and Pamela von Hutten excelled; Max, in fact, was pulverised by the sudden discovery of his own talent in this direction. "Really—I have to tear them up and watch them well on their way to the sea before I can regard myself as fit to mix with decent society!" he is reported to have said. The method of production of these works of literature was each player alternately to contribute a line; unfortunately, they are quite unreproducible. Their quality may be judged from a few surviving stanzas of the *Lines to be Hung in a Hotel Bedroom at Charing Cross*. It was the year of Blériot's flight across the Channel, when Monsieur and Madame Blériot were reported to have spent the night at the Charing Cross Hotel.

The first line runs:

> "Remembered Cupid taught dull Man to soar:
> I do not wish to but I *must* say more:
> Behold the bed on which the Blériots . . ."

—after which William's memory discreetly fails him, but for the concluding fragment:

"Union of adamant with adipose,
Accentuated by a lack of cloes.
(The cloes, neglected, lay upon the floor
And passed into the keeping of George Moore.)
So love two earwigs in some battered rose

.   .   .   .

While Emily, sweet creature, gently smiled.
The disproportionate result—one child."

3

These trips, to Portofino and Dieppe, were not the only ones
taken by the Nicholsons while at Woodstock. William was
commissioned by the Harper brothers to go to the United States
and make some drawings for their magazine: a prospect which
filled him with delight, for the New World with all its allure
of freshness and its springing energy of a "young" country
offered a powerful attraction to the adventure spirit within
him.

His wife travelled with him. They arrived in New York on the
hottest day of the hottest August within the memory of any
living New Yorker; people were sleeping out in the parks, and
cab horses falling dead with the heat along Fifth Avenue.
William established Mabel in the Brevoort House with an electric
fan, and went to find out exactly what the Harpers wanted from
him.

He was told, portraits of politicians. William, uninterested
in politics, even English ones, had no interest whatever in
American politicians, and said so. Impressed against their will
by this young English artist who had crossed the Atlantic to work
for them, and now said he didn't want to, they kindly offered
him a choice of subject, and William, making the *amende honorable*,
said that he would like to draw Theodore Roosevelt and the
famous (or infamous) Boss Croker of Tammany; then named,
among others, Mark Twain, Joseph Jefferson, Thomas Edison and
the Chinese Ambassador. A promising list; unfortunately, none
of these people proved very interesting as sitters. All busy men,
they looked on William as a reporter, because he came from
Harper's. Roosevelt, in his office, practically ignored the young
artist, who sat modestly sketching in a corner, and Edison slept
most of the time, his relaxed hands deeply stained with chemicals,

the cuffs of his shirt looking as if they belonged to a very old, grimy pair of pyjamas.

William took Mabel to see Jefferson in *Rip Van Winkle*. It was one of the great performances of theatrical history; she watched it through practically without comment. It was not her adored Lyceum, her darling Irving and Terry. And what was happening to the children? . . . This was almost her only outing; when William tried to interest her to the point of accompanying him on his short, sight-seeing trips about this wonderful new city, which, to him, was a revelation, she lay exhausted on her bed at the Brevoort, only waiting to go home. Painter as she was, the new scene, which was like an electric current to William, meant nothing to her.

At the end of the sittings, Jefferson sent William a pair of the white gloves he wore as Bob Acres, and a "rag" from *Rip Van Winkle*, which were brought home to add to the collection of treasures—to Irving's dagger used in *The Corsican Brothers* (used also in our burglary in the first month of the war, to prize open the locked drawers of a rent table which contained, unfortunately for the thief, only some hundreds of our letters), to Henley's hat and Marie Tempest's little bonnet and all the rest of the precious junk which was to repose and ripen in Apple.Tree for many peaceful years. He (Jefferson) had touched William's heart by showing him his watercolours—tender little landscapes in sepia, with a different type of brushwork for each separate class of tree; like most amateurs, Jefferson was immensely serious and conscientious about them. (A crack of Ben's comes to mind: "My tutor does watercolours; they are like the work of a girl of fourteen when she was twelve.")

Of the Chinese Ambassador William retains a bright memory; it was His Excellency's pleasure to go about on a tricycle, his heels on the treadles, with his magnificent robes tied up out of harm's way with broad white satin ribbons.

At last the portraits were finished, and William watched the Statue of Liberty fading on the skyline with mingled feelings of relief and regret. New York was such a wonderful place, and he had seen hardly any of it; his work aside, he could not leave Mabel alone for long at a time. Still, there was always the future. . . .

As for her—she was radiant; her face was set towards home.

4

A thing so tragic that it was almost unbelievable had happened. During their absence, William had let Chaucer's House for twelve months. On their return, he was horrified to discover that the kitchen garden had been turned into a tennis lawn, trees planted by his mother had been cut down, and the interior had been redecorated throughout, in a style very far removed from the owner's ideas. Last, and most outrageous of all, Chaucer's chapel had been converted into a servants' hall.

William was furious, but could get no compensation: the tenant replying, through his lawyers, that he had spent £1,500 on the property during his year of tenancy. William retorted that there was no more dangerous weapon than money in the hands of a man with bad taste, and that Mr. R—— had used it to the full. Years later he sat next to a stranger at dinner, who presently introduced himself as the late Mr. R——'s lawyer, and said that perhaps William would like to know that he (the lawyer) had never seen a man so angry in his life as R——, on receipt of William's letter! Gratifying; but all the gratification in the world could not restore its vanished charm to poor little Chaucer's House. William was heartbroken, Mabel angry, and even the children a little stunned by the changes that had come over their familiar home.

For they had been long enough in Chaucer's House to feel it was unchangeable; even Ben, who had been hurtled from Denham to Bedford Park, Bedford Park to Avonmore Gardens, Avonmore Gardens to Mitcham, had forgotten those restless beginnings; Tony and Nancy remembered no other home. Even for them the place was packed with memories.

While they were at Chaucer's House an old century had died, a new one dawned; they had celebrated the end of the Boer War with free beer to the village at large and torchlight processions which ended in the bursting of the big drum. (Later on, when he came to know Smuts, William suffered from qualms about this celebration; was it possible the Boers had been right, and we had been wrong, about the whole affair?)

And there was the New Year's morning when it was suggested that he and Sandy Merrill should climb the Blenheim Orange-tree and plant some mistletoe. Sandy, who always knew the right way of doing everything, said the berries must be pressed into the bark, underneath the boughs, where the birds could not get at them. William had forgotten all about that, until they were leaving Chaucer's House; he had forgotten it again, until more than ten years later, when, revisiting those scenes of bygone happiness, he found the Blenheim Orange almost obliterated beneath a great mass of mistletoe.

From Chaucer's House he had gone up to watch Queen Victoria's funeral—twice over; he was on his cousin's ship at Southampton when the *Victoria and Albert* came up the Solent with her flag at half-mast, and had seen the gun carriage with the very small coffin jolting its way along Piccadilly. He, at least, had some cause for sentiment at the passing of the great Victorian age!

He might in time have got over the violation done to Chaucer's House, have settled down and removed as far as might be the traces of his tenant's vandalism; but by now Mabel had got her itch to move on. A doctor, called in for some minor ailment, conveniently gave it as his opinion that the low-lying country of Oxfordshire was no healthy dwelling-place for a young woman reared in the astringent airs of Edinburgh, and she was off like a bird.

William was to see no other Spring creep golden in buttercups across the lush Oxfordshire meadows; to ride no more across the frost-rimed grass of Blenheim Park; to visit no more Fair Rosamund's bower, or the old Trout Inn on the river. *Nous n'irons plus au bois—les lauriers sont coupés.*

They found a small house in Hampstead, Sandy was called in—Sandy who, in removals, was indispensable: he enjoyed them nearly as much as Mabel—and at number one, Pilgrim's Lane, as it were to clinch the matter, Mabel produced her fourth baby, Kit, in December, 1904. She nearly paid for it with her life; the doctor was in the house for twenty-four hours.

CHAPTER NINE

*Introduction to the theatre—" Bloomsbury Family"—Portraits
—" Those were the days"*

I

WHEN J. M. Barrie wrote to William, suggesting he should design the costumes for *Peter Pan*, he (J.M.B.) was living at Leinster Corner; William found him in the preposterous setting of an ornate Edwardian drawing-room, sitting with his knees drawn up in excruciating discomfort on a short Empire settee with gilded ends. It was with obvious relief on both sides that they quitted this inappropriate *decor* for the little summerhouse in the garden, where he lived and did most of his writing, surrounded by his big dog—the original of Nana.

Nana had been taught an impressive trick which delighted Barrie as much as it mystified his victims. Whenever he had a call from one of his literary friends, Barrie skilfully led the conversation to one of the visitor's books, which presently Nana was told to fetch: whereon she walked solemnly to the bookshelves and returned with the volume in question in her mouth. The secret of the trick was, of course, that it had been planted beforehand; Nana had learned to fetch a book—any book—from a certain place on the shelves, and Barrie had seen to it that the book was there before the visitor's arrival.

Barrie's suggestion delighted William; it was his first opportunity of coming to grips with the theatre, which exerted over him the powerful fascination it must have for all imaginative and creative natures. He had already a good working knowledge of it, thanks to the many times he had watched Irving's rehearsals— to whose vast apocrypha he could, if he chose, add richly. His prettiest Irving story concerns an occasion when Gordon Craig had to make an entrance. Teddy, always shortsighted, visibility reduced—for him—to a minimum by the blaze of the battens, come nosing out of the wings with the hopeful, helpful expression of one who thinks he may evade notice. It was too much for Irving.

"No, no, no, NO, Teddy! Go back, go back, go *back*. You look as if you were coming out of a urinal ! "

William's approach to the theatre was—and is—highly

romantic; the stage stripped for rehearsal, the yawning flies, the ponderous dimness of the scenedock are invested, for him, with a magic that is populated with the bright ghosts of the past; but the romanticism does not blot out his critical capacity, as any one who has accompanied him to a rehearsal must know. He has an instinctive understanding—not always present in those who work for the theatre—of the relationship between the actor and his setting; he views his own contribution not as an isolated and all-important element, but as part of the completed whole.

Alongside of the vein of fantasy, to which he was able to give free play in such productions as *Peter Pan* and *Polly*, runs the illuminating sanity and scrupulous respect for balance and justice which appear in his Still Life. His love of the drama and instinctive perception of its requirements make him a natural workman of the theatre, through which he weaves his little way, unperturbed by personal contacts, intent only on his own province, though conscious in every pore of that which concerns other people.

Perhaps this is the place to say that William, as member of a theatre audience, is an uncertain quantity; his reactions are quite unpredictable and sometimes sensational. On one occasion Barrie sent him a box and he took Mabel and the children—to what play he cannot remember—when he was so carried away by a speech of the leading lady's that the tears poured down his cheeks. Thoroughly ashamed of himself, and not wishing to draw attention by using his handkerchief, he leaned with his elbows on the ledge of the box. Something, however, made him look down, when he saw the drummer of the orchestra, in a frenzy of rage, shaking his fist at him. William was crying on to the big drum.

Another equally disconcerting occasion arose out of a box at His Majesty's, sent by Tree to William and his family, who, that night, were going to a ball at Covent Garden, and were in fancy dress. About half-way through, William became so bored with the performance that he retired to the back of the box, lay down on the floor and went cosily to sleep. Tree, graciously coming to visit his guests during one of his waits, must have regarded with mixed feelings the prone figure over which he stumbled in entering the box. William does not seem to remember how he extricated himself from this situation, but, knowing him, it seems likely that he emerged with aplomb and even grace.

These two stories must not be taken to imply that William

THE HUNDRED JUGS.

was a Barrie addict and allergic to Tree as an actor. On the contrary, Barrie's whimsy made every tooth in his head jump, and apart from *The Admirable Crichton*, he never willingly went to a Barrie play; while for some of Tree's work he had a considerable admiration.

But William in the theatre is always a little unnerving; if we go to the play, or are invited to join a theatre party, he always makes the provision that, if bored, he may come out—hardly an encouraging note on which to accept an invitation. It is only fair, however, to add that he rarely avails himself of his own proviso: although it took all my persuasion to keep him in his stall at *Mourning Becomes Electra* (actually, it was the *entr'acte* music which got him down —and no wonder either), he sighed with regret, like a small child, when the curtain came down on the last act of *The Duke in Darkness*, which satisfied his every sense, pictorially and dramatically, although he recognised that it was not a great, nor even a *very* good play; but it was most beautifully acted, it fulfilled the astute criticism which he makes on so much modern acting: "They say their lines as if they had learned them by heart; you never see the thought pass through their minds first." You could see the thoughts pass through the minds of the duke and his prison companion.

To return to Barrie and *Peter Pan*—the collaboration went well from the beginning. They attended rehearsals together, and often lunched at a little "local" nearly opposite the Duke of York's Theatre, where the rehearsals took place. One morning William asked Barrie why he always ordered Brussels sprouts, as he never ate them. After a short pause, Barrie explained, shyly and confidentially, " Because it's such a nice thing to say—Brussels sprouts!"

It was Sidney Pawling who suggested that William might paint Barrie between rehearsals. Barrie's reply was characteristic:

"*Leinster Corner, Lancaster Gate, W.*   *February 13.*
"MY DEAR PAWLING,—On the one hand I have long ceased to be on speaking terms with my face, so why have it painted? On the other hand I do have such an admiration for Nicholson's work that if he really wants to paint me, and would do it here, so be it. This *is* a sort of studio, tell him, but with the north light painted out, and I'm always in it in the mornings, ten to one.
     "Yours sincerely,
         "J. M. BARRIE."
          G

William started a small head of Barrie, looking rather like a
sparrow after a dust-bath; when Barrie's sister saw it, she burst
into tears. It was placed very low on the canvas, with a lot of
space up above. Max, to whom Barrie and all his works were
anathema, and whose pencil, as well as his pen, was like a
scorpion, made a caricature of it, reducing Barrie's head to the
size of a pea, at the foot of a waste of background. For all his
reputed sensitiveness to ridicule, Barrie stood up to it manfully,
though there is a certain lack of enthusiasm in his letter to
William about the portrait:

"My dear Nicholson,—I think it is first rate now and by all
means exhibit it. I still dislike the blue cheek and all who have
seen it do so—looks dirty as if I hadn't shaved to our thinking,
but follow your own feeling. There is a general opinion also that
the arm is still short. These are the only criticisms, all else is
eulogy.

"Yours sincerely,

"J. M. Barrie."

During rehearsals a little, unknown, American actress distinguished herself in the Pillow Dance; this was the future, and
perhaps the most famous, of all the Peter Pans—Pauline Chase,
who, when the play was revived, stepped into Nina Boucicault's
part of "the boy who never grew up." William designed a special
dress for the Pillow Dance girl, who, at the end of a long and
tiring dress rehearsal, came down to the floats and called out to
Barrie: "Say, Mr. Barrie, I can't go on like this. My hair's too
long and my boots are too big." Barrie (in the stalls) thought
for a moment, put his little arm behind his head and said, "Well,
my dear, put your hair into your boots."

One of the points on which Barrie was most insistent was that
the pirates should be *real* pirates, not Gilbert-and-Sullivan
travesties. William carried out his wishes with zest. He found an
enormous buck nigger for one of the pirates, put him into a great,
tattered, green silk dressing-gown, and gave him a club as big
as his head—with the result that some of the children in the
audience were scared into hysterics on the first night, and the
nigger was withdrawn. The pirates, as the play continued on its
way down the ages, gradually became more and more Gilbert-
and-Sullivan, and finally ended up as Sullivan-and-water.

For Du Maurier William designed a superb wig of purple

chenille, arranged to look like snakes; it was darker than the darkest thing imaginable, and was the focusing point of the scene. Du Maurier refused to wear it because his wife said it was unbecoming, and went on looking like a cross between Charles II. and a fourteen-year-old schoolgirl: in spite of which he gave an exquisite performance, elegant and *stylisé* to the last degree, and bearing as little relation to latter-day performances of Hook as the proverbial chalk to cheese.

All William's designs for the costumes were stolen from the theatre, except one or two which William gave to Du Maurier. "Do you feel drawn yourself to do a poster of the Esquimaux boys looking thro' legs at wolves?" wrote Barrie—but apparently William was not "drawn," and the poster was not done.

A high spot of the first night was the final scene, in which the lost little boys' mothers were supposed to turn up and claim their missing offspring. Although this scored a success with the more naïve section of the audience, the sophisticates (according to William) "laughed like hell": as the management had put on a crowd of supers and it looked more like the Empire promenade, prior to the activities of Mrs. Ormiston Chant, than a family reunion. This scene was very soon removed, when the meaning of the sniggers from the stalls had penetrated to the management.

A few years later, William went to see the play again, and found his costume designs unrecognisable; he therefore wrote to Barrie, asking for his name to be removed from the programme.

2

The next move—why or wherefore no one seems to remember, but, at a guess, it may have been that the house in Pilgrim's Lane was too small for a growing family: there was nowhere for William to work, and he had had to take a studio in The Boltons— was to Mecklenburg Square. From the world of Keats into the world of Thackeray; they were almost under the shadow of the Foundling Hospital, and the plane-trees brought green into the old-fashioned rooms—not the singing green of Woodstock, but the subtle, blackened green of a London square, which has a magic of its own. There was nothing particularly distinctive about Mecklenburg Square—just a solid, well-built quadrangle that retained (in 1906 or thereabouts) some traces of its former well-to-do occupation. The comfortable (although basemented) houses had not been split up into "maisonettes"; one could still enjoy the privacy of one's own front door. Mabel was not enthusiastic about the address; she had aspirations to Chelsea, which was then the "fashionable" artistic quarter, and was presently to be annoyed with Orpen for labelling his portrait "Bloomsbury Family." But she had a drawing-room with a magnificent dragon carpet and a black satin sofa. She had great taste in interior decoration, and each new house presented itself to her as a canvas on which she could execute her fancy.

The dining-room (William is partial to dining-rooms; across a dining-table—especially his own—he is always at his brightest and best) was William's creation: a charming little room with meerschaum-coloured walls, on which were displayed his beautiful Dighton prints. Dightons, jugs, silk scarves, bilboquets; through how many antique shops, at home and abroad have we rambled in search of these? Apple Tree, the flat at Hove, and my studio were crowded out with jugs; less than six months before our war-time odyssey started we had added some lovely pink lustre to the collection started away back in Woodstock days. We shall see those, perhaps, after the war; the Dightons have accompanied us on our pilgrimage, and have helped to make "home" of some unhomelike places.

When the Nicholsons took up residence in Mecklenburg Square, Orpen had just exhibited his *Accident in Fitzroy Square*, William saw and admired it tremendously, and wrote to him, asking the Orpens to dinner.

Those were Orpen's pre-collar days; he smothered his throat with a muffler and was hardly known to utter in public; when he did, it was in a thick, barely intelligible Irish brogue. His wife was a distinguished-looking young woman, with the unusual beauty of a mass of blonde hair and very dark eyes. She and Mabel became friends, almost on sight.

Orpen said he could not get enough light in the house where he was then living (in Ebury Street), or afford another studio, so William offered him the use of The Boltons, as he (William) was now settled down in an upper room in Mecklenburg Square. When Orpen demurred, on account of the rent, William said he could give him a picture, if he liked, to square the agreement. This was how *Bloomsbury Family* came to be painted—Mabel's very minor rôle in this important picture being due to her dislike of the tedium of sitting.

(This was not the only occasion on which William was painted by Orpen. In *Café Royal*, William may be observed, making a very "chesty" entrance on the left, while George Moore is leaving, in what seems to be an extremely pointed manner, on the right. Augustus John and James Pryde figure in the foreground. William was not too pleased about his own unauthorised appearance in it. "Why on earth didn't you ask me to sit for you?" he asked Orpen, who mumbled something about "not wanting to bother him with sittings." Orpen alone of the portraitists captured that elfin quality in William's appearance which is notably missing from the grand full-length by John.)

3

Success in full measure seemed to have followed the Nicholsons to Mecklenburg Square. Suddenly—it seemed—William was in demand as a portraitist. It was not surprising, for, in addition to his power as an artist, he has that indispensable gift of the portrait-painter of "loving his fellowmen." His relationships with his sitters are, with a very few exceptions, of the happiest; the exceptions have been, at least in his own estimation, failures. "I don't want to paint any one who doesn't want to be painted by *me*," he says: which means that the cold and businesslike commission which occasionally comes along, from someone who wants to buy "a portrait" as he might buy a piece of furniture, presents no attractions to him, although financial necessity may oblige him to accept it. It is only fair to add that, from such uncompromising premises, happier relationships have been known to develop, and that the sitter is usually infected in the end by the painter's own attitude to his work.

The nightmare of all portraitists, and of William in particular, is the reluctant sitter, whose portrait had been commissioned, perhaps, for presentation purposes; who arrives sheepishly and indifferently at his sittings, and sit with his eye on the clock. The atmosphere of tension and irritation which results from such sittings cannot bring satisfaction, either to subject or to painter, and there is no hope of establishing the basic understanding on which is founded the difference between photography and portraiture.

I have never known William deliberately to indulge in an analysis of character; I have a shrewd suspicion that he would not know "which end to begin." Yet some of his work in portraiture might well rouse the envy of psychiatrists. There is even a psychic quality, a suggestion of control, about it. I have in mind a particular portrait which might well be described as an *exposé* of its subject; we only recognised it as such long afterwards, when certain facts came to light. Yet there they are, as plain as print, on William's canvas! I think these truths emerge through William's wholly uncritical outlook on life, just as I believe he is incapable of a deliberately cruel piece of work. His occasional cruelty is a facet, of which he is unaware, of his own simplicity and truth. His portraiture, in fact, the spiritual side, as opposed to the technical side of it, reminds me of Ellen Terry acting, of Nijinski dancing: neither of these great artists could explain or analyse their effects, which were born out of their subconscious.

In 1906 he painted a Mrs. Curle: the pretty, red-haired woman sits with her elbows on a table, her cheeks resting lightly against her clasped hands. The table itself is spread with a Still Life of crystal, among which are carelessly dropped the lady's gloves. Gloves always fascinate William; he has collected them for years, he loves to give them and to design them. For Ursula Lutyens—now Lady Ridley—on her wedding day, he designed a pair of gloves of which the ring-finger was detachable, and on each finger of which he inscribed a line of the verse written by Peter Quennell for the occasion. *Mrs. Curle*, *The Girl With the Tattered Gloves*, *The Crystal Horse* are only a few of the paintings or sketches in which gloves play an important part. A pair of gloves is flung into the corner of a flower-piece, on more than one occasion; and he indulged his fancy to the utmost in the large Still Life which shows a handful of gloves, faïence blue, candy pink, greens and yellow, with a lustre jug in the background. E. V. Lucas always considered the portrait of Mrs. Curle one of William's loveliest paintings; it was followed by another, of the red-haired Curle baby on a green lawn.

On morning he received a letter with the Galashiels postmark, saying that the writer had seen the portrait of Mrs. Curle, and would like to be painted by the same artist. A large full-length was suggested, as it was to go into the family gallery, which, as William was later to discover, included Raeburns, Knellers and Jamiesons. And a few weeks later the door of Mecklenburg Square opened to admit a young Scotswoman with wide blue eyes, the clear, bright colouring of the Northerner and a strong

Scottish accent—our dear and constant friend, Ada Pringle—
"Pring."

It must have been an eye-opener to Pring—that entrance into
a Bloomsbury Family! Born and bred among the stiffest Lowland
"county," her acquaintance of London limited to that which goes
by the name of "Society," she found, even in the early days of the
sittings, plenty to fill those big blue eyes and plenty that would
have caused a Sassenach tongue to wag. In the course of the next
twelve years she observed everything and stored everything away
in that phenomenally exact memory of hers, and without her help
this part of the story would hardly be worth writing; for she did
not, as many a young woman in her place would have done,
concern herself only with the amusing and trivial, but recorded
faithfully all the work on which William was engaged while he
was painting her portrait.

When people complain, as they do sometimes, that William
wants too many sittings, they might be reminded that Pring
gave more than a hundred sittings, and that the painting of her
portrait was spread out over the greater part of eleven years. This
must, I think, be a record in perseverance, both for sitter and
painter. Her friends used sometimes to say, "How on earth can
you put up with sitting so often?" To which her answer was,
"You don't know Nicholson!" Her small boy added a testimonial
of his own. While William was painting him, Pring, thinking
the child might become bored and restless, one day suggested
bringing a book and reading aloud while the work was going on.
Her son scorned the suggestion. "You don't want *books* with a
person like that!" Children do love being painted by William;
he has exactly the right approach, never makes the least attempt
to "entertain" them, but talks to them as if they were grown-up,
his equals in intelligence and their opinions valuable.

There was plenty of work on the easels when Pring arrived.
There was Lady Kitty Somerset, in a little black hat with mercury
wings; there was little Miss Hannay, a girl of thirteen, in a
powder-blue dress with a long string of beads round her neck.
This portrait received, for some reason, enormous publicity, and
William instantly began to suspect it—as he suspects any of his
works which happen to achieve a general popularity. He was
finishing *The Little Baron*, the Baroness von Hutten's boy, which
was started at Portofino: a portrait interesting because it is the
only one painted by William in this particular *genre*—flat, pale,
almost like tempera, the child in a holland blouse, with holland-

coloured hair and light blue eyes. The only high light in the picture is in one eye; if this is covered over, the whole portrait goes dead.

Pring went out and bought herself a white chiffon gown at Hayward's, and a large black hat loaded with ostrich feathers— the last sort of thing, as she was later to realise, to appeal to William's fancy as a painter. However, the sittings started, and not the least pleasant feature of them was the luncheon interval, when Pring, "stark mad in white chiffon," and William in the white ducks which by then had become as much of an institution as the spotted shirts, mounted the steps of the Russell Hotel, the cynosure of all eyes—a piquant experience for a young woman who had been brought up in the belief that the attraction of public notice was a mark of deplorable taste.

Pring was enjoying herself enormously. Her horizon had broadened, and she was discovering that there were other standards—and much more entertaining ones—than those of Galashiels. It was not long before she was absorbed into the lively saraband that pranced in and out of the studio in Mecklenburg Square: Dolly Mann and her legion of admirers, the Orpens, George Belcher, and, of course, the ubiquitous Jimmy. They all liked the cheerful young Scotswoman with a house in Savile Row, nurse, nursemaid and babies all complete, to give her the background of pleasant domesticity which Bohemia is supposed to scorn but secretly envies—and no objection to being knocked up at odd hours of the night when the pubs were closed and studio supplies had failed.

It was arranged between Mabel and Grace Orpen that the two families should go to Margate for the summer; four adults, six children and the Nicholsons' buxom, red-haired nurse—who, on the one occasion when she was induced to dabble with Planchette (a temporary craze of William's), produced such a flood of obscene writing that she burst into tears, and would never touch "the horrid thing" again.

William and Orpen used to paint in "The Hall by the Sea," a derelict circus which had once belonged to Lord George Sanger, and was later used as a skating rink. It had a theatre and bar, and, outside the main building, the cages where the wild beasts had been kept. Orpen painted the bar—florid with tarnished gilt and fly-spotted looking-glass—and William the skating rink, round which were Græco-Roman statues with gilded hair, and deers' antlers festooned with the jaded remnants of coloured paper streamers; here was the baroque touch beloved by him at this particular period, which breaks out now and again in a *City Banquet* (1937) or *The Discreet Diner* (1931). *The Hall by the Sea* was afterwards bought by Constance Collier.

While the men were thus soberly employed, their wives went on the spree. It was singular, how these two young women, sedate and reserved when apart, went crazy whenever they got together. Before they met Grace Orpen was among those who favoured the pre-Raphaelite, trailing around in classic draperies with a volume of Ruskin under her arm. Mabel soon made short work of that, and the pair of them had gone off, before leaving town, and ordered quantities of clothes from the most expensive houses; William and "Orps" were left, with wry faces, to foot the bills—neither of them having a penny to bless themselves with at the time.

One evening after dinner the four of them went for a walk along the beach. Deep in their conversation, neither William nor Orpen noticed, at first, that the dusk was drawing in rapidly; they made the discovery simultaneously that it was nearly dark, and that their wives were missing.

Knowing Mabel, William thought they were only up to some prank or other among the caves that fringed the beach, but Orpen grew anxious, and it was only after some whistling and shouting that shrieks of laughter were heard from out at sea. Mabel and Grace had walked in up to their necks in the new (and unpaid-for) evening gowns. Their husbands, not so certain of the joke, had to wait for the moon to rise before taking them home—Mabel in the ruins of something by Lucile and Grace in almost non-existent black chiffon—both dripping like a pair of Undines.

Shortly after this William and Mabel had a serious talk on economy, which ended in their cutting off their subscription to *The Daily Mail*. On the same afternoon, Mabel walked out and ordered a new pianola.

4

Covent Garden balls were then the delight of the art world, not having yet been invaded by suburbia and the Bright Young Things of Mayfair. William had a Georgian costume in which he looked extremely well, and lent Grace Orpen a beautiful crinoline from the chest of dresses which he had already started to collect.

(This chest, which will be Liza's some day, was a *pièce de résistance* of Apple Tree; at one party we gave, the dresses were taken out, pressed and hung carefully in the alcoves, the bright blues, candy-pinks, rusts and yellows of the Hogarthian period making a memorable décor; and there is also a bright memory of another evening, and Edith Evans Millamanting about in a self selected hotch-potch of all the more fantastic garments.)

Mabel had a Persian outfit, Orpen went as Chardin and Jimmy in a fine, fantastic get-up as Macaire. "Also present" were Max, who had elected to have an enormous *papier mâché* replica of his own head, and went round with this balanced on his shoulders, and Reggie Turner, who, in his not so original costume of Father Christmas, was blissfully convinced that he was unrecognisable, in spite of the fact that everybody rushed up, clapped him on the back, and cried out, "Hallo, old chap, I haven't seen you for ages!"

When the ball was over, and the last dancers drifting away, the Nicholson party sat on the stairs, blandly refusing to depart, and chaffing the officials who tried to move them on, pretending to take them for characters of the ball. They were at last ejected, only to go and hammer on the doors of Bow Street, whose officers, accustomed to the playful ways of Covent Garden revellers, were so tolerant that the joke palled. So they spent the rest of their money on flowers and fruit and pranced back to Mecklenburg Square, where Mabel immediately sat down and started to play the new pianola, while Grace pulled off her crinoline and danced like a mad thing in her petticoat.

Orpen, who by now was very tired, kept saying to William: "Get hold of Grace now—she won't do a thing I say—Grace, come on now an' get your hat!"—until William, who was equally sleepy, went out and found a fourwheeler, when the two men managed to get Grace down the stairs and into the cab. Just as they were ready to start, Mabel struck up again on the pianola, and Grace was out of the cab and up the stairs again like a streak of lightning, dancing like one possessed.

By mutual effort she was again thrust into the cab, and while Orpen held her in, William raced up the stairs again and down with the crinoline, hung it round the horse's neck, yelled "Ebury Street!" to the driver, and gave the horse a slap on its rump which started it off at the gallop with the crinoline swinging from its collar.

As we have already remarked—those were the days! But even for painters and their wives, life was not one grand sweet song of Covent Garden balls and wading into the English Channel in twenty-guinea gowns.

Pring was one of the few who realised the enormous drain on William's strength and his resources caused by their extravagant way of living and the expensive way in which the children were being educated. When she arrived for her sittings at eleven, William had been at work since half-past eight; he was as thin as a lath and as pale as a ghost, overwhelmed with commissions and not daring to turn any of them down, for he was burdened, not only with the cares of his own family, but with those of the Prydes, who had a bland way of taking it for granted Mabel's husband should look after them all.

Pring, by now, was established as a seemingly permanent feature of the home; when not sitting she was doing little jobs about the studio—adding up accounts, writing occasional letters, keeping her eyes open and her mouth shut. Sometimes she would pose for an absent sitter—she "sat" for Lady Phillips's hands: which, as William's future mother-in-law was very fat and Pringle's arms were very thin, was not so successful, the gloves falling into wrinkles; and spent patient hours in a sheepskin coat and tin hat for the portrait of a soldier. She was the rare and ideal sitter who does not carp at unpunctuality, who is always ready to make allowance for a painter's moods. Although a busy woman, with a full domestic and social life, she never seemed to be hurried, never forced her own time-table on others; was equally ready to talk about domestic problems with Mabel or to divert the children's attention from their father when work had arrived at some uncomfortable crisis. (Ben and Tony were away at school, but Nancy and Kit were at home.)

She says the studio was "like a reception-room"—an amusing reception-room, in which you might meet any one from duchesses to dustmen.

William is a very sociable painter; conditions which would paralyse many artists seem to stimulate him, and if the work is going well he is perfectly serene and undisturbed by half a dozen people carrying on cross conversations above his head. (Naturally this does not apply to portraits, when both painter and model must concentrate; but even over portraits, Pring's genius for self-effacement served her; she was often present, dealing un-obtrusively with the chaos of William's correspondence, when a sitter was there.)

Her sister, Mrs. Mitchell, had commissioned a portrait of her little boy, and there was some sisterly manœuvring for sittings.

"Alec is only good in the mornings," pleaded the anxious mother.

"Mrs. Pringle is only good in the mornings," was the calm retort, with a lowered eyelid towards Pring, who, with her Scots blood by now thoroughly roused about the portrait—which was not going quite as well as might have been expected—was ready to sit at any hour of the day or night.

This portrait was at last considered finished, and was despatched to Torwoodlee, where William accepted an invitation to see how it looked in competition with the Raeburns. He was not at all satisfied, and insisted on bringing it back to town—at first to retouch it, but when Pring turned up at Mecklenburg Square in a little flowery Paris hat, he took such a fancy to it that he insisted on scrapping the original and started off on a fresh canvas.

I don't think any portrait ever caused both painter and sitter such *Sturm und Drang* as Pring's! It was surely no fault of hers; there could have been no more amenable and gracious a sitter. When the new one was well on its way, somebody said it was not a good likeness, and the hat was painted out. Then William had a new conception, and started on a third canvas—this time posing his subject in a Chinese coat lined with white fur, which he happened to find lying about the studio. They were about half-way through, when the owner of the coat turned up, was furious to find someone else being painted in her property, and swept it away. Reasonable, but disconcerting. Tiresome, too, because the sittings had temporarily to be suspended; Pring was about to have her second baby.

It was curious, that willingness of William, in the case of the portrait in the flowery hat, to accept the criticism of an outsider on a matter of which, after all, he must have been the final judge. He did it once again, with a still life, *Mauve Orchids*, which was seen and bought by an artist named Stewart. Un-fortunately it was also shown to a visitor, who passed the remark, as stupid as it was futile, that it was "just about fit to hang in the Ritz." William took this so much to heart that he painted the mauve out and made the orchids white. When the buyer came back to claim his picture he very naturally would not take it.

This readiness of William, to accept unintelligent criticism, is sufficient proof of the state of his nerves at that time.

More and more the need had been growing on him of a place of refuge apart from his home. Ben (by now the Child Champion of Diabolo) and Tony were uproarious schoolboys of twelve and nine respectively; Nancy, at seven her mother's daughter, was already chalking up VOTES FOR WOMEN over the kitchen sink. Their occupations, their games, their noises, their presence, invaded the studio at all hours of the day. William adored his children, and would have disciplined them after his fashion; Mabel adored them, and would not have them disciplined. The natural result was that they worshipped her and were off-hand about him. William had neither time nor energy to spare in showing them that he was not a person to be off-hand about.

It was by a happy chance that he discovered a studio to let in The Pheasantry—that strange old rabbit-warren of studios that stands in the King's Road, Chelsea, set back in a flagged courtyard guarded by a florid stone archway over which, in gilt letters, was blazoned the legend, AMÉDÉE FRÈRES.

William acquired a good studio, with living accommodation; he also acquired peace, isolation and quiet, for the first time since he got married.

Mabel was not interested in the Pheasantry; she had just realised her heart's desire. She swept the family away to Chelsea, where, in The Vale, she had discovered a charming Georgian house, with oak panelling in the rooms on the ground floor. It was no longer a Bloomsbury Family.

CHAPTER TEN

Rottingdean frivolities—The Pheasantry and Marie—Paris

I

It WOULD hardly seem sane, that, with the fag-end of the lease of Mecklenburg Square on his hands, the rent and upkeep of The Vale and The Pheasantry, William was at this time responsible for a fourth house—the old Vicarage, Rottingdean!

He had always been in love with Rottingdean from the days when he visited it to draw Kipling, and when Mabel, in the throes of one of her restless moods at Mecklenburg Square, suggested their hiring a car and driving down to have another look at it, he jumped at the proposal. The truth was, he had never given up fretting for Chaucer's House; the urban life which satisfied Mabel was not enough for William, in whom is imbedded deeply that love of the good earth which seems peculiarly an Englishman's heritage.

There would seem always to be some diabolical agency at work when the Nicholsons sallied forth to sample a new neighbourhood; *of course* the Vicarage was empty, and *of course* the vicar, for whom it was much too large, had got permission from the Ecclesiastical Commissioners to sell it, and *of course* it represented exactly the type of country residence for which (it now struck William and Mabel) they had been looking ever since they left Woodstock. William, whose genius for spending money was only equalled by his genius in finding it, managed to "raise the wind," and down went the whole caravanserai for the summer holidays.

Rottingdean of those days was an adorable place, with its duckpond surrounded by the little clutch of mellow houses—the Kiplings', the Burne-Joneses', the Noyeses' and, now, the Nicholsons'; with the beach within easy distance and the downs folded softly behind; a peaceful, paradisaical sort of place, undiscovered by the vulgarian builder and land agent who has now made that stretch of the English coast hideous.

The Trees were renting a house there. Tree, who was the worst rider in the world, subscribed to the local fashion for riding, until one day the Nicholsons' ass got loose, joined the

cavalcade and let out an ear-splitting bray at the heels of Tree's
mount. The horse bolted, Tree clinging on like a sack of potatoes
—to the joy of the young Nicholsons, who had no conception of
the deference due to the owner and manager of His Majesty's
Theatre.

There was plenty of affinity between the Nicholson and the
Tree children: so much, that Mrs. Tree called to complain that
they were in bad odour with the local farmers, having inaugur-
ated a private " hunt," which streamed out in the early mornings
across the farmers' lands. The " hounds" consisted of all the local
mongrels, rounded up for the purpose under the leadership of
Mrs. Tree's black poodle, Bingo, a charming animal whom, on
leaving Rottingdean, she presented to William. Bingo became
the love of the Nicholson household, and years later, when Lady
Tree came to call, she could hardly believe her eyes when she was
greeted by the sight of Bingo, apparently not an hour older than
when he ran with the Rottingdean " hounds."

" Bingo dear, Mother's Bingo!"

" Gr-rr," said Bingo.

" Mother's baby Bingo—come to Mother, darling Bingo!"

" Gr-rr-rr," said darling Bingo, who evidently preferred his
present quarters to his old ones, and found this evocation of the
past in the worst possible taste.

During one of their sojourns in town, William and Mabel
dined with the Trees, and were asked by Viola Tree if they could
possibly lend the Rottingdean house to herself and her husband
for a short holiday, as they had both been ill and had been ordered
to the seaside. William said Yes, if they didn't mind Kit and his
nurse, who were down there at the time; so all was satisfactorily
arranged, the Parsons went down to Rottingdean, and William
got on with his work in the Pheasantry.

After a few weeks a letter arrived, asking if one of the sitting-
rooms might be turned into a bedroom. As there were plenty of
bedrooms in the Vicarage, this seemed to call for investigation,
so, without replying by letter, William and Mabel went down the
following Sunday, to find eight horses grazing on the lawn and
the Vicarage presenting every aspect of a flourishing seaside hotel.
Not only Viola and Alan Parsons, but Lady Tree, the Duchess of
Rutland, Raymond Asquith, Edward Horner and Lady Diana,
with their maids, valets and hangers-on, were in blissful residence,
and extended a warm welcome to their unsuspecting hosts.

Having enjoyed the hospitality of their own house very much

William and Mabel returned to town, from which in due course a discreet note was despatched, to say they would be needing the house very shortly. This drew a frenzied reply from the duchess: she was so sorry, but Diana was ill in bed and they thought it might be pneumonia.

To cut a long story short, Lady Diana had pneumonia—in the famous Magda Heinemann bed. It was collecting quite a tradition; the Baroness von Hutten fainted one night when dining with the Nicholsons, and was deposited in the golden bed until removed next morning by her brother and someone whom every one took for the doctor, but who turned out to be a reporter —but that is another story. To pile Pelion on Ossa, the duchess's Pekinese was seized with sudden indisposition, and the local doctor, who attended the Nicholsons, and was called in for Lady Diana, was roused from his bed at midnight by the duchess's imperative command to come immediately and see her little dog. After inquiring the dog's symptoms, he said, " Give it a dose of the medicine I sent round for Lady Diana," and briskly rang off.

Mabel sold a picture and built a small studio for William: a sign of permanence which might have boded well, but for events beyond the control of both. There was also one great drawback to the house at Rottingdean, from William's point of view; it was "the fashionable thing" to drive down to Brighton on Sundays, and a visit to William Nicholson at Rottingdean had unfortunately become the vogue. William, who is the most hospitable soul on earth, took it all for granted, until it dawned on him that he was getting no good out of the place he had bought for rest and retirement after his hard week's work.

Marie Tempest came down to stay, and sat on the lawn, doing exquisite needlework and making conquests of Ben and Tony. The Princess Bariatinsky arrived, complete with husband and Press photographer, announcing her intention of being photographed with William—an honour he gracefully but firmly declined. Lady Tree brought Mrs. Patrick Campbell and Lord Charles Beresford—" Dear Mr. Nicholson, I brought these two sweet people down specially to see your beautiful ship!"

(Every one who has visited Apple Tree knows *The Pandora*, the original working model of the ship which went out in search of the mutineers of the *Bounty*. He acquired this magnificent model (six feet over all) for a few pounds in Edinburgh, and when, a few years ago, he gave it to me, he sent for a charming old man called Mr. Beaufort, who knew every inch of block and

OUR WINDOW.
By courtesy of Miss C. Bell.

tackle, and had her refitted. Mr. Beaufort worked in the studio for weeks, and the result was a triumph of restoration. He was then over eighty years of age, a mine of general information, particularly in regard to the Victorian theatre, of which he was a great patron, and among his many accomplishments was that of a beautiful script. He printed and illuminated the history of the *Pandora* for me on a sheet of cardboard, which was glazed, and replaced the worn old record, which we put carefully away.)

The ladies' comments, Lord Charles's demonstrations with Mrs. Patrick Campbell's parasol, and Mrs. Campbell's horrible little hairless dog which went for Lord Charles's heels while he was demonstrating, belong, alas, not here, but to the theatre. It was one of the many Rottingdean scenes which might have originated in a Coward comedy.

2

Pring came back from the business of "giving another little Pringle to the light," to find significant changes. Mecklenburg Square was no more, and in charge of The Pheasantry was a keen-eyed young Frenchwoman with a tattered Shetland shawl over her head, who was a lioness in defence of William's privacy. On her Pring managed eventually to impress the fact that she (Pring) was qualified for admission to the studio, and went in to greet William, and to learn the history of Marie.

One morning, from the top of a bus in the King's Road, William noticed on the pavement the neat, fresh, Spring-like figure of a young woman, obviously bound on her household shopping. The driver of the bus caught William's eye and pointed with his whip. "There's a pretty thing to see on a May morning!"

But the vision and the incident had slipped into the back of his memory when, in answer to a request, Newstubb, who was then the proprietor of the Chenil Gallery, and Grace Orpen's brother, sent to his studio as model a young woman who introduced herself as Marie: a thin, pretty, sharp-faced young Provençale, with a pair of dark-blue eyes full of feminine slyness, and exquisite colouring. She presented herself as a model for the nude, but William soon found she had no experience and could not hold the long, exhausting poses to which the trained model is accustomed. She had a reserved, secretive manner, spoke English

H

haltingly, with a strong accent of the Midi, which added to her charms. She admitted eventually that she had never posed for the nude before.

He eventually got Marie's history from her: that she had been married to a German husband, from whom she had been separated, and had taken another name. She took William's life and ran it with all the economy, neatness and ability of her race and class; she gave him peace, stability and organisation where formerly had been chaos, and the strength and volume of his output from now onwards was in no small degree due to Marie. She only made one mistake—from her own point of view: she fell in love with him. At this time William was only capable of loving one thing—his work. Marie's devotion was to last over thirty years, and if finally it dissolved in bitterness, it was no more than was to be expected by one who for so long had supported herself on a delusion. She at least could say, with another, " *Ronsard me célèbroit*," for with her as model he painted two of his most famous pictures, *Le Tricolor* and *Déjeuner de Marie*.

For his nude he found an excellent model and painted the beautiful *Carlina* which is in the Glasgow Gallery. This girl was tireless, and could hold the pose for hours on end; she never wished to rest when William, himself a little weary, offered her the opportunity.

Another model who came to him at The Pheasantry was the immortal Lottie, the original of *Lottie Stafford of Paradise Row* and of the equally well-known *Girl with the Tattered Gloves*. Lottie was a sunflower grown in a slum; she sat for all the contemporary painters—William, Orpen, Sickert, John—and her comments on her employers were frequently illuminating.

" You've been sitting for X, haven't you, Lottie?" " Yes, I 'ave. My word, 'e's little, that one, but 'e's sorcy!" " And how do you get on with Z?" " 'Im? I don't sit for 'im agine—no fears! W'y—'e doesn't even *arsk* yer!"

Whatever the conversation, it always ended with the same formula:

" Well, I must be puttin' on me 'at an' get back to Paradise!"

Poor Lottie; she had children every twenty-five minutes, and came, as is the wont of her kind, on hard times.

Another model, whom William found through Eric Kennington (of whom more hereafter) was the original of *Lizzie with Fish*. This was an excellent model, of a coarse, heavy type, thick-lipped and sluttish in the right, garish, paintable way. He painted her behind a table heaped with lobsters, crabs and crayfish, and this, oddly enough, is one of the canvasses we have been unable to trace. He enjoyed this kind of work much better than portraits; one could work on it with freedom and lightheartedness, with no cramping consciousness of the commission to take the joy out of one's labours.

He was also painting Marie's daughter, a really lovely young woman, with all her mother's beauty of colouring and the fortunate addition of black brows and lashes (Marie's were so fair as to be almost invisible)—an etherealised version, probably, of the father's blonde, Teutonic type. She was sitting in a black taffeta gown with little bunches of coloured flowers sprinkled over it.

On one of the walls of The Pheasantry hung the fine, belligerent portrait of William by John, who had just painted his *Smiling Woman* (now in the Tate), and had said he would like to paint William, but could not afford to do it unless commissioned. William commissioned it for a very small sum, making the stipulation that if any one bought it he would give the difference in price to John. William, overcoated, yellow-gloved, the picture of a Georgian buck, glares from the corner of an overdark eye at the beholder: a superb piece of coloratura painting, ranking with the Suggia as one of the finest of John's portraits, though not quite convincing as a likeness of the sitter. Still, perhaps in those days William did look like a gentleman pugilist, or perhaps this aspect of his personality was called out by their mutual fondness for the Ring.

William lent the portrait, when finished, to the Fitzwilliam, where it lingered so long that the Trustees began to feel they had proprietorial rights in it, and Sydney Cockerell actually wrote to William, suggesting he should present it to the Gallery. William very rightly replied that painters could not afford to give their works away, and asked John to fix a price. They decided to ask a thousand pounds, and when the cheque came William asked John to lunch and gave him the cheque. With characteristic generosity, John insisted that William should keep half.

The unexpected five hundred pounds was very welcome, for those were lean days. William's household expenses were far beyond his means, even without the ever-increasing burden of the children's school fees. Some of the extravagances were inevitable; Ben was a martyr to asthma, and, hearing that the climate of

Madeira was good for this complaint, William resolved to send him there with Mabel.

3

In order to pay for the Madeira expedition, he accepted a commission from Edward Knoblock, to decorate the latter's flat in the Palais Royal. This was his first visit to Paris since the days of Julian, except for a brief sojourn on the way to Portofino.

Marie, who, by now, was indispensable (she not only cooked and mended for him, but looked after his correspondence—she wrote English much better than she spoke it—and ran his life in general), was established at a little hotel in the Palais Royal, which looked like a little gambling hell but was the neatest and cleanest place imaginable. There she installed her birdcages, her flower-boxes and all the neatness and order which surrounded her wherever she went.

William stayed in Knoblock's flat, and worked out an elaborate scheme to be painted on glass, and set in a frame like that of a large-paned window, which was to be fitted to the walls.

Those were the days of the great *bals masqués* at the Opera. One night Marie rang him up and asked if he was not going to take her. He was just going to bed, and Knoblock was away, but he thought he could fake some sort of costume, and, looking among Knoblock's theatrical properties, he found a Venetian mask. He blackened out one eye with a patch, tore two pale blue feathers out of a feather duster and fastened them on either side to simulate side whiskers. With a Gibus, black cape and white duck trousers pulled down under the insteps, he looked like some sinister creation of Aubrey Beardsley's. So macabre, in fact, was his appearance, that when they went into the Café de Paris at about four in the morning, a woman who came in with two Americans took one look at William, shrieked off into hysterics and had to be carried out by her companions.

William painted this scene—of the empty café, the great mirrors reflecting the few dim lights and the waiter drowsing beside a pile of plates. Right down at the end, among the farthest reflection, you may see (if you happen to be in Venice) the tiny figures of William and Marie.

She was a delightful companion, unexigent, ready to be pleased with anything—so long as William did not spend too much money. One of her naïve pastimes was to sit in the gardens of the Palais by moonlight, making sand-pies in the children's sandpit. All the dwellers in the Palais Royal had keys to the gardens, and nothing delighted Marie more than to woo William away from more expensive diversions to this blameless occupation.

They came home, to find a letter awaiting William, about an exhibition of painting to be held in Amsterdam; two members of the exhibition committee wished to call upon him, to consult with him about a choice of his works to be sent to Holland.

Expecting these visitors, he was not surprised one morning at The Vale, when the maid came up to say that two gentlemen were waiting downstairs: and only glimpsed that something had gone wrong when he recognised the identity of his visitors. There is something unmistakable about a bailiff, even if you have never had one in your house before, and William had no trouble in placing a big, hulking individual who stood at the foot of the stairs, or a little one who was leaning against the front door. If there had been any question of mistaken identity, the big one would have corrected it by saying gruffly:

"We've come to take you."

It turned out that a writ had been issued in William's absence for the small sum of seven pounds, and that William—who now heard of it for the first time—was to be arrested for contempt of court.

"Have I got to be arrested, or can I settle it now?"

"You can settle it," was the surly reply, "but we've got to take you all the same."

Not quite seeing the force of this, William said he would go round to his club and get the money, but his visitors shook their heads.

"We ain't got to let you out of our sights!"

As he did not see himself arriving at the Savile with two bailiffs in attendance, William sent a messenger with a note, and, making the best of a bad job—he was in his dressing-gown, but was evidently not to be allowed to go upstairs and dress—asked the men to sit down and have some refreshment.

This they accepted, with the melodramatic preliminary of putting their revolvers on the table, and under the influence of the "refreshment" the atmosphere mellowed perceptibly, so that by the time the messenger got back from the Savile, a good time was being had by all, and William had learned quite a lot about the technique of arrest.

"If folk won't open their doors," he was told, "we goes on hammering; then, when they gets the door just off the latch, I buzzes my pal in by the seat of 'is pants; 'e's a little chap, but 'e knows 'is job."

When William produced the money, there was so much good feeling on both sides that there was no further mention of his being "taken," and he was obliged regretfully to decline a warm invitation to accompany them further on their rounds and see the system in action.

But the affair at The Pheasantry was not so easily settled. William had to go to the Jews to get out of that one; meanwhile, no one could have been pleasanter than "the man in possession." From the first day he was one of the family, acted as butler and general factotum, and put the crown on his helpfulness by posing in heraldic garments for the portrait of a nobleman on which, at that time, William was engaged. William had to pay fifty per cent on his loan for years—which troubled him less than the subsequent theft of Lord Plymouth's robes. It looked very much as if the charming bailiff had made use of his opportunities to acquaint himself thoroughly with the lie of the land, before taking his unregretted departure.

CHAPTER ELEVEN

The War, 1914—Visit to India

I

WHEN the war broke out, Tony was seventeen; Kit was a school-boy at Gresham's, and Ben's asthma put him outside military service.

Things looked very black for William. Unless he was content to stay in town and paint brass hats, he could hardly make a living as an artist. He was young enough, at forty-two, to join one of the services, but there was no immediate talk of conscription, everybody said it was going to be a short war, and he knew—none better—that artists do not, as a rule, make good soldiers. (Eventually he was to join the Artists' Rifles, where he drilled alongside of "Bunch" Keys, who kept them all in fits of laughter on parade; but military organisation seemed not to set much store by the Artists, and recruits were informed that if they wanted uniform they must buy it for themselves. Feeling, quite rightly, that if he was not worth a uniform to his country he was not worth anything else, William very coolly "deserted.")

It was now that Edwin Lutyens came forward with a solution of what seemed a desperate problem. Lutyens had been commissioned to build Delhi—he was working on the plans in his studio in Apple Tree Yard, nearly next door to William's future home; and it was he who undertook to arrange for William to paint the Viceroy's portrait.

There was an instant hurly-burly of preparation. It is always William's boast that he has made money out of any of the houses he has ever owned; he had so improved the Rottingdean house that a buyer was immediately forthcoming, and they arranged to let the house in the Vale. Mabel announced her intention of moving into the Pheasantry. Her interest in painting had recently revived, and a very good study of a dog belongs to this period.

Mabel with animals was adorable: when she spoke to them her voice softened and warmed in a fashion unknown even to her family, and over cats, notoriously the least biddable of domestic beasts, she had an influence which could only have come from deep love and understanding. Her animal paintings, and particularly this little study of a Pekinese, are full of the sentiment (*not sentimentality*) which, in her other works, is controlled by her critical sense.

They were a gay party on the voyage to India. Edwin Lutyens and Herbert Baker, on their way to superintend the foundations of their work at Delhi; George Lloyd, going to Bombay, Leonard Woolley, who left the ship on a hush-hush Egyptian commission, and Aubrey Herbert. Lawrence (not yet "of Arabia") was also on board, but held himself aloof from the lively company.

There was an odd incident passing through the Suez Canal—whose banks were lined with the wreckage of the Turkish ships our Navy had put out of action. The attention of the party was presently drawn to a good-looking young officer who rode along the bank, keeping abreast of the ship, from time to time shouting something through his cupped hands.

"Is anybody going to Lahore? Is anybody going to Lahore?"

When he saw he had got the attention of most of the passengers, he shouted:

"Because if anybody is going to Lahore, tell Mrs. X you have seen her husband."

Whereupon he swung his horse round and rode back at the gallop.

Amused by the incident, William recorded it in ink and chalk, addressed an envelope to Mrs. X at Lahore, and, in due course, posted it in Bombay.

The sequel is not, perhaps, so strange to those who know their India, and the inevitability of such encounters. Months later, when the heat had driven him up to Simla, he found himself at the viceregal dinner-table, placed next to a pretty woman whose place-card he leaned forward to read. It was, of course, Mrs. X. . . .

From Bombay they went straight up to Delhi by sleeper, William in the berth below "Ned's"; they wiled away the tedium of the journey with a pocket chessboard, which they passed up and down from one to the other. They arrived in Delhi on Christmas Eve.

The "Ned" stories must be legion, and rival in quantity, as they surpass in quality, the Goldwyn apocrypha which has filtered across the Atlantic. Our favourite concerns his letter to Lady Hardinge, who died shortly before William's arrival in India: "I wash your feet with my hair. I have very little hair,

CARLINA.
By courtesy of Glasgow Art Gallery.

but you have very little feet!" His début in the mess, with the bells chiming midnight, must be remembered by many. Rushing up to the padre, he slapped him on the shoulder. "Have you heard?—It's a boy!"

The portrait of the Viceroy was started at Delhi, and William says it was the most difficult problem in painting he ever had to tackle. Had he known in advance the peculiar obstacles that he would encounter, he would never have accepted the commission. The Viceroy, who had specified a full-length, life-size, could only sit for an hour a day, and there were many days when he could not afford even this meagre allowance of time to the painter. The light was impossible—because everything was shaded, verandas and screens preventing any direct light from ever reaching the sitter or the canvas. It was a discouraging start.

He made the discovery also that there was nothing in India that he wanted particularly to paint. This may seem a strange statement to any one who is not familiar with William's approach to his work. I have never known him to set to work readily in any foreign country we have ever visited; in fact, harsh words have passed on his almost invariable habit of embarking on "a little something" after the reservations have been made at Cook's. The Lido paintings, all of which save one (in my possession) were sold at their first exhibition, were begun at the end of a month on the Lido: when the summer visitors had departed, the sirocco was blowing up, the beach was deserted, and the black clouds piled across the Dolomites were disgorging their contents upon the terraces; the Segovian group after we had been in Segovia certainly more than two months. The luggage was labelled for Avignon and packed to the waiting car when William sat down to paint the loveliest of his Carqueiranne pictures, and the Margué was painted from notes long after we returned to England. We spent a month in La Rochelle and he produced nothing; it was not until several weeks after our return to the *appartement* on the Cours Wilson that he began, tentatively, to "make notes" for the paintings which later came along.

I think the depth and truth of William's vision of the foreign scene is due to his refusal to accept it on face value. It is only when he has learned a place by heart, has absorbed, not merely its shape and colour, but its spirit, into his subconscious, that he can begin to paint. A slick, superficial rendering of the obvious is not within his range; neither have I ever known him satisfied with anything less than the truth: that is, the truth *as it appears to him*. This applies in an even greater measure to his portraits, and explains his frequent refusals to do "just a quick sketch," which some sitters ask for because they have not the time or the patience for protracted sittings. A successful portrait, he says, must be an act of collaboration between painter and sitter, and the only times I have known a portrait to be (in William's estimation, although probably not that of his subject) a failure have been when this collaboration is lacking; when the sitter's mind is given to other matters, when he is watching the clock, counting the minutes to another appointment—and, therefore, giving out nothing.

As for the Still Lives—I have known William arrange one and have it about the studio for days before setting to work. This, in its time, has given rise to domestic contretemps, as when I absent-mindedly ate the greater part of a bunch of grapes which was ripening, in more senses than one, under the painter's eye. (It must be added that there is not a sweeter-tempered creature on earth, or one quicker to see the joke, when an accident of this sort occurs.)

It is obvious that William would not find the Indian scene paintable, for, confined within the hidebound circle of viceregal etiquette, the chatter of British society drowning whatever opportunities he might have had of hearing the temple bells, he had no time in which to absorb it, to get beneath its surface. The India which flings itself at one in terms of aniline-dye sunsets and eternal red sandstone does not readily yield up its subtleties, even to those who have time and opportunity to seek for them. He saw one landscape, right at the end, when the rain had started, and he had gone down to Bombay to wait for his ship.

At Scandal Point, a hook of land bordered by a low wall runs out into the sea. There, at sundown, came the Parsee women, to wait for the breeze that comes across the water, while behind them, squatting on their haunches, were the white-clad bearers, and the fantastic variety of their vehicles, ranging from the Rolls Royce to the tikka gharry. The light was too dim for painting, but he made notes of it—of the sunset across the water, and the moon behind them, throwing their opposite shadows, and the rocks that jutted out like coal reefs on either side of the wall.

While he was jotting this down, a soldier came up and asked him to explain his business. As William's notes are illegible to any one but himself, consisting largely of various systems of cross-hatching, which, as in heraldry, stand for the different colours, he could not explain them to the soldier, nor, when he was conducted to the barracks, to the officer in charge. It was not until he had the happy inspiration of telling them to ring up a judge he happened to be painting in Bombay that all ended well—with cocktails in the mess.

There was nothing to do but get on as best he could with the Viceroy's portrait—a task lightened somewhat by the frequent visits of the little Maxwell girls, who, like all children, had taken a fancy to William. He gave them paintbrushes and allowed them to scrawl about on the foot of the canvas—horrifying certain members of the viceregal entourage, who regarded this as no less than an act of *lèse majesté*. And at night he went out under the stars and smelt the dung fires and wondered if he had made a mistake in coming to India.

The best painting he did out there was of the Viceroy's orderly, a magnificent specimen of a Sikh, about six feet two in height, which was later bought by Mrs. Kinnell.

2

When he got home in 1916 (he had broken the journey at Marseilles, and taken a holiday at Avignon with Marie, who came down to meet him; a holiday which included two days in bed, suffering from a bad attack of *bouillabaisse*), soldiers were marching along the King's Road, Tony was in the army and Nancy on the land.

Mabel, without telling him, had let the Pheasantry, and taken herself and Ben (whose asthma was very bad indeed) to Meisenadd in Wales—and the first thing to be done was to find somewhere to live and to paint, as the house in the Vale had been let to two ladies who, as it turned out, refused to pay any rent or to vacate the house when requested. As a moratorium had been declared, William was without means of redress, and the old problem of ways and means, which had been happily in abeyance during the Indian adventure, once more " lifted its ugly head."

As it fortunately happened, Dolly Mann's husband, Harrington Mann, was going to America, and offered William the use of his studio in Eaton Square. William was grateful to accept, though Harrington's red brocade curtains made him feel ill, but it was a charming studio, and it was pleasant to have Dolly coming in and out. (She had taken, for the time being, a little

apartment near Buckingham Gate.) Dolly was the ideal companion, gay, lovely, too much used to compliments to mind
whether she received them or not. Where Dolly came the string
of her admirers was bound to follow, and there was laughter and
good humour and indifference to poverty or wealth, so long as
one was "*de bonne volonté.*" The Eaton Square studio became a social
centre, people turned up for sittings, or simply because they
enjoyed good company, and seemed to forget to go away. For so
"fashionable" a part of London, it was all very simple—as if the
spirit of the Pheasantry had been transported a few hundred yards,
and settled comfortably into its new surroundings of red brocade.

This is perhaps the place to observe that "Bohemian" society,
in the accepted sense of the term, never attracted William. He had
long since left Bohemianism to Jimmy. He never cared for the
casual, often squalid life of the studios, for the drinking,
promiscuity and general disorder which is popularly supposed to
be the life of the artist. It was less a moral objection (although
I suspect the Newark background was not unaccountable for some
of what certain people regarded, inaccurately, as William's
"puritanism"; he was, in fact, very far from puritan in many of his
notions and his "goings on"), than a rooted objection to disorder.
This statement any one who has seen the chaos of his studio may
reasonably question; but any one engaged in creative work
understands the difference between the disorder of the workroom
and that of the household. The studio itself might be strewn
with the indispensable litter of a full creative life, but the foundations must, for William, be clean: floors polished, woodwork
shining, no soiled cups and glasses standing about. After work is
finished, there is no sitting down to a cleared corner of a work-
bench, or eating out of oddments of crockery. A well-laid table,
a well-served meal; napkins once used must not appear again—
that, at least, was the rule before this second war. Everything
neat and correct in the kitchen, in the bedroom: Marie saw to all
that, and Marie's example is a hard one to follow. It was, I think,
largely this material fastidiousness that set William apart from
the "Bohemian" world in which he mingled but rarely: this, and
his instinctive recoil from anything that could be described as
orgiastic, and, therefore, damaging to his work.

War-time license disgusted him, because it seemed graceless
and tasteless. The truth is, that William has one of those hair-
spring natures whose electrical reactions gain nothing, and lose
much, from the false stimulus of alcohol. William, sober,

is fifty times gayer, more fantastical, more wildly imaginative and inventive of word and action than the average person drunk, and he very reasonably resents a condition which robs him of half his perceptiveness and a great deal more than half of. his power of enjoyment.

Pring tells a charming story of a day when William had been working very hard on a large canvas—a commission—with which he was not at all satisfied, but had decided at last, in despair, that it must "do." The studio kitten sprang to the top of the easel, slipped over on to the canvas and slithered down it, leaving the scratchmarks of sixteen little claws as a souvenir of its enterprise. William whooped with laughter.

"Oh, my God! The cat knows best!"

3

The return from the fleshpots of India to the simplicity of home life gave its usual impetus to William's work. He adores luxury—for a limited period; the reaction sets in suddenly and hard, and six months of India had given him enough of the "pukka sahib," club gossip and the ever-burning question of social precedence to serve him for a lifetime. (I rather fancy this Indian trip must have been responsible for the germ which broke out in 1938 or so, on a wet afternoon in Santander, in the following:

> "There once was a colonel from Quetta
> Who went to High Mass in a swetta.
> When he went on his knees,
> The priest said, ' Per-*lease*! '
> And fanned himself with his biretta.")

War or no war, he had *real* light, his time was his own, and he was going to paint all those subjects which the Indian interlude had obliged him unwillingly to abandon.

He had brought back with him the portraits (with the exception of that of the Viceroy), the picture of the Viceroy's servant, a few landscapes (one of the fort of Delhi) and a study of a banyan. Pringle now produced her little boy George, whom William started to paint in a white fur coat, round about Christmas, 1916.

Little George Pringle was very pale, and the white fur made him paler. When the portrait was exhibited, his fond mamma had the pleasure of overhearing the following conversation:

"How terribly ill that child looks!"

"My dear, haven't you heard?—He's *dead*!"

It was during this Eaton Square period that William painted the well-known Walter Greaves, to which reference has already been made. He also painted General Smuts (who wanted him to do camouflage work for him); he painted *The Roseate Cockatoo*, which found its way to the Luxembourg. An interesting piece of décor came his way—and William loves décor: décor of the theatre, décor of rooms. When first I went to live at Apple Tree, he was always planning out schemes for the redecoration of my room—schemes which mingled peacocks with Hogarthian gowns, with slippers, with gloves: wonderful schemes, which, alas, there was never time to do more than indicate on large sheets of paper.

Two years after he left Eaton Square he was to do his *chef d'œuvre* in this style: the famous *trompe l'œil* decoration at Folly Farm, which Lutyens built for Mrs. Merton. This masterpiece in fantasy reached its apex in the lovely dining-room, with its imitation windows, its birdcages and shadowy frieze of china plates. It seems incredible that, owing to the indifference of a subsequent owner, the only record which remains of a valuable and beautiful work of art is in an old number of *Country Life*, which published an article, and photographs, of William Nicholson's work at Folly Farm.

One morning, when William was lunching at the Ritz, it flashed into his mind that he was due at the White City for his medical examination for the army. He leapt on his bicycle and tore off to Earl's Court at full speed, arriving breathless and with his heart pumping—to be ordered immediately to strip and take his place in the line with the other examinees.

When his turn came, he started to explain to the doctor the reason for his breathlessness, and was promptly told to hold his tongue. William, who does not take kindly to dictatorship, but who recognised that in parting with his clothes a man parts with his authority, held his peace, while another doctor was summoned and proceeded to add his investigations with a stethoscope to those of the first. But as the examination seemed to be unduly prolonged, he tried again.

"Look here: I've just come down here on a——"

"C3," snapped the second doctor, and William, who, for insurance purposes, is a first-class life, was dismissed as "unfit for military service."

CHAPTER TWELVE

Apple Tree Yard—Dark days: and the end of the War—Second marriage

I

IN 1917 Tony got his commission and went to France: a great blow—for all his pride—to William. Nancy was on the land, Kit still at school, and Ben, no better for the Welsh air, was sent to Los Angeles, to see what the Californian climate would do for his complaint. And word came from Harrington Mann that he was returning, and would want the studio in Eaton Square.

Through his visits to Lutyens, William had become acquainted with Apple Tree Yard, that unnoticeable little *cul de sac* a few yards down on the eastern side of Duke of York (which was then simply York) Street. In those days there was something still pleasant and even picturesque about the little yard which, according to local records, was a bowling alley in the days of the Georges; the porcelain-faced atrocity of Eagle House had not reared its pseudo-American ten stories at the far end, or the service doors of restaurants filled it with dustbins.

At that far end, on the right-hand side, was a derelict, half-broken-down stable belonging to Lord Stafford. Through his friend George Muntzer (who had been responsible for the house-decorating commission, and was Lord Stafford's agent), William made contact with his future landlord, who agreed to put the stable and the loft over it in order; Lutyens designed a very good window for the studio, and number eleven Apple Tree Yard gradually assumed the aspect by which it was known to William's friends and visitors for the next twenty-three years.

It was a considerable work of reconstruction, although nothing was attempted save to make it into a practical workshop with some living accommodation. One of its charms, in William's eyes, was the ramp which led down from the front (and only) door to the stabling for six which he was anxious to preserve, as far as possible, in its original form, with the old Georgian iron grilles surmounting the wooden divisions of the stalls. Two of the divisions, on one side, had to be moved, to make room for a rather ramshackle little kitchen; the others were left, and became ideal storing places for canvasses.

The saddle-room was made into a tiny dining-room; William did some ingenious work there. Besides covering the walls from head level to ceiling with bookshelves, he built in a long narrow cupboard of glass, which ran under the lowest shelf, and besides holding special pieces of china and silver, gave an illusion of thickness to the wall, which, in point of fact, was no more than matchboarding between the dining-room and kitchen. It is pleasant to think of the entertainment enjoyed by the domestic staff (of one) when William regaled his guests! William had really all the fun of the fair over that dining-room: it was his doll's house. He painted spotted muslin curtains on the windows and coloured the very high ceiling black, which when varnished, increased the illusion of height and reflected the candles on the table. (There was also another means of illumination: a green-shaded light slung from the ceiling, which, at a certain stage of revelry, it was William's pleasure to set swinging. This, together with an artful rocking movement imparted to the table by William's knees, brought pallor to the cheek of many a guest.) He left the blocking for the saddles in place, and also the original colour of the walls (as much of them as was visible), which was cosily described by one of the house-painters who came in to do a little work as "purple-brown," and disposed his treasures where they would catch the eye of the visitor, and, incidentally, promote conversation, in the unlikely case of its stagnating. I never heard conversation languish in that little dining-room: mainly because no one was invited as a "social duty," and no one who was a bore.

What a jumble of odd and precious things there was in the tiny space!—An assortment of the "hundred jugs" (the rest were where one could find space for them: plunging into some forgotten cupboard, one would pull out some lovely piece of lustre, and the top of the kitchen plate-shelf was enough to make a "fancier's" mouth water), Jefferson's gloves, the original of Max's *Lord Tennyson reading In Memoriam to His Sovereign*, a fine sporting print (*Randall and Turner Sparring*) which took one back to the palmy days of Covent Garden, a beautiful little primitive madonna in black wood—lost, alas, against her dark background, Queen Victoria in needlework over the fireplace, the yellow-bordered bandanna that celebrated Polyphemus's Derby, a set of lovely papier maché trays, painted with flowers upon a pale buff found-

PROFESSOR SAINTSBURY.
By *courtesy of Merton College, Oxford.*

ation, which Mr. Nicholson had bought at the Crystal Palace Exhibition in 1851—many of these could not be seen for the overcrowding, but the feeling of them was there.

A steep staircase led to the upper floor, the larger part of which was covered by the loft—now studio, with its two deep alcoves on either side of the well which lighted the kitchen, one alcove with a tiny window which was claimed as Elizabethan. The studio, of course, was whitewashed; on the floor, with infinite pains and consideration, William laid out a beautiful design in squares of black and white linoleum. The beauty of this floor, its wide and shining scope, its multiple reflections when polished, must remain in the minds of many of his sitters. Across an angle of the room was the wide, old-fashioned fireplace, whose brick façade he colour-washed pale-blue, with a handsome old bow-fronted brass fender. When it was finished, the windows hung with their crisp white muslin curtains, it was a model of work-manlike simplicity, and the kind of thing William had been looking for all his life. Some of his delight in it was due to the fact that it was all of his own making, with no intervention from any other source, and entering it for the first time, seventeen years later, I remember a thought that flashed into my mind: it was as much *him*—as much *William*—as though no other foot had ever crossed its threshold. No one, past or present, could leave his impress on Apple Tree except William.

There was none of the hard glare of light that meets one in the average studio. Through the muslin curtains the sunlight fell sheer across the shining black and white chequer which reflected every gleaming Chippendale surface and the great bouquets with which he had chosen to celebrate my arrival. The whole effect was of dancing, glancing sunshine, mellow and summerlike, which came from white walls, from Empire mirrors and from the round-bellied jugs of pink lustre which flanked the clock on the mantelpiece.

It was the most perfectly beautiful studio I have ever seen—let's admit that, apart from party occasions, I was never to see it so tidy again. But even at its wildest, with the great round walnut table heaped with sketches, the rent-table in the corner smothered with unanswered letters and bills, paint smeared across the immaculate flooring, a kitten or two chasing bits of rag and cottonwool among the chairs, and every available surface of chest, chair and sofa covered with the débris of William's search for a little vanished something (which was under his eye all the

I

time)—it held its own beauty and we shall not look upon its like again.

There can have been few who, privileged to visit it, were not impressed by Apple Tree: for it was the complete record of a life of more than common richness. Simply, with a gesture or two—a gesture as clear as one of his own woodcuts—it summarised the great Victorian age, brushed lightly over Edwardian opulence and lampooned (as far as a good loyalist may lampoon) the primness of the Georges. At a glance, you knew the character that had created it. There was nothing haphazard—none of the usual studio junk—in that mêlée of easels, paint-tables and pochade-boxes: nothing that had not been chosen for some quality that endeared itself to William as it endeared itself to those who enjoyed his hospitality—with some pleasing notes of fantasy (worthy of the inventor of the Aspidistra Class) thrown in.

A top hat held his brushes (of which the favourites are always those which have been worn down to a sixteenth of an inch of bristle), and an assortment of military drums the sherry glasses, Balkan Sobranies and coffee cups from which he regaled his friends. Under the mantelshelf, a neat row of painted numerals, and a seal sliding on a string, testified, at least, to William's good-will to keep his appointments. He wrote the name and hour of the appointment in charcoal, and, if he happened to remember, moved the seal along the string to the appropriate date. The snag was that a newspaper, or Sid, the houseman, were not always at hand to tell him what day it was. . . . This, however, was William's only engagement book, when we lived in Apple Tree.

The soaring *Pandora*, with her noble spread of canvas, on the top of one of his high sea chests; the Callot maps; a certain beautiful old banner of golden silk, picked up in one of the old deserted kitchens of Blenheim—these also linger in the memory: and William in the midst of them all—very "dandy" in spotted shirt, snow-white slacks and socks the colour of a very young duckling . . . I had yet to discover that this was William's painting uniform, and that no thunderbolt of laundry bills would induce him to violate his samite with the useful necessity of a painting-smock.

2

Nancy had got engaged to Robert Graves, and the natural sequence of war-time engagements was a quick marriage. Mabel wanted a "smart" marriage, at the church of St. James's: disconcerting William, whose views on marriage were, like those of the majority of men, "the less to-do the better." Nancy, with her little head and long, slender neck (she had the physical elegance of the Nicholsons) rising from the picture gown of checked silk, was "a lovely bride." "Everybody" was at the wedding, and there was champagne and a tremendous reception afterwards at the studio. Although fathers are popularly supposed to resent their daughters' weddings, William was pleased. He liked his new son-in-law and the pair of them had much in common; he liked the type of physical and intellectual vigour which Robert Graves, in those days, stood for, and appreciated his poetry and the liveliness and humour of his mind.

The Zeppelin raids on London started. When the warnings sounded, the Nicholsons went down to the little dining-room and played cards. The housekeeper, who joined them, enlivened proceedings by shaking her fist at the ceiling and cursing the Kaiser each time a bomb came down. Sometimes they went out to the Piccadilly Hotel, where a few refugees, tramps and ladies of joy took shelter in the underground ballroom. The great, pale room with its crystal chandeliers, the gleaming floor, the rags and tatters of humanity sitting about on the gilt chairs and a young woman who suckled her baby, crouching on a roll of red carpet, which remained from some bygone wedding banquet, were recorded the following morning in his studio by William in a picture called *Air Raid in a London Ballroom*, now in the possession of Martin de Selincourt. Another war-time picture of great beauty and poignancy which he did about this time was a coloured sketch of a little boy, standing by the high broken window of an empty room, holding the tattered relics of the Belgian flag. This was reproduced in *King Albert's Gift Book*, one of several publications which appeared in aid of war charities.

Late one evening Tony came home on leave. William telephoned to Mabel, who caught the last train and arrived from Wales in some pale hour of the dawn. They spent a few days "painting London as red as they could afford" (to use William's own words), then Mabel and Tony went off to Wales—Tony

unfortunately developing influenza, which Mabel caught, became
seriously ill, and had to go to bed. William was wired for, and, on
his arrival, found Mabel delirious.

Tony's leave coming to an end, Mabel naturally wanted to
see him off to France, but, as she was still evidently very ill,
William forbade her to get up. Again, unhappily, as after the
birth of Ben, her will was stronger than her common sense; she
said, Could she get up if the doctor gave her permission? Think-
this was a safe gambit, William said Yes; he was taken aback
when the doctor, on his next visit, agreed that she might leave her
bed (it was long after this that William found out that Mabel had
taken all the aspirins she could find to bring down her temperature: hence the doctor's permission), and the three of them
returned to town, and Tony said Good-bye.

The same night, at Apple Tree, Mabel's delirium returned;
complications set in, and the only nurses they could get were two
women who were totally unable to control their patient. All the
good nurses were with the troops, and the burden of the nursing
fell upon William and Jimmy.

One day she seemed to rally. She asked for a cup of coffee and a
cigarette, and scrawled something on a sheet of paper they left
beside her. "Bingo." She died on the 13th of July, 1918, in her
forty-eighth year.

3

Armistice. William was in Lutyen's workshop, when the
maroons went off.

"Another raid?" said Ned.

"No, by God!" said William, who had flung open the window,
and caught the meaning of the shouting crowds who were
surging past the end of the Yard before it penetrated to his
companion. "It's *peace*, my boy!"

For William it was an empty peace. For the second time
within three months he had received a heartbreaking blow. On
the 16th of October he had received a letter from the War Office:

"The Military Secretary presents his compliments to Mr.
Nicholson and begs to inform him that a further report has now
been received at the War Office, which states that 2nd Lieutenant

J. A. Nicholson, Royal Field Artillery, died in 49 Casualty Clearing Station on the 5th of October from gunshot wounds.

"The Military Secretary is desired by the Secretary of State for War to express his deepest sympathy with Mr. Nicholson in his great distress."

From his earliest childhood, everybody loved Tony; he was such a rosy, cheerful, little boy, with "big wide-open eyes and a big wide-open mouth," according to Edward Knoblock: with a simple, friendly manner and a lack of pretension that endeared him to people older than himself while he was still a boy at his public school. All those who knew him well speak lovingly of him to-day, as the least "clever," but the most intelligent and sympathetic of the four children; affectionate, sincere, and winning friends wherever he went by force of a character disposed to friendship. Max Beerbohm wrote him a charming letter when he was going to the Front:

"MY DEAR TONY,—Your father told me that you are going to France to-morrow. When one is as old as I am one finds a certain difficulty in keeping pace with things; and, though I have twice seen you lately, I still *cannot* help thinking of you as a child in knickerbockers and with a nurse!!—so that your going to France at this moment seems to me rather odd. But with an effort I bring myself up-to-date and I send you my best wishes that you shall have good weather and an interesting time and plenty of triumph and frequent leave and everything that soldiers like to have.

"My wife sends her best wishes and thoughts too.
    "Yours affectionately,
       "MAX BEERBOHM."

Gay, extravagant and reckless, Tony was of all the children most completely William's son. Kit was too young, yet, to be a companion, and between Ben and his father there had grown up the rather tragic tension that sometimes occurs between father and son who are engaged in the same art or profession. It was unfortunate for Ben, now showing great promise as an artist, that he was the son of a famous painter ; he was still too young to dismiss the question of rivalry, and to realise that there was room for two Nicholsons in the world of art. He was very earnest, and like many young men, very humourless about his future. It was to Tony that William turned for laughter, and, with Tony's death, it seemed as though all laughter had been drained out of the world.

However, like many others who had lost "all they cared about" in the war, William was swept into the celebrations of Armistice night. He and Marie went to the Café Royal, which was packed from wall to wall with blithe spirits, who imposed their conviviality on the (slightly) soberer section of the community. Among them a charming young officer lurched from table to table—"A toash'—a toasht—we've gotta have a t-toasht!" When sufficient attention was focused upon this reveller, and every one was laughing and all glasses were lifted, he brought out his proposal in a triumphant explosion: "La'zh an' zhen'lemen—I give you—a toash! The dear—ole—Kaizher!"—a toast which was honoured as it could only be in an English restaurant at the end of four years of war; "the rafters dirled" with shouts of "The dear—old—Kaiser!"

William and Marie were swept into Piccadilly Circus, which was a mêlée of traffic, surging in all sorts of directions, of service men trying to find their girls, or their buses, or both, of excited, tipsy, happy people. William, assuming all the authority of which he is, at moments, disconcertingly capable, leapt into the traffic stream, checked it by imperiously holding up his hand, wrenched open the door of a Rolls-Royce filled with fat women in sables, thrust in a couple of Tommies while others swarmed upon the roof, slammed the door and shouted "Drive on!"—a pleasant jest, which he repeated until there was quite a perceptible thinning of the foot traffic in his part of the Circus, while liveried chauffeurs, who must have shuddered for their coachwork, bore onwards into the purlieus of Mayfair and Belgravia the beaming proletariat who, for that night, were kings and queens of London.

So much for Armistice Night. Next morning the gutters piled with paper streamers, the carnival caps trodden into the mud, the whole miserable air of "after the party" brought back to many beside William the cold realities of "after the war."

As usual, he flung himself into work as a panacea for his unhappiness, and once again Lutyens came to the rescue with a new proposal. He was designing a house in the country for a Mrs. Merton, and he suggested that William should undertake the décor.

Unhappily, no record but a photographic one remains of the charming and original motif of that dining-room, with its painted frieze of plates, its *trompe l'œil* bell-pulls, windows and birdcage, which mingled fantasy with realism in the fashion dear to William's heart. Pring went down and picnicked while the work was in progress, and returned full of enthusiasm for the scheme and the manner in which it was being carried out.

Shortly before Mabel Nicholson's death, she had written to a friend in China:

"We have found some new friends, Major and Mrs. Stuart-Wortley, with whom we go about a good deal."

Major Stuart-Wortley was reported missing at the time of Mabel's death; news came through later that he was killed. In 1919 William married his widow.

CHAPTER THIRTEEN

*" The Owl," and some important portraits—An adventure in
stained glass, and some changes of scene—Back to the theatre*

I

WHILE William was working down at Folly Farm, an idea was
born which was later to blossom into one of the most interesting
artistic and literary adventures of "after the war." The few
existing copies of *The Owl* are now collectors' treasures, and its
history, known then to only a limited public, is probably forgotten.

It was during his midday rest out-of-doors that William,
playing as usual with pen and paper, worked out the cover design
of an owl with six (and a half?) little owls somersaulting round
him, against a background which might be snowflakes, or falling
leaves, or what you will. ("Now, Mr. Nicholson, will you tell me
what your picture *means*?" "Well, supposing you tell me what it
means to *you*." "Oh . . . I suppose it means . . ."—*long and
confused explanation.* "Of course, you're right. That's it!" How
often this conversation takes place, and how tired he is of explain-
ing that a picture means just what it conveys to the spectator's
eye.)

When completed, he showed the design to Robert Graves.
"Here's an idea for a book, Robert, which starts, just as it ought
to start, with the cover." He went on to describe his idea of what
such a book should be; that it should be called *The Owl*, that it
should be an anthology of all the best in drawing, in prose and in
poetry, by contemporary artists and writers, and that it should
appear periodically, at no settled dates, but only when its com-
pilers had collected enough of the right kind of material to justify
its publication. Like many of William's ideas, it was thoroughly
idealistic and uneconomic in conception, but he communicated
his enthusiasm to Robert Graves and W. J. Turner, who agreed to
make himself responsible for the letterpress, while William
looked after the illustrations.

William, moreover, undertook to finance the venture, and
between them they succeeded in interesting a remarkable list of

artists and authors, who professed themselves willing to accept the lowest possible rate of remuneration to contribute their work to *The Owl*. Among them were Max Beerbohm, Edmund Blunden, John Masefield, J. C. Squire, John Galsworthy, Robert Graves. T. E. Lawrence, Siegfried Sassoon, Robert Nichols and W. J, Turner. The editors also got permission to reproduce unpublished work by Thomas Hardy, R. Caldecott, Sir Edward Burne-Jones, and Pellegrini (a brilliant sketch, on blotting-paper, of Swinburne. I do not know whether this blotting-paper effort inspired William's caricature, also on blotting-paper, in green ink, of Max, all starry-eyed, frock-coated, beside a cactus. Mr. Nicholson and Mr. Beerbohm made a feature of caricaturing one another. During the present war, William, strolling down St. James's Street, came across a group of Dominion soldiers, convulsed on the pavement outside the Nicholson Gallery. Going to see the reason for the mirth, he was confronted by one of Max's caricatures of himself, balancing a little cane on the tip of an outstretched finger. It is not recorded that the soldiers recognised the original in their midst. William had never seen the work before, but thought so well of it that he bought it at once.)

The list of artist contributors also included, beside William Nicholson, Eric Kennington, William Orpen, George Belcher, Joseph Crawhall, Frank Dobson and Pamela Bianco. There is a very charming line and wash illustration by Nancy Nicholson.

The Owl achieved three numbers. Even at the price of twelve and sixpence, which was low for the standard of the publication, it could not pay for itself; it had no publicity and reached only a very small public. William hoped to recoup himself by calling in all the unsold copies and selling them later to collectors. He had no regrets. It was just one of those optimistic and beautiful adventures which in a world governed by commercialism are "their own reward," and he had the satisfaction of having contributed something new and valuable to a post-war world which needed some such leadership to regain its standards and to set new ones.

To all those who were part of his former life, the years immediately following William's second marriage are something of a blank, which is not easily filled in because so much of it is domestic. New interests had swept him temporarily out of town, and after Liza's birth at Meisenadd, he made a brief return to Rottingdean, where he took the Burne-Joneses' house. Recently in her book called *Three Houses*, Angela Thirkell made rather acrimonious reference to the "destruction," by William Nicholson, of one of her grandfather's frescoes, which, when the Nicholsons took the house, adorned one of the nursery walls. Far from this being the truth, William, who had a great regard for Burne-Jones, and who recognised in the fresco one of the finest examples of the work of the painter he regarded as the best of the pre-Raphaelites, took infinite pains for its preservation. The wall was in a bad condition and the painting was in danger of obliteration. With great care and skill, he managed to "lift" the fresco from the wall with a knife, afterwards mounting and glazing it; he eventually gave it to Lady Horner, the great admirer, friend and some-time subject of Burne-Jones.

Edith Nicholson's father, Sir Lionel Phillips, gave her the Manor House at Sutton Veny, under the Wiltshire downs which William always loved. He loved the house too, long and low, with a high, raftered hall which was the living-room; it had an enormous chimney, in which the bees nested, regardless of the fact that they were smoked out each time the logs were lighted on the hearth; and here, at Sutton Veny, he enjoyed a hard-earned peace, painting the things he wanted to paint—small landscapes and Still Life, with an occasional portrait thrown in only as a make-weight.

As always, the place was swarming with children. Edith Nicholson had two by her first marriage, and there was Liza, a baby. Nancy's first baby had been born a few months before her Aunt Liza ("Here comes Aunty in her pram" was a favoured witticism with the young), and then there were three more in quick succession. They were often down at the Manor House, and the broad lawn was scattered with lovely children, who found it an ideal playground. Kit came in his holidays, and Ben—to play tennis, as he had played Diabolo, always a little better than any one else. Kit was growing into a schoolboy whose high spirits needed sometimes a little wholesome correction.

"If you don't behave, Kit, you'll have to come and sit by me," said William, in a burst of fatherly discipline.

Kit's answer summarised the relationship between William and his children. Beaming, he carried his chair round to William's side of the table.

"Oh, Father! *May* I?"

But Liza was her father's idol. It had been nobody's fault that, in the childhood of the others, the responsibilities and anxieties of keeping up a home and family had a little damped down his enthusiasm for his first brood. His second wife was not dependent on him, and he had only Ben's and Nancy's allowances and Kit's schooling to pay for. And, although frequently surrounded by children, he was no longer in a whirligig of them.

Liza came into his bed in the morning; the "Blokes" were drawn for Liza, which, later, were published by Faber & Faber; for Liza and the grandchildren he wrote and illustrated the two charming books for children, *Clever Bill* and *The Pirate Twins*. Nancy designed the first pirate twin, who was made out of an old sock, and he "modelled" for his own portrait and that of his brother. These books also were published by Faber & Faber, and in U.S.A. by an American firm; but the American colour printing was so execrable that William would entertain no further proposals from this house.

There was Gipsy too: the lovely silver-grey Alsatian bitch which came to William from Mells. He was staying with Lady Horner, and making a pencil portrait of her grand-daughter, Perdita (now Lady Perdita Jolliffe), and in return was given one of the newly-littered Alsatian puppies to which he had taken a fancy. Gipsy was the perfect companion, as wise as Minerva and as gentle as a fawn; with grain scattered along her back, she would stand shivering while the chickens flapped and fluttered and pecked their way from her ears to her tail.

Among all this peace and happiness, which had been lost to William since Woodstock days, work flowed from his brush. London saw little of him, but an occasional sitter came down to Sutton Veny, to be painted in ideal circumstances—from the painter's point of view—away from the hundred and one distractions of the London scene. An interesting and famous portrait of this period, commissioned by Sir Edwin Lutyens (but not painted at Sutton Veny) was the *Miss Gertrude Jekyll*, now in the Tate.

Miss Jekyll, known to her friends as "Bumps," (a nickname invented by Lutyens—of course), was a genius and revolutionary of gardening, and one of the people who emphatically did not want to be painted. What, she inquired bluntly, did any one want with a portrait of an old woman like her? It was one of the few occasions when William, out of his affection for "Bumps," as much as on account of the commission, persisted against a sitter's unwillingness, and every difficulty was put in his way—not out of malice, for a more charming personality never existed; but "Bumps" just did not want to be painted, and was not going to indulge in any sitter's antics for the benefit of the painter. Her reluctance provided William with just the kind of problem in which he delights, since it transpired that the only time at which "Bumps" could be painted was in the evening, by the light of a single lamp, which William placed between himself and the sitter.

Dodging the lamp, no less than the old lady's objections, William produced one of the most charming and human of his studies of old age—a valuable record of a valuable person. The hands, placed finger to finger, the silky bandage of white hair and the solid, contemplative modelling of the features must be known to all who pretend to an interest in William's work.

Less well known, because it is in private possession, is his Still Life of *Miss Jekyll's Gardening Boots*, which he painted for Sir Edwin Lutyens. The old pair of army boots in which she trudged about her gardens are invested with so much of their owner's character that they seem to have a life of their own.

(At the National Gallery Exhibition in 1942 this was exhibited together with the beautiful and brilliant study called *Miss Simson's Boots*: an elegant Victorianism in white satin, picked out from among William's collection of footwear, nearly as various as his collection of gloves. Who Miss Simson was no one knows, but she had a charming foot and a pretty taste in clothing it. Such paintings show William as the romantic. He used the shoe motif once again, in one of his rare watercolours—a little pair of black ballet shoes, whose scattered ribbons twine about the stem of a green wineglass.)

Also belonging to this period, although it was not painted until 1925, is the well-known portrait of Professor George Saintsbury —which was painted in circumstances nearly as unpropitious as the Miss Jekyll: a tiny, crowded room, and William crushed up against a window, to get as far as possible from his subject, and from the famous Saintsbury nose. It was a nose of vintage and came near to defeating William, to whom truth is all, but his sense of chivalry almost equally sensitive. He hit at last on the brilliant idea of treating the nose like a Still Life: which relieved him of his embarrassment and relegated the aggressive feature to its proper place in the scheme of the portrait.

Miss Jekyll and *Professor Saintsbury* are admirable examples of William at his happiest in portraiture. Smooth and conventional beauty is less grateful to him than character. The very young and the very old are his favourite subjects; "pretty"

women are his bane, although he has made some beautiful portraits of beautiful ones—notably that of the Countess of Spencer;
but here was something much deeper than physical beauty, which
the painter's vision has captured and recorded on the canvas.

Portraitists have some odd experiences now and again. A
Society woman asked William to do a nude of her, and William
agreed, thinking she might make a good nude. After a few visits,
however, she asked if her current lover might be present during
the next sitting. As William does not hold with the mixture of
the amorous and graphic arts, the sittings came to an untimely
end.

2

Another "new adventure" came through Lady Horner, who,
asked William if he would design a memorial window for her
husband, Sir John Horner, in the private chapel at Mells. William,
who had never worked in stained glass, jumped at the idea, and
worked out the simple and beautiful design based on the legend
of St. Francis—both Sir John and Lady Horner having Francis
(Frances) among their names. The saint stands on the right, his
hands extended towards the shoal of fish that sweeps, partly
submerged, and partly clear of a deep-blue wave, up and towards
the hem of the robe of the Virgin, whose halo swings out and
collects the upper part of the design.

There are all sorts of curious and interesting things to observe
in this window, of which one of the most important is that the
design ignores the mullions, and carries on from wall to wall,
an idea which, so far as we know, had never previously been used,
the common plan of the designer being to break the window space
into panels, with a separate design in each. The value of the
continuity appears in the lofty and noble effect of the design.
Another interesting point is the ties themselves, which, instead
of being arbitrary strips of lead, support the birds which swirl
around the figures of the Virgin and Child. The haloes of the two
Holy figures form separate centres for the circles which suggest a
diffusion of light and the rays of both haloes, prolonged, follow
slightly different angles of projection, and, in William's words,
"Give life to the design."

Many designers of windows hand their designs over to the
worker in stained glass and leave them to it, but not so William,

who, with the assistance of a student who had some experience of window-making, proceeded to cut out and set up every piece of his own window. Apple Tree was ankle deep in glass splinters, and every now and then "one got a funny feeling in one's feet," and looked down, to see them covered in blood, as the glass dust worked in everywhere. The effect, when finished, paid for such discomforts, and on sunny days the light streams blue and brown and silver across the equestrian tomb designed by Lutyens to commemorate the two sons who were killed in the war.

Those were years full of variety and change of scene. Visits to France resulted in a rich harvest of landscape, and the Carnegie Institute invited William to Pittsburg, to judge an exhibition of contemporary art. He is one of the few visitors who have something good to say of Pittsburg, for he arrived, by a happy accident, during an industrial strike; Pittsburg, relieved of its pall of smoke, had beauties unsuspected by many of its inhabitants. (This was his third visit to America; he had been over to paint a portrait, and came back beglamoured by American hospitality, but found the States, as a working milieu, useless to him. He could not paint there. It is one of William's favourite tales against himself, that, if he had no use for the States, the States had no use for him. He was asked to send over a collection of his works, which, at the end of twelve months touring, returned to him intact—not one picture sold! The organisers of the exhibition wrote to him very regretfully, that it would doubtless have been different if William had accompanied his work into the States. This, however, is the last thing he could have been persuaded to do; the continental custom of putting the artist on show with his pictures has always seemed to him vulgar, stupid and beneath the artist's dignity.)

He and his wife went for a holiday to South Africa, where they stayed with her parents, and William delighted in the new landscape and the beautiful painting light, but did no work of importance. India, America, South Africa; for all their individual drama and significance, they failed to kindle the creative spark in one whose source of inspiration is essentially European. One may be sure he had eyes for all their beauties, but the desire to record them was absent.

In his introductory remarks to the Nicholson-Yeats exhibition at the National Gallery in 1942, Sir Kenneth Clark writes:

"William Nicholson is one of those rare and fortunate artists who have recognised the nature of their talents. He handles his sensations with the fastidious economy of a Max Beerbohm; in fact, some of his finest pictures may be compared to essays in which the subject is slight—a black swan, a china bowl, a pair of boots—and success depends on delicacy of perception and coherency of style. Like all good essayists he looks at his subject, animate and inanimate, with a kind of humorous sympathy. His comments are so tactful and urbane that some of his pictures may seem at first sight to be plain statements of fact; and probably he would claim no more for them. But we are not long deceived by this half-ironical reticence. The ordinary eye can no more select and arrange the data of sight with Nicholson's perfectly-balanced taste than it can reduce them, like Yeats, to lumps of molten colour."

The expression "half-ironical reticence" is particularly good. "Give them Pity and give them Irony . . . just a little Irony— O give them Pity!"—that is one of Hemingway's drunks; Hemingway, one of William's favourite modern writers, as Irony and Pity are two of his favourite qualities. But one cannot be ironic about the unknown, one cannot pity that which commands one's wonder and one's veneration. In forbearing to record those foreign countries—foreign in a sense that no European scene is foreign—William was "recognising the nature of his talents." He was unable to identify himself with the scene; this, in an artist whose approach to his subject is highly subjective, rarely, if ever, and then only on occasions of what he himself would call "failure," objective, is sufficient to explain the matter.

3

Just how or why William swung back into the orbit of the theatre no one seems to remember. It must be understood that for an artist who had reached William's point of eminence in his work, scene-designing could never "pay," in the financial sense of the word. It could have done if he had belonged to the class of theatrical craftsman who dashes off a sketch and tosses it over to the scenic artists to get on with, but this was not his way. Such work as he has done for the theatre has been truly a "labour of love," for the offered terms have never been commensurate with the amount of time and trouble he has given to the task. He enjoyed his theatre work for he said, "One can make such experiments and all will be destroyed in a short time if it fails or not"; and he liked a big brush.

Between 1920 and 1930 he was connected with three important productions: *Polly*, the ill-fated successor to *The Beggar's Opera*, whose run it would probably have rivalled, but for the sudden illness of the leading man and his withdrawal from the cast; *On With the Dance*, which many people remember as the most brilliant of all the Cochran revues (what a cast!—Alice Delysia, Hermione Baddeley, Ernest Thesiger, Douglas Byng, Nigel Bruce and Leonide Massine were only a few of the stars who sparkled in that galaxy), and *The Marquise*, with Marie Tempest, at the Criterion Theatre.

Polly, with its charming sets and its charming costumes, requires no description to recall it to the thousands who crowded the Savoy Theatre for its too-short run. One amusing incident lingers in William's memory. On the night before the production, the Act Drop was still unpainted, and, happening to meet that fine sculptor, Frank Dobson, William in his despair, begged him to lend him a hand. Dobson good-naturedly consented, and the pair of them worked all night. William had painted two tall palm-trees, which swung from the lower corners of the curtain, crossed in the middle, and burst into foliage in the top opposite corners from those from which they sprang. At the foot of these trees, on either side, was to be piled the luggage belonging to the fair castaways—trunks and bandboxes, partly disgorging their contents, hats and sunshades, all the feminine impedimenta of travel. They had plenty of fun in inventing all these trivialities, and Dobson, on William's instructions, added an enormous powder-puff to his corner, and "called it a day." Looking at the results of their labours, William insisted that Dobson, as well as himself, should sign the finished product, so Dobson put a neat "Frank Dobson" near the powder-puff and they both went home.

On the following night, when the curtain was lit for the first time, the full glory and force of the lighting focused, for some reason, on the powder-puff, and William was left to wonder about the emotions of a serious sculptor, on seeing his name trumpeted from a powder-puff.

In *On With The Dance*, William was commissioned by Cochran to do the décor of two of Massine's ballets, *The Rake* and *The Tub*. *The Rake*, billed as "A Hogarth Impression," gave full scope, not only to William's sense of period, and his love for this period in

MISS JEKYLL.
By courtesy of the Trustees of the Tate Gallery.

particular, but to his power of creating an atmosphere which contributes to the actor's impersonation. The great candles rushing upwards which he painted on the backcloth, each candle swinging slightly out of the "true," and the confusion of the divergent rays, set the stage for riot, for the dissolute, for all the rich redundance which the choreography suggested. It made the spectators a little doubt their eyesight and their balance—even as the Rake himself was doubting his.

William became very friendly with Massine, for whose work he had a great admiration, and on several occasions Massine went down to Sutton Veny, taking William in his car, which he drove with the same exquisite sense of rhythm which he exploited in his dancing.

For *The Marquise* William designed and painted a grand set in what he describes as "rather a wonderful red," of an octagonal room with the floor painted to represent black and white marble. His association with the management was not a wholly peaceful one: there was trouble over a chandelier, and, with Marie Tempest, over a superb costume of sulphur yellow and black which he had designed for one of the actors, and which she declared was going to "kill" her own appearance. Strange that so supreme a mistress of her art could not realise its value as a challenge; stranger still that she should have so little confidence in her own powers as to fear the rivalry of a dress. William stubbornly refused to alter his design in any way, and she had to accept it; long acquaintance had probably shown her the imprudence of arguing with William on his own subject!

One of the backers "treated" the production to a beastly brownish brass chandelier (William's description), heavy and graceless, which, without William's permission, was hung in the middle of his scene. He immediately had it taken down—to the disapproval of the management, who thought that his unusual set would be disliked by the audience. "But it cost *so* much!—and So-and-so (the donor) would be so offended!" William did not give a damn for So-and-so's offence, but he was so infuriated by the attitude of Marie Tempest and Graham Browne that he would not go near the theatre on the first night. When Graham Browne rang him up, after the show, to tell him what a success it had been, and how much his décor had been admired, William was very frigid, and actually did not return to see the effect of his set for some time.

When he did—or at any rate, shortly after—he came near

K

to causing a personal furore: as, like many people who are not used to the wings of a theatre (which William *was*), he managed to fall foul of one of the flats, and discovered himself on the stage in full view of the audience. The sudden appearance, in a period set, of a character in gents' evening suitings must have been sensational; mercifully, Mary (at the height of one of her important scenes) had her back turned. The only person who appeared to notice was the stage manager, who, from the prompt corner, made hideous faces and gestures at William, who proceeded to do the only thing possible: which was to stroll calmly across to the opposite exit, where he was met by the stage-manager in a state approaching apoplexy. William took the words out of his mouth.

"Don't you ever say one word about this!" he threatened him: and left the theatre—this time for good. So far as he knows, Mary was never told, and as for the audience—they probably thought they dreamt it.

That year—1927—was the year when William, returning home after an absence, found a letter to say that he had gained an award—at of all places—the Olympic Games at Amsterdam, and was invited to come over and receive—of all things—the Gold Medal for his Almanac of British Sports. He had never heard that the Olympic Games had any connection with the Arts, and, not unnaturally, thought there must be some mistake. However, he decided to go and, looking at the date of the letter, saw that he ought to be in Amsterdam already; so he rushed out, booked reservations on a plane (his first flight), and arrived in time for lunch on the penultimate day of the Games.

Having lunched, he made inquiries about his prize, and discovered that Heinemann had sent over some originals of his Almanac of Twelve Sports. Two good seats had been put at his disposal, and he and his companion enjoyed all that remained of the Games: after which he had the sensation of his life on hearing his name called on the loudspeaker, the flag of his country was flown, and the enormous stadium thundered with applause for William, and the work he had done some twenty years ago.

This was the second time he had gained a gold medal; the other time was at Munich, for his *Queen Victoria*. It could not have arrived at a more opportune moment, for William was "broke." He instantly pawned the medal and devoted the proceeds to the solution of his embarrassments.

CHAPTER FOURTEEN

*Some " True Travellers"—An experiment at the Zoo—First
visit to Spain*

I

WILLIAM has a *tendresse* for tramps. It began with W.H.—"Bill"—
Davies, the poet and "true traveller", who, at the time of William's
first meeting with him, was just entering on that curious little
social phase of which he has written in his biographies. Strange
compact of vanity and simplicity, there was a "borderline"
streak in Bill's mentality that charmed William, who is always
drawn by the element of fantasy. Bill had an artist's reverence for
other artists, and a naïve fancy for having himself immortalised
by their brushes or chisels; William painted an excellent head of
him.

In his contacts with society, Davies had all the touchiness of
one out of his social depth (there was a disastrous meeting with
Max Beerbohm, of which Davies has given his own version in the
second volume of his autobiography: the truth being that Max,
the most courteous creature on earth, having "cracked himself"
to say the right things to the poet, from whom he was separated
by the deepest gulf that ultra-sophistication and ultra-simplicity
could devise, made some unhappy reference to "helping lame
dogs over stiles," which the hyper-sensitive Davies interpreted
as a gibe at his physical disability): yet the most flattering
attentions from lion-hunting ladies—this was a period when a
poet in one's drawing-room was supposed to confer social *cachet*
on the hostess—left him unmoved and unspoilt.

Foremost among the lion-hunters was Lady Cunard, who
invited Davies to lunch with her in Grosvenor Square. Bill,
probably expecting a *tête-à-tête* with his hostess, was ushered into
a company of titled guests, ambassadors and the like, whose names,
when they were introduced, conveyed nothing whatever to the
tramp poet.

Meeting him a few days afterwards, William said:

"Well, Bill, I hear you've been lunching in Grosvenor Square!
Who was there?"

Davies considered the question before replying with the utmost simplicity:

"I think—just some of the neighbours."

His relationships, even with his closest friends, were all beset with little mysteries. William had asked him down to Rottingdean, where he stayed for a few days, apparently very happily, until there came a morning when he announced rather abruptly that he must go back to London. William asked why; Bill was evasive; William pressed him to stay; Bill was insistent on departure. It at last came out that he had come to the end of his nightlights. When William assured him that nightlights were procurable, even in Rottingdean, the matter settled itself peaceably and Bill contentedly unpacked his baggage and remained with his friends.

William's second tramp was Mr. Bohun.

It was a wet and wretched night of winter, and William was walking back across Hyde Park Corner, after dining with friends. The derelict specimens of humanity huddled on the park benches touched him deeply, and he commented on them to a policeman.

"Isn't there anywhere for these people to go? Do they have to stay out-of-doors on a night like this?"

The policeman shrugged his shoulders.

"There's plenty of lodging-houses. They'd sooner be outside than under a roof and four walls, most of 'em. We got no orders to disturb 'em, so long as they behave themselves."

After the policeman had gone, William went up to the nearest bench, and touched a bundle of rags on what might have been its shoulder. A deplorable head withdrew itself from the shelter of a collar.

"Look here: can't you find somewhere better to sleep on a night like this?"

After a pause . . .

"Thank you; I am quite all right, I am used to sleeping here."
—An educated, even a dignified voice. There is no dignity like the dignity of a tramp.

"Come now, you'll catch your death of cold in this rain. Go and find a lodging of some sort—here's half a crown——"

The half-crown was put aside with a courteous gesture— good God! thought William: what sort of a tramp is this, refusing half a crown?

"No, thank you. I am really quite comfortable."

" . . . Tell me," said William presently. "Isn't there anything I could do for you—anything you'd like?"

A deprecatory movement or two; when William persisted—

"Well . . . I hardly like to mention it. There *is* one thing I should like. I should like a bath."

"Very well. You shall have a bath. I live in Apple Tree Yard—do you know where that is?"

"Oh, yes, very well indeed. As a matter of fact, I get most of my food there."

When William expressed surprise, as well he might, his companion explained that he scavenged the dustbins of the Apéritif Grill. "The food is of very good quality; of course, it is a little mixed. . . ."

"Come to Number 11, Apple Tree Yard in half an hour," said William hurriedly, "and I will have a bath ready for you. By the way, what's your name?"

A hand fumbled in the recesses of what might once have been a pocket: brought out a bundle of papers, extracted from them a visiting-card. Under the light of the nearest lamp William read the inscription, "Mr. Bohun."

"I'm descended from the Knights of Woodstock," said Mr. Bohun, as simply as if it was quite a common knightly custom to sleep under the trees of Hyde Park.

While waiting for his visitor's arrival, William collected an old suit, some underclothing and shoes, and put them in the bathroom. When the bell rang he went down to open the door.

"Come in, Mr. Bohun."

"Well . . . have you got any newspapers? I'm rather wet—I'm afraid I'll spoil your stair carpet."

Standing on newspapers, Mr. Bohun dripped conversationally for a while beside the stove.

"Your bath's ready, and I've put some clothes in the bathroom for you. When you've undressed, pitch the others into the yard."

The Mr. Bohun who emerged from the bathroom an hour later was hardly recognisable, and considerably less romantic-looking in William's discarded suit. Pleasant, calm, and completely master of the situation, he smiled when William offered him a batch of illustrated papers, light novels and so forth which he had thought might beguile the hours on a park bench.

"Thank you very much, I'm afraid I can't manage that sort of reading. As a matter of fact, I'm studying the French classics."

"Mr. Bohun," said William. "Tell me: what sort of life do you look forward to? Are you always going to be as poor as you are now?"

Mr. Bohun appeared to consider the matter.

"Well . . . no. As a matter of fact, I am expecting some money: some money which is due to me through my family."

"How much? A hundred pounds? Two hundred?"

"Oh, no. I wouldn't like to tell you—" Mr. Bohun smiled slowly. "You wouldn't believe me. But, really, a great deal of money. Meanwhile, as everything is very unsettled and uncertain, I prefer to do nothing. I always find it better, when things are uncertain, to do nothing whatever." He looked at William. "May I ask why you have been so very kind to me to-night?"

"Oh . . . well, I'm not having so good a time myself," said William, "and I thought perhaps you might bring me luck."

This was not the end of Mr. Bohun. Many months afterwards, William was crossing the park, to dine with the same people with whom he had been dining on the night of his strange encounter. On the end of a bench—it was again raining—he recognised Mr. Bohun, still wearing his suit, which by now was in almost the same sorry state as the previous rags.

After dinner he asked his host if he happened to have an overcoat to give away, and left the house with a good coat which he duly delivered to Mr. Bohun. A few days later the housekeeper at Apple Tree came upstairs to say there was "a person" at the door. It was Mr. Bohun, who had called to return some small change and a silver cigarette-case which he had found in the pockets of the overcoat.

Only one word more of Mr. Bohun. He was arrested for having no visible means of support. Seeing an account of it in a newspaper, William wrote a note to the magistrate, describing Mr. Bohun as an estimable person: which got him his discharge.

Many people must know Mr. Brazil, who sits like a black-bearded Father Christmas in one of the little passages between Jermyn Street and Piccadilly. There is a stiff nor'-easter in those whiskers, and Mr. Brazil's conversation, when he can be persuaded to talk at all, smacks of the high seas. Some time able seaman, the descent of a bomb on Babmaes garage, where he happened to be sheltering for the night, had left him quite unmoved when we came across him the following morning. He was a little angry; one sensed sailorly invective withheld out of deference for feminine company behind those angry brows. But nightfall found him nesting, as usual, in his little self-made bunk slung to the railings. A modest curtain of sacking preserved Mr. Brazil's slumbers from the irreverent, but William or I, passing, invariably caught the twinkle of a bright brown eye, and a friendly mumble of " Good-night, sir—good-night, ma'am." Why the police had to interfere, and remove Mr. Brazil's little bunk, we do not know; we certainly resented it quite as much as its owner did.

One summer William asked Mr. Brazil to sit for him; but, alas, he spoiled himself by changing his suit and having his beard trimmed for the occasion. A strangely neat and tidy Mr. Brazil, with a complexion we had never, up to that moment, suspected of being as fresh as a girl's, turned up for the sittings. William made the best of it, but Mr. Brazil—he pronounces it, by the way, *Braz*-il, with the accent on the first syllable—in his state of trans-figuration, was heavy going: by no means the cheery soul of Jermyn Street.

Mr. Brazil and Mr. Bohun, by the way, had one thing in common: they changed their underwear every day. Newspaper, explained Mr. Bohun, is very warm, clean and comfortable.

2

Apple Tree, which, for a little while had languished, had virtually come to life again. Not that Sutton Veny had lost its power of attraction; it might even be said that this grew more poignant as William's visits there became more limited by the demands on his time and his brush. Have we not said somewhere that William's first and his last love is his painting? Apple Tree, for him, was the home of his mistress: a place dedicate and immune from domestic intrusions. It was never, at any time, a "woman's place," and I do not think he ever wanted women there: not, at any rate, the kind of woman who is not dismissable at whim—the paid housekeeper, the sitter, the occasional visitor. Apple Tree was in no way adapted to domesticity, as both his wives discovered; as I was later to discover, but perhaps it was easier for me, with very little time to spare for domestic con-siderations—and those I was content to leave to the houseman who had learned the art of looking after William in the way that suited him best.

It was not many sitters, after all, who could take time off

to stay in the country, while William painted their portraits, and one of the many conveniences of Apple Tree was its situation within a bow-shot of Piccadilly Circus. So, gradually, he settled back into his nest, and Sutton Veny became a week-ending place. Soon after dawn on summer mornings he and Gipsy were on the Great West Road, her wet black nose bobbing against the windscreen of the little M.G. A couple of days of delight, with Liza and Gipsy, and back to town again, where there was plenty of work to be done. Portraits again were in the offing, and, although they represented the least agreeable side of his task, they had to be undertaken. William was not minded to become a pensioner—and in Apple·Tree he sought for, and found, his independence.

Among the portraits of this period was the one of Diana Low, about which Robert Nichols wrote lyrically after the exhibition at the National Gallery in 1942:

"One can delight and delight and go on delighting in the wonderful painting . . . the masterly freshness of the flesh tones in her sunlit face and the amazing rendering of the eyes with the light coming *sideways* through them. One can delight in all that, and the whole thing, while staying strictly within the medium, is crying—I should almost say shouting—something at one. And what it's shouting is that youth and courage and character— such as this young woman has—that the mere sight of these things is *happiness*. In token whereof you have hung out a yellow (golden?) banner. You know, William, when I saw the picture I could have shouted for joy."

It is seldom that the painter is rewarded with coherent, yet absolutely spontaneous and sincere appreciation such as this; no "phrase-making," but a "shout" from a poet's heart. The portrait of Diana Low is, of all William's portraits of youth, his masterpiece.

A very amusing new departure came in his way, while he was working hell for leather on portraits that summer. Many years previously he had designed, at the request of Sir Peter Chalmers Mitchell, then Secretary of the Royal Zoological Society, a kind of scroll, introducing all the beasts, birds and fishes, which was intended for reproduction, as a form of acknowledgment to all those who contributed animals to the collection. Now, one morning, he was rung up, and told that the tiger-pit, which had

DIANA LOW.
By courtesy of Mrs. Warren Low.

just been constructed at Whipsnade, looked like "nothing on earth": could he suggest anything about it?

To cut the story short, William became responsible for the décor of the tiger-pit: a fact interesting because its invention has been claimed in other quarters. It was William who made the design, suggesting earth and rock strata, which runs round the sides of the pit, and William who, with his usual dislike for delegating the working-out of his designs to other people, carried out most of the painting: swaying on a scaffold above the pit, now using brushes, now a spray, to reach the outward-curving parts that were not within arm's-length of his board. When the wind was in the wrong direction the paint from the spray blew back and covered the painter. It was also William who invented the colouration of the pool, which was afterwards copied in other enclosures: a gradation from dark indigo to clear light blue, which, from above, gave a beautiful effect of deep water to the shallow basin. The tigers grumbled behind their bars at the end of the pit, waiting for their housewarming; the original tiger-pit, it will be remembered, was one of the sensations of Whipsnade.

Down at Sutton Veny, William, "his blood up" after this experiment in Zoo-decoration, was improvising with a birdcage. It was a shabby old cage, but when he had graded the colour of the bars from deep to light indigo, it was as if they vanished, and one saw through clear to the bird inside. He suggested that something of the sort should be done with the great enclosure that held the cheetahs, and was told to go ahead. All through an August Bank Holiday he painted away, with one of the keepers as his assistant—affording the maximum of pleasure to the holiday-minded proletariat, who deserted the animals to come and exercise their wits at the expense of William and his companion. This, when finished, was as much of a success as the tiger-pit, and it may fairly be said that William had earned his Fellowship, with which he was presented in acknowledgment of his efforts.

3

Back on the scenes came Pring. She was one of many who had felt themselves exiled since William's second marriage. She had also had a hunting accident which had threatened to cripple her for life, but, with her usual intrepidity, scorned the prospect of invalidism which would have daunted any less courageous. Between her journeyings from specialist to specialist, she drifted into Apple Tree, and rejoiced to find that it had come to life again.

Pring had discovered a new interest; she had been to Spain, and had become a rabid *aficionada* of the bulls. She dreamt bulls and talked bulls, and anything which kept her away from her beloved Andalucia she considered a sheer waste of time. Even the care of her garden—the chief delight before she discovered the *corrida*—faded a little in importance beside this dazzling new adventure; to accounts of which William listened with all the interest he always brings to a new subject. She had a present for William; a novel called *Matador*.

Pring was going back to Sevilla, and insisted that William should accompany her. He needed a holiday, and he needed something to take his mind off affairs at home. She swept him off his feet with her insistence, and away they went, the pair of them— Pring semi-invalid, and obliged to spend much of her time in bed, but dauntless as ever, and William relieved, for once, to leave the English scene behind him, and to plunge into "a new adventure"—for which he had plenty of opportunity, his companion's illness leaving him free to do very much as he liked for the greater part of the evening.

He did some charming work, during this first visit to Spain, on hot mornings in the gardens of the Alcazar, where the light was so brilliantly clear that it was some little time before he could adapt himself to it. The whole atmosphere of the place excited and stimulated him, and through Pring he had a unique experience, such as does not often come within the range of the casual visitor to Spain.

She took him out to a ranch to see a *tentadero*—the testing of the young bulls for the ring, which is one of the most interesting and exciting of the processes of cattle-rearing. On this enviable occasion William could not, unfortunately, speak a word of Spanish, and so was unable to make much contact with the great *matador* whose name, to any Spaniard, evokes all of the beauty of the *corrida*: who succeeded Joselito as the hero of the bullring, and whose fame, since his retirement, has never been challenged. Belmonte, like many ex-bullfighters, had taken to bull-breeding, and his ranch was one of the finest in the country that lies between Sevilla and Jerez de la Frontera.

They stood on a wagon to watch the proceedings, and had the excitement of being jostled at times by the rush of the charging bulls. Pring's injured spine was forgotten, and William caught excitement from her. He no longer wondered at her taste for Spain; he had acquired it himself.

4

In the imperceptible, yet shockingly sudden way of children, Liza had grown up and had been sent to boarding school. Suddenly it was no longer "home" at Sutton Veny. Strange faces were there, that did not "belong," although they were familiar. Conversation ran on subjects that seemed boring, when they were not sordid, and Apple Tree had become, not merely a workshop, but a spiritual, as well as a material, refuge. That desire to swoop homewards across the downs had lost its meaning, since Sutton Veny stood no longer for the spacious Manor House, with the shutters William had painted, the great hall whose floor he had designed and the garden with children scattered like daisies about the lawn, but for a little workman's cottage up a lane, which, although prettified and modernised, had small attraction as a domicile from William's point of view. There was no sense of privacy, nowhere to sit and work, or just to be lazy.

He accepted it all as a new phase in the pattern of his life. There was always Apple Tree, and one went forward to "the next thing." *Good-bye to All That*, as his son-in-law (whose domestic affairs were also in a tangle) had recently written: and—"Nicholson loves houses more than he loves people." It was for the Manor House that he mourned, when he went back again to Spain—this time as the guest of Sir Peter Chalmers Mitchell, to spend Christmas at Malaga. Pring was out there too, at the Caleta Palace, and very Scottish and independent about not accepting hospitality from the Villa. There was plenty of diversion to be found during the daylight hours, but, lying in bed, with the distant wash of the Mediterranean sounding through the silence, the Manor House replaced the white walls of the Villa, the night sounds were those of a Wiltshire garden, and Apple Tree shrank, in retrospect, to the size of a little box.

For the first time for many years, William had no country retreat from his workshop, and no one, if he had found one, to lend it meaning. Even Gipsy was gone, for she was "too big"—so it was said—for the cottage, and William knew he could not imprison those long, fleet limbs in a little London house. Gipsy was with a veterinary surgeon in Salisbury; the silver lay heavy now on her beautiful head; she was too old to course the downs, or fetch his slippers, or follow the flight of his boomerang.

This was, I think, the saddest and emptiest period of William's life—empty except for work.

CHAPTER FIFTEEN

Back to Spain—The Bulls—Flamenco—A visiting card

I

WHEN William returned to Malaga he had just finished the Chalmers Mitchell portrait, which was commissioned by the Royal Zoological Society for presentation to the retiring secretary. Sir Peter, overworked and preoccupied by all the business attendant on his retirement, could only sit in the evenings, and although he proved a perfect sitter, both sitter and painter became obsessed with the time-factor—with the usual disastrous result.

During the night before the presentation ceremony, William scraped the whole head down and repainted it from memory, and when the men came to frame and remove it to Regent's Park, he was still working on it, and in two minds whether to throw the whole thing up and, to use his own idiom, "bolt for the woods."

By a merciful accident, in carrying the frame upstairs to the studio the glass was broken, and this gained William a short respite, in which he worked like a maniac. Eventually the frame and glass were put over the still wet paint. The portrait, as it at present hangs in the board room, was actually painted in six or seven hours, and is, to my mind, one of the most brilliant of William Nicholson's later portraits, and a notable example of the way in which he gets "under the skin" of his subject.

Perhaps there is no such thing as a "holiday" for the artist; perhaps the word itself holds a different meaning. A "holiday," for those who paint and for those who write, is not a cessation from these occupations; it only means that they are carried out in different circumstances. The commission, the contract—bane of painters and writers—have no place in a holiday, whose very essence is in doing the thing you want to do at the moment you want to do it. We were three tired people at Malaga, but William's pencils and coloured chalks were never out of his hands, Sir Peter was working on his first translation of Ramón Sender, and I was on the third book of my Spanish trilogy, *The Tavern*. The fourth member of the house party was Lena Ramsden, who had come out

157

with me to see the Easter *feria* at Sevilla; it was lovely to have somebody around who had really nothing to do but ride and swim and abandon herself to the general feeling of holiday.

William brought out with him the sketches for *Paul and Mary Bright*, a book which was to follow *Clever Bill*. (It was never finished; in our many wanderings, we never happened on a *milieu* where there were children, and William says, to write children's books, you must have children about you.) We posed and were photographed by Lena, in various helpful positions, as Mr. and Mrs. Bright. One day when he was in the *sala*, painting a little Still Life of plumbago and dark crimson and golden primulas in a lustre jug, I made the pleasant discovery that William does not mind being watched while he works. It had never before occurred to me to paint the shadow before one paints the object which throws it. . . .

In the evenings, towards sunset, he would vanish up the hill, from which he was making sketches for the *Malaga Bull Ring* which was later bought by Lena. Those who were accustomed to the general lowness of tone in William's landscapes invariably exclaim on seeing this, which glitters with pale light. "Why," I asked him one day, "do people paint Spain in terms of screaming blue and orange?" He smiled, as if he found the question childish; his vision of Spain was the same as mine—pale, pale and glittering: silvered, not gilded, by its heat. "The colour," he pointed out, "is all in the shadows."

On an afternoon of our brief visit to Granada he captured the sunlight and threw it on to the canvas in flakes like fish-scales. This was the much exhibited *Granada Window* which he afterwards gave to me. It was painted quickly and gaily, during the hour of the siesta, and is one of the very few pictures he was never impelled to touch again.

One day it was a cactus plant, another a group of old country-men, hunched on the hillside, watching the corralling of the bulls down in the ring, which was afterwards worked into the bullring landscape. In between there were bursts of sheer fooling—"The Aspidistra Class," invented for Lena's and my benefit: a composite effort in landscape, to which we each had to contribute some feature, and "Cup-Tie Final," which started by William's covering a large drawing-block with egg shapes, which we had to convert into faces by the addition of the fewest possible lines.

How trivial it seems . . . and how pleasant it was! After dinner we played poker, or simply sat and talked. I often wonder if the art of conversation died out with William's generation. He has, it may be said, a technique of his own. "William's a marvellous raconteur," I observed one day, when the display had been more than usually glittering. "William's a marvellous whisperer," came the retort, and I accepted the amendment. As the story unwinds, approaches its climax, his voice sinks lower and lower, the listeners find themselves hitching farther and farther forward on their chairs, in their anxiety not to miss what seems to be a deep secret between William and his God. He hands one the whole bouquet of the nineties in a sentence, and draws a portrait as neatly in words as he does with his brush. One feels that the portraits are always a little flattering, but that is part of their charm. The jacaranda-tree on the terrace, the perfume of tobacco plant that drifted through the *rejas*, the grave dance of the large night moths, did not lend themselves to the sharpness of drypoint, nor, quite, to realism. It was an atmosphere of romance, and there was, one felt, just a gossamer of romance over William's reminiscences. I had my first glimpse of that world delicately apart from reality which is William's natural element, with persons and properties tastefully arranged, as on a well-set stage.

2

It was a good year for the bulls, and the *corrida* at Cordoba was the best, save one (that at Antequera, in 1934, with Belmonte), that I have ever seen. Armillita was fighting, and Ortega, and— I think—Vicente Barrera.

There is only one thing more intolerable than not going to a bullfight: it is going to a bullfight with a person who is in-different to what is happening in the ring. I have several times been to bullfights with people who were antagonistic, and this is interesting: but to sit beside someone who is bored, and who carps at that which he does not understand, is not to be borne.

I knew within ten minutes that William was a natural *aficionado* of the bulls. Sitting beside him was like being close to a live wire. He was silent and still, but with an electric stillness. Absolutely unconscious of everything that went on in his im-mediate vicinity, the whole living part of him was out there on the sand. He knew nothing, or next to nothing of bullfighting, but all that panorama of colour and movement, that mystic relationship between the man and the bull which is the drama of the bullfight, was as if it existed for him alone. To explain anything, I saw, would have been to spoil it for him. He was lost in his own vision.

That *corrida* was valuable for the beautiful *suerte* of the horse, which I wrote about in *The Sun Is My Undoing*, and for being one of Armillita's best days, when he worked with coldness and calmness very close to the bull, and showed by a kind of contemptuous certainty his superiority to the other fighters. (One of them had been fighting too much that season, and was stale, and the other was unlucky with his bulls.) Although he did not kill well, his work with the *banderillas* was impeccable.

Cordoba was packed for the *feria*, and we could not get accommodation at any of the hotels, so we had to drive back to Antequera for the night. William crawled into the back of the car, curled up in a corner and went fast asleep. I remembered a drive back to Granada, when, after seeing Belmonte, all my companions, emotionally exhausted, slept from door to door.

3

William told me he was not very much interested in music. It is true, up to a point; I have never known him to express enthusiasm at the prospect of any musical entertainment; we have never been to a concert or to the opera together, and at the ballet he shows no interest in the orchestra. This indifference is partly self-protective; it proceeds, less from a dislike for the combinations of sound which we of the western hemisphere have agreed to regard as music, than from excess of sensibility. On him this western music, this music of civilisation, has an enervating influence; he sometimes expresses himself as "good for nothing" after listening to it. (There is one exception to this generalisation: he loves the old English and old Scottish songs which Mabel Nicholson sang in her beautiful, untrained voice, after they were first married.) He had already told me it was too "emotional," by which, as I came to recognise, he meant emotional in a sophisticated way.

I was doubtful of *flamenco* in Malaga, a bastard city, assembling the worst elements of the province and smeared with the unpleasant influence of cabaret and the venal characteristics of a tourist centre. When our host—sacrificing himself, I am sure, for he is no lover of *flamenco*—offered us an evening of *cante jondo*, I was almost as apprehensive as I was delighted.

They started with the trite little local songs which are considered "good enough" for the foreigner; a gipsy danced—in slovenly fashion—a *fandanguilla*. We applauded politely, but taking courage from a gleam in William's eye—that bright, alert look that comes when his attention is captured—I asked if there was not any one who could sing a *solea* or a *martinete*.

The singers' faces were a picture—first of incredulity, then of beaming pleasure. So these foreign villa-dwellers knew something about *flamenco* after all!

We had two *soleas*—not of the first quality; then I drew William's attention with a nod to the man who was going to sing the *martinete*. A thin, little, undersized creature, with a voice like a thread, his clutch on the *guitarrista's* shoulder was like the clutch of a dying man, and, as canto after canto dragged itself from his lips, the exuberance of his companions was hushed, their "Olés" and "Andas" came more and more faintly, as though he had drawn them after him into his tragic impersonation.

I had forgotten to explain to the others the significance of this song of the chain gang in the mountains, but when I looked at William, his face was like the face of the singer: the same pallor, the same blindness. *Flamenco* had gained another addict—a word used advisedly, for the cult of *flamenco* is much the same as the cult of opium to its devotees.

He was to hear it again, in Granada, in the perfect setting of an Albaicin tavern, where the large stars shone through the meshes of the quince-trees, and the delicate splash of the little fountain cooled the heavy air. That night we were all very gay and in a mood of celebration. That night there was blind Manuel. . . . There are many blind *guitarristas* in Granada and most of them are very bad, but there was something profound and evocatory in Manuel's playing, and in the faint, sweet sound of his voice, that went beyond technical skill. He sang that night my favourite, of Nuestra Señora de las Angustias, and it seemed as though the night and its stars must go on for ever; that time stood still in that little *patio* under the shadow of San Bartolomé.

William's willing surrender to the emotionalism of *flamenco*, and his recoil from the emotionalism of concert music are logical enough. It is the response of the spirit to the primitive and spontaneous, and its rebellion against the artificial and conscious. I have often remarked that self-conscious or ultra-conventional

L

people dislike *flamenco*, are in some way even offended by it, and I have seen some strange hysterical reactions, and some of an unbelievable stupidity—usually from people who have tried to put up a resistance to that which, accepted naturally, is irresistible.

The greatest thing, apart from his painting, that William got out of Spain was *flamenco*, and from the unashamed simplicity of his surrender I learned more than I might have learned in months of companionship.

4

There came a day when nobody appeared at the window of my workroom with a plateful of cherries, and no clumps of paintbrushes lay on the balustrades to dry. As William is the quietest of individuals, with a natural gift for moving like a cat, and as he has none of the humming and whistling habits that constitute one of the minor blemishes of his sex—it was odd, how very quiet the Villa Lucía seemed to have become, since we all gathered in the *sala*, at some hour before dawn, to speed the traveller on his return to England.

I looked at the card he had left me:

MR. WILLIAM NICHOLSON

11 Apple Tree Yard,
Duke of York Street,   *Savile Club.*
S.W.1.

—on the back of which he had written, "An invitation more permanent than any wave!"*—and wondered how much of a joke it was, and what he would say if I put it to the test.

* A tilt at my solemn weekly journey down the *arroyo* to the hairdresser, with which, according to William, not even the most solemn considerations of art and literature were allowed to interfere.

CHAPTER SIXTEEN

"A new adventure"—Segovia—The gathering storm

I

DURING the following autumn and winter, we had plenty of opportunity of finding out who were our real friends. For both of us, life had assumed a new, and at times difficult, pattern. We were harassed by overwork, and worried by our professional commitments. We rushed about a great deal, in William's car or in mine; he had a little M.G., which he adored and drove like a demon, I preferred the superior comfort of my Hillman, which, although he admitted its convenience, William did not care for, because the coachwork limited his vision of the countryside.

It was the most exquisite autumn; sometimes, when the sun was patching the black and white squares of the studio floor, William would jump up, throw down his brushes and say, "Let's get out into the country!" We threw a handful of things into a little bag, William yelling from the window to the garage across the way to have the car ready. Sid, the houseman, a hardened philosopher after years of William's little ways, did not bat an eyelash when we said we were off "for a few days."

I grew to realise, in those pleasant driftings about the lanes, the woods, the orchards and pastures of England, that William, like all good Englishmen, is a countryman at heart. In every village we came to there was some house which, we both felt, was our potential home. Apple Tree was only a workshop; we both wanted old turf and old trees and a little Georgian manor we could fill with our possessions and with my cats, and with an Alsatian bitch who would remind William (but not too closely) of the angelic Gipsy.

The most unfortunate thing was, of course, that both William and I were equally bad about money. If we had had the sense to economise, if we could have altered the extravagant standard of our London living, that country home would have been a reality, instead of a dream. But William, at least, has a great capacity for living on dreams. It is a blessing; for his generosity has probably robbed him for ever of living on anything else.

(Apropos of which, his epitaph comes into my mind—one of several written by the poet Geoffrey Taylor, to whom William one day expressed his opinion that a man ought to be able to choose his own epitaph before he died; so Geoffrey "obliged" with the following, whose bitter-sweetness rings true in our ears to-day:

W. N.

Here lies the painter Nicholson, Alas!
But to posterity his genius sends,
A monument "more durable than brass,"
Of which he kept but little—having friends.)

He showed me eagerly all his favourite places: Cerne Abbas and the swannery; a certain yew-tree wood up on the Wiltshire downs, where the twisted trunks and matted branches enclosed one in an under-sea deadness, and the ground was strewn with white owls' feather: places of "magic"—another of William's favourite words. He took me to Mells—where Lady Horner, bending over her flower borders, had no conventional greeting for us. Holding my hand, she said to William, "Are you happy?" —and then, looking from one to the other of us, "Yes, I see you are." We swam in her pool—William a pretty spectacle in my pink silk culottes (we had not brought swimming-suits) going in off the diving-board. Later we drifted on to see Liza at her boarding school, and to Nancy, surrounded by her brood, at Sutton Veny.

It was all very irresponsible and unsettled, but William managed to do some of his loveliest small landscapes when we were down in Cornwall, and, to my reading aloud of *General Opal and Mrs. Camber*, a study of black and white cattle in a pasture near Arundel, which I always envied, and which was bought by his niece, Nancy Bridgeman.

William and I were one in our love for Meredith; I remember a charming story he told me, of an occasion travelling down to Woodstock, when he was reading Meredith in the train. He had come to the description of a storm, and, having to change at a wayside station, he electrified the other occupants of the carriage by buttoning his coat up tightly and turning up the collar, before stepping out into the balmy sunshine of a perfect summer afternoon!

For William, living with someone who was, like himself, a

worker, was "a new adventure," and he found it stimulating; but one of the most complicating features of our mutual household was to strike a happy mean between William's liking for company while he works, and my own almost ferocious need for solitude. Only when he wrote letters (which he took very seriously, and was never satisfied until he had made of them almost as much works of art as some of his Still Lives) did he appear to feel the need for silence, and he said that he often saw his own work more clearly when he looked at it, as it were, through the web of someone else's conversation.

An exciting commission came along, which helped in no small degree to stabilise the situation: Lord Harewood wanted his portrait painted, in the Garter robes. He was, obviously, a marvellous subject, and William was at once full of schemes for the portrait, a full-length life-size. The Reynolds tradition got to work, as the "pattern"—so essential a part of William's portraits— evolved itself in his mind. When we dined out, as we did almost every night, nothing was talked of but the Harewood portrait, and I would hesitate to say how many of Quaglino's tablecloths, menu cards and cabaret notices were sacrificed to the thick pencil and restless play of William's fancy.

There was a crackle in the studio air; as always, when a "major work" was in process of evolution, dozens of other ideas germinated with it, side by side.

People seemed to pour in, that winter: people who were fond of us both, and came to wish us well; people who came out of curiosity to see how the new ménage was working; friends of William's, coming to make my acquaintance, and friends of mine, coming to make William's; friends who came to eat the classic Apple Tree herring at luncheon (Sid cooked them like blue trout, and served them with lemon and mustard sauce, which made a dish "fit for a king": that at any rate was the opinion of Lord Oxford—then Mr. Asquith—who was among the many who delighted in an invitation to Apple Tree lunch), and friends who dropped in for tea or sherry and a "private view" of the current work.

One of the first, and ever the most welcome of those visitors was Pring, who arrived on a black winter afternoon, with her blue eyes full of lively curiosity. It was just luck that Pring was already, through *Matador*, a "fan" of mine, and William's only complaint about our friendship is that, when Pring and I get to-gether, it is impossible to get a word into the rapid crossfire of

Spanish reminiscences, of bulls and bullfighters and the *corridas*, *novilladas* and *capeas* that each has attended.

"Max," too, materialised mysteriously from Italy, and "Gus" —purposely I give William's names for them—from Chelsea; E. V. Lucas, who became, of them all, perhaps our most constant and faithful visitor—and, naturally, Hugh Walpole, because he was a "best friend" of mine, and his loyalty and friendship helped us over some hard times; Lady Horner, trailing clouds of pre-Raphaeliteism, but with a most unpre-Raphaelite wit and charm, the lovely Julia Neilson-Terry, whose beauty and whose mere manner of sitting in one of the Napoleon chairs transformed it into a throne and the studio into an audience chamber. . . . I remember an afternoon during which, by chance, Julia Neilson-Terry, Dolly Mann and Mabel Nicholson's friend, Dolly McCleod, came, one after another, to Apple Tree; I remember feeling rather discouraged about my own generation, for it did seem as though all the vitality, all the charm and all the beauty had been concentrated in theirs.

One could go on stringing names—almost for ever; people of the studios, people of letters, people of the theatre. William was extremely hospitable; to like a person was to invite him to lunch—and an invitation to lunch was a timeless, leisurely affair which went on long after the last glasses of beer were emptied, the last crumbs of cheese consumed and the dregs of the fourth or fifth relay of coffee cooling in the cups. As William "sped" his guests from the door, Sid would, as likely as not, be coming up from the kitchen with the tea-tray, the visitors, on William's urgence, would turn right instead of left, up the stairs instead of out into the Yard, and over Earl Grey and muffins the threads of conversation would be gathered up again, the tea-party would turn, perhaps, into a picture show, or to an exhibition of bil-boquet, which went on until Sid's appearance with the sherry—when we all generally "woke up" to realisation of the fact that half a day had worn away, and all sorts of engagements and duties had drifted away on the smoke-wreaths of William's charms as a host.

There were days when the bell never seemed to stop ringing—and all this apart from necessary visitors to the studio of a well-known painter: buyers, sitters, would-be sitters, the working personnel of the studios and galleries—of whom ever the most faithful was Sandy Merrill of the Leicester Gallery, whose career in the world of art had run parallel with William's. (He owed to Sandy his first exhibition.) I remember a day when, William not having yet appeared, Sandy and I were looking at some of the landscapes, which were being framed for exhibition: and Sandy's comment—"Kid's the only painter who knows how to paint a horizon." He meant, the only painter who realises that a horizon is not invariably flat, but curved, and its edge not sharp, like a silhouette, but melting.

There was, of course, my own little train of professional callers, and the situation was not eased by the fact that I, at that time, had no private place in which to work, and was wildly trying room after room—one day the dining-room, another the loosebox, another a bedroom, and coming back time after time to the big rent-table in the corner of the studio, where at least I was near enough to the telephone to take my own calls, or to bolt when someone came to see William on business.

It is hardly surprising that shortly after Christmas we began to feel desperate.

Soon after our return to England, we had had a warm invitation from my friends, Paul and Joan de Castro, to visit them in Segovia, and although the Castillan plateau in winter did not offer a particularly alluring prospect, I could not but realise what an experience Segovia would afford to William, who had never seen it. Things were looking black, too, in Spain, and I had a feeling that, unless we went at once, we might not be able to get into the country for some time: a presentiment only too unfortunately true.

It is curious to look back and to see how, from our first year together, our plans and our work were shadowed by wars and rumours of wars. We met Ramón Pérez de Ayála in the Mallorca restaurant, and he was not optimistic: but he furnished us with papers that eased our passage through the Spanish customs. William, as usual, was radiant at the prospect of going abroad (he is equally radiant at the prospect of coming home), we sent off wires, embarked on a whirlwind packing, and, abandoning the Harewood portrait for the time being to its fate, we set our faces towards the freedom and beauty of Spain.

2

We stood in the corridor of the train, and the plain flowed around us in immense waves, like a slow sea. Now in the trough of one wave, now in another, Segovia, like a floating island, mocked our eyesight and gave us that sense of hallucination which never quitted us until we went south. The railway, following the concentric folds of the valleys, showed us the cathedral, and sometimes a glimpse of the Alcazar, now from one aspect, now from another. At one moment we seemed to be speeding away from them, at the next rushing towards them, only to be defeated by some fresh altitude of the indomitable land. Suddenly we saw the snows of the Guadarramas, and then we were stepping out on the wind-blasted platform of Segovia, with the icy Castilian gale cutting into our cheeks. Everything was grey, or iron-coloured, and the sky was wild with flying scud. A strange, a formidable Spain, in which, for the first and only time, I felt a foreigner.

William is the perfect companion on an adventure of this kind, because, for one thing, he brings to it the will to be excited, and, for another, his approach has the freshness and gaiety which he conjures from his palette. The least methodical of people in his day-to-day life, he has a talent for organising a journey, he conjures comforts and conveniences seemingly out of thin air, and produces a thousand little devices of his own invention for tiding over the tedious patches.

The house was wonderful: it had the beauty of pale, gleaming light throughout—light from the whitened walls, from the pale wood floors inlaid with beautiful designs, from the balconied windows which, on one side, looked across the plateau and on the other into the *patio*, surrounded by beautiful, crumpled roofs, on which the Segovian cats paraded and mocked the *sereno* with their high, erratic *flamenco*. There was a room full of canaries, flying about in exquisite freedom, or spreading the little golden fans of their wings against the window netting, to warm their breasts in the morning sun. The house was full of the singing of birds and the scent of olive wood fires, and from the wooden gallery where the washing dried we could look over the great deserted pile of the Sacramento, and over the Templars' church, and over a score of little churches, belfries and convents.

Before we left, we were to watch many of those little buildings go up in flames, but on that day of our arrival, when the warmth of Paul and Juana's welcomes was seconded, in the graceful Spanish fashion, by that of their staff, revolution seemed very far away.

3

Only a painter can appreciate the joy of escape from the blackness, the half-light of London in February to that pellucid Castillan air, and the delight of tuning a palette to a note which is never sounded under our overcast skies. Even on days when the sun did not shine there was a delicate clarity over the landscape.

Paul was gritting his teeth and tackling the Cathedral for the— I forget how many-th time. The Cathedral is the bane of Segovian painters: if they once start, they cannot stop painting it. In the course of a day it passes through a cycle of colour which reaches its climax at sunset in a singing gold, while the windows of houses around and below it burst into flame.

It was the Matadero which captured William, grimly mounted on its pale golden bluff above the Eresma and Clamores rivers: a thing so complete in placing, in design and in dramatic values that his enthusiasm took me by surprise.

It is William's little way to choose an unpromising subject, and, by his treatment, to reveal qualities which are concealed from the uninstructed eye. I had seen him conjure beauty from a derelict shed, a heap of old scrap iron and the pink backsides of a cluster of pigs, and was more used to this form of impishness than to his choosing an already complete and beautiful thing. I had often observed the ease and certainty with which he performed this act of painter's magic, while the obvious "picture" tormented, eluded and sometimes even defeated him. He was to pay for his addiction to the Matadero; it took him the better part of a year to complete his painting of it—which was done in England, long after our return.

It was still sheltered enough under the pines to paint out-of-doors. Joan and I, like a couple of dutiful wives, made up baskets with crusty bread, cheese, black olives, figs and red wine, and took them out to our men at the hour of *almuerzo*. But with sundown the air grew glacial. At night we sampled the cafés; the house of Juan Bravo, on the *plaza*, became our rendezvous, but we soon found the difference between an Andalucían café and one in

Castilla Vieja. The peasants coming in, with their faces of iron,
their cold, northern gaze, their reluctant acknowledgment of our
buenas noches, had none of the welcome of the genial Andalucían
for the strangers. It did not matter to William; he only saw in
them wonderful types to draw. We played dominoes and drank
a bitter manzanilla. No, the Segovian night-life was not gay.

Paul and Joan did their best to hold the shadow away from us,
but as time went on it was not to be ignored. Little things
brought it home to us: a morning when two nuns called to ask if
we could give shelter to some novices "in case of trouble";
shots after dark; Juan Zuloaga's little son coming home from
school with blood streaming down his face; the *plazuela* behind
the Cathedral which, on my last visit, was like a rookery with
its clusters of religious, now deserted, save for the hooligans who
stoned each other round the base of the Zuloaga statue.

Every now and than a shrinking figure, a pale, evasive face,
attracted attention by its evident anxiety not to do so. A knitted
shawl, too closely moulded to the wearer's head, and, above all,
the betraying gesture of hands which sought wide sleeves no
longer there to offer shelter, told of the nun driven from the life-
long sanctuary of her convent into a terrifying world.

All sorts of small, inconvenient things had started to happen:
important letters were lost in the post, some proofs of mine
disappeared, our telegraphic account soared into astronomical
figures—and so did the cost of registering packages, which took
weeks before reaching their destination. Yet, on the whole, the
current of life behind the high walls of Daoiz went on gently, as
though the match were not already laid to the trail which was
to blaze from end to end of Spain.

We had each, of course, our means of escape. For William it
was threefold. He was protected by his ignorance of the language
from hearing many unpleasant and disquieting things. He is
indomitably non-political in his outlook, believing that the art-
politics liaison which a certain section of the art world would
force upon its members is essentially sterile. And he had the
pinewoods and the high plain that rolled to the white fringe of
the Guadarramas and the little Templars' church and, of course,
the Matadero, and a score of other subjects, to set between himself
and the spiritual darkness of those evenings when we sat in the
sala and listened to the lamentations of Juan Zuloaga.

Zuloaga, cousin of the painter Ignacio, was a frequent visitor;
his head of an El Greco, his haunted eyes, the restless fever of his

movements, showed that he had already entered on the first stage of the long martyrdom which took him, by way of prison, to his death in an asylum before the end of the civil war. He was a burning idealist of the Left Wing, and he despaired, even then, of his country's future. With his entrance the air darkened, and when he spread out his thin, narrow hands in some gesture of frustration, one looked instinctively for the stigmata.

I have never been more thankful that the whole of William's life is his work than during those ominous weeks.

Paul was painting a *patio* somewhere in the town; Joan, sitting among her birds, had started that diary which I hope may some day be published. I was working on *The Lost One*, which E. V. Lucas had commissioned for Methuen—in two fur coats, with a hot-water bottle on my knee and another at my feet. In spite of central heating, there was no keeping out the cold that crawled through the old, warped window-frames and shutters. One day we heard the wolves had come down and plundered some dwellings on the other side of the river. Then the snow came.

I began to find it difficult to write. I envied William, peacefully painting *La Ropa* from the bathroom window. (Hygiene went temporarily by the board; there was no climbing over or around William and his impedimenta.) Not that his calm was, by now, totally undisturbed. He too was conscious of the creeping melancholy about the place; Juan Zuloaga's visits were a recurrent nightmare; the irritant effect of four people living at close quarters under abnormal conditions, trying for the sake of each other to repress their personal anxieties, broke out in small, gusty quarrels.

The rational thing would have been to leave. But there were the paintings to be finished. No personal consideration will move William when he is working, and, although Paul had gone to Paris, and we were as uncomfortable a party as a trio is traditionally supposed to be—Joan and William, for some reason rooted primarily in the prevalent atmosphere of strain and worry, got thoroughly on each other's nerves, and I was far too edgy myself to act as peacemaker—*La Ropa* had to be finished. We huddled over the fires, or pressed ourselves against radiators, discussing what to do next.

When I think of that holiday now, I think of it as the holiday without laughter. We must have had jokes, because it is not possible for four such people to be together and not to have jokes: yet, somehow, they contributed no perceptible pattern to the sombre texture of our days.

William has the priceless gift of only remembering the pleasant things, for, for him, the most pleasant things are those of the eye. No wonder he succeeds, against all reason, in recalling only the loveliness of Segovia: storks dancing their grave dance upon the ruined archways; the moment at sundown when the whole of the town that looked towards the west, and the Matadero on its rocky bluff, turned to rosy gold; the dark plantation of the Alcazar, where the white peacocks paraded their silver robes; the gold leaf and azure and vermilion of a Cathedral ceiling, and the complicated beauty of its ironwork; a palace whose outer wall was also the wall of the town, and from whose ramparts one looked across the Guadarramas; its deserted *sala* with relics of beautiful furniture and brilliantly painted rafters. We could have had all that for three pounds a month, but it was a summer palace, and there was no provision for central heating.

How delighted William was when he found, in one of those grand deserted chambers, a billiard-table with the baize eaten away by rats, and twisted cues flung on the board as the players had left them, on the interruption of their last game! The framework was crusted with pigeon-droppings and the board warped with leakage from the roof. It was *The House by the Sea*— it was *Air Raid in a London Ballroom*—it was another of those subjects, fantastic, rococo and full of dramatic significance, which he has always loved to paint.

Coming in one afternoon, I found a telegram from Matheson Lang, saying that he wanted to meet me, and to discuss a dramatisation of *Matador*.

Of the two, William was the more excited. He at once made up his mind to do the sets. What scenes did I want? Where should we go to get sketches? There must be a bullring: which bullring? We had seen some beautiful bullrings, of which the Sevilla one, queen of all bullrings, was the most beautiful, and the old wooden ring at Antequera the most interesting—or, as Hemingway might say, the most "emotional." The obvious choice was Sevilla, and it was William who, almost before I had begun to plan coherently towards a meeting with Lang, had booked our seats on the plane for the south.

CHAPTER SEVENTEEN

*Sevilla, and the sets for " Matador"—Farewell to Spain—
" Sir William"*

I

OUR FIRST stroll down Sierpes revealed to us the astonishing truth:
that Sevilla was still its changeless and charming self, that the
sevillano still found it easier to smile than to preserve a non-
committal gravity, that hospitality and courtesy were in the
Sevillan air and that the stranger was, as always, the object of
the sevillanos' most friendly solicitude.

We found an excellent wine bar, crowded with *ganaderos*. It
seemed incredible there could be such a place—with no mutter of
politics, no whispering in corners, no suspicious glances, no
antagonism roused by the presence of a stranger. One after
another the ranchers, with the utmost politeness and formality,
invited us to drink with them. We drank to Joselito, and to the
ganaderías, and to certain bulls by name. Then we drank to
Belmonte, and again to Joselito, and to great bullfighters one
after another—but always coming back to Joselito. And we
talked about bulls, and the bulls of last season, and the bulls of
the season to come, and the glasses were never empty—and
whenever one failed for a toast there was Joselito.

Were we going to see the bulls brought in at Antequera la
Venta? A car was at our disposal. Were we going to the
apartado? Had we got our seats for the fight? *Los palcos—no?
—La barrera! Olé, los ingleses! Olé, los aficionados! Hombre, una
copita conmigo!*—At the sight of William, bashfully beaming as
he was smitten on the shoulder by brawny fists, toasted in a
language of which he knew next to nothing, and hailed as a
kindred spirit by half a dozen agreeable toughs in leather chaps
and broad-brimmed sombreros, I knew we were " on the up and
up." Ignorance of a language is never, for William, any barrier
to making friends. He has a shy, polite and engaging manner
which foreigners seem to find irresistible, and not a trace of the
national superiority which makes one cringe when one is obliged
to meet one's compatriots on foreign soil.

Matheson Lang had not said definitely that he would do the play, had not arrived at the Cristina, had not even replied to our telegram to Malaga; but every bit of the scenery was planned in William's mind, and on the next morning we went out to find what he wanted for the three sets. (Eventually there were four: but what we then had in mind were the *patio* of Don José's house in Granada, the house of Doña Mercédès, and, of course, the bullring.)

William found a beautiful *patio*, which we agreed was the perfect setting for the loves of Juan and Pilár, and the more sombre relationship of Don José with his mistress. (The latter aspect was finally cut out; Lang, obsessed by the squeamishness of the provinces, scrapped what should have been the finest scene in the play. We both tried to make him see how much it contributed to the build-up of his own character, but it was no use; Lang did not "see himself" like that.)

Sevilla is a city of silver; there are none of the rose-red façades which are characteristic of Granada. So it was decided we should pay a flying visit to Granada, for the old Carmen de los Array-ánes, where Doña Mercédès lived. So far had the war shadows withdrawn that it did not occur to us we might not be able to make such a journey, although it was said casually at the Cristina that there was trouble in the Malaga direction: there was always trouble in the Malaga direction—we made little of that. As for stories that the 'buses between Sevilla and the coast had stopped running—they were malicious inventions, circulated by the *malas lenguas* who were always manufacturing scares for the tourists. It seems incredible, now, how lightly we accepted such assurances.

Meanwhile, we would wait for Matheson Lang's arrival, and take in Granada on our way back to Segovia. So off we went to the bullring, where William made friends with the porter, and we were left to wander at our leisure behind the scenes. I had not realised, until I saw them through William's eyes, the decorative possibilities of an empty bullring. We went through the chapel, the infirmary, the *patio des caballos*, and into the dark pens behind the *toril*, looking at shadows, at angles; and I knew that, whether Matheson Lang chose to do it or not, I must get *Matador* on to the stage, for the sake of William's sets. He bought me one of the great pink percale fighting capes, "so stiff that it would stand alone." (There was later on a little acrimony, when, on our return to Apple Tree, William insisted on displaying to visitors "*my* fighting cape and *my* banderillas." I managed to impress on him

THE BULL RING.
By courtesy of Miss Lena Ramsden.

that, while he was at liberty to claim the whole of the rest of Spain, anything belonging to the bullring was *mine*—and please not to forget it!)

When night came there was laughter and singing in the wine-bars and the music of guitars and lovers pressing themselves against the *rejas* of old houses behind the Giralda . . . and still William made drawings in the *patio*, and round and about the town. One day we found a tramp sleeping in the shadow of the Torre del Oro, and William pressed a *duro* into his unconscious hand—a *propina* to the gods.

The first intimation that we were living in a dream came in a telegram from Malaga; I was asked to ring a hotel, and learned that Lang's party had met with "trouble" on the way along the coast, and the visit to Sevilla was abandoned.

It was like Musical Chairs, when you allow yourself to be carried away by the music, and find yourself "out" when it stops. Only two of us were "out." We no longer had any excuse for our pleasant extravagance of lingering in Sevilla, and our illusion that we might now go on to Granada was dispelled, when we mentioned it, by the reception-clerk. Granada?—No. That was perhaps a bad idea. Things were not so good in Granada—it was, after all, not so far from Malaga. Why not stay in Sevilla, where, as the *señores* could see, all was pleasant and peaceful? Wherever in Spain there might be trouble, it would not be in Sevilla—the sevillanos having too much good taste to mix themselves up with politics.

Much to our tastes as this naïve propaganda might be, it was important we should get, if possible, to Granada. At the consulate we were told that the "trouble" along the coast was certainly exaggerated; there was no reason why we should not go to Granada—if it was necessary. Something in the use of that word *necessary* made us prick our ears. I asked bluntly if there was going to be war, and was made to feel I had committed a serious diplomatic gaffe. It was obvious that if we chose to go to Granada nobody was going to be responsible for us, and that if, as William had mentioned, we were obliged shortly to return to England, it would be prudent to make plans for our return.

2

Spring had taken advantage of our absence to sweep across the Castillan plain.

"Good God!" said William. "All my pictures will be different!"

He rushed at them as soon as we got in. It was almost ludicrous—the change in the Segovian scene: a piping green where had formerly been steel colour, almond blossom blowing across the gardens. The poplars in the middle distance of *La Ropa* had changed from purple-reddish witches' brooms to plumes of jade, and new grass sprang lively through the winter stubble.

Fortunately the pictures we had left behind, with the exception of *La Ropa*, were almost finished; but a new range of subjects now tempted William and lured him out on the green hillsides. Paul was back from Paris, was painting with a stubborn determination in which one detected the race against time; I tried to pick up the disconnected threads of my book; Joan, looking terribly ill, spent much time walking the dogs and brought back ominous reports of local feeling.

The housemaid's nephew was murdered. A man's body was found in the street close to our doorstep. The Archbishop of Segovia dared no longer sleep in the palace, but fled like a rat from hiding to hiding among the houses of his supporters. Night after night the skies were lit with the bonfires of blazing convents. Segovia *el noble*, thanks to corruption and terrorism at the time of the elections, was for the first time in its noble history represented in the Cortes by Communists and Anarchists. Maria the cook came in from the market with news that there was to be a house to house search for arms throughout the town: all firearms were to be commandeered by the military, who gave receipts whose value was probably a little less than the paper on which they were written.

The house was full of guns—the property of Joan's father; and it was William who suggested we should hide them. He had no political motive; it was merely that a hint of coercion drives him berserk. We spent a morning oiling them and wrapping them in sheets of newspaper, and William found the hiding-place, which involved the removal of boards, the disposal of the guns, and a careful replacement of dust and cobwebs after the deed was done. All this was safely accomplished before the searchers arrived. They were polite and apologetic, and seemed to regret their task.

At the end of May we left for Santander, begging the de Castros to come to England if there was trouble. We had twenty-four hours to wait before the boat came in, and planned to visit the Altamira caves; but the rain came down in torrents, and our driver said it was impossible, part of the road was washed away with the spring floods.

We sat at the window of a cheerless hotel on the waterfront, and watched the rain and the grey sea and the endless processions of Communists filing past with raised fists, to the tune of the Internacional. What a farewell to Spain.

3

On our return to England I had to go into a nursing-home, and when I was better, William made use of my enforced inactivity by starting to paint me—in a pale blue satin dressing-gown, lying on the pink glazed chintz cover of my bed. The walls were yellow, and he brought in the daylight lamp from the studio, which picked up every variation of the blue satin and the pink quilting, and reflected them in the yellow varnish. It was the second portrait of me he had started; I sat for him in Segovia, for head and shoulders—but the saddest thing in William's and my relationship is my complete failure as a sitter.

A portrait, says William—very rightly—must be a collaboration; but it is, unfortunately, temperamentally impossible for me to sit for hours concentrating upon having myself painted. With all the goodwill in the world, a hundred things flash into my mind—things that I ought to be doing "at once": and to ask William when I may be free is mortally to offend him. Except for a few pencil sketches, there is no portrait of Marguerite Steen by William Nicholson: a great disappointment to him, a great loss to me. In fact, the subject is so painful a one that it is now seldom raised between us.

It was getting on for dusk. Sid came in with the letters and told us our solicitor had called. William shouted to W. P. T. to come up, and the letters were forgotten, until William asked if there was anything for him.

I shuffled them over. Bills, bills, bills. I threw each one as it turned up to W. P. T. to put in the wastepaper basket. We hadn't

M

any money to pay bills with, so what was the point in opening them? "Here's something that looks like a sales advertisement; wastepaper basket . . ."

W. P. T. was holding a large envelope thoughtfully.

"Do you often get sales advertisements from Downing Street?"

. . . We sat for a long time, discussing the knighthood. W. P. T. and I were much more moved than William, who, true to himself, was "getting on with the next thing." The knighthood was of less importance to him just then than getting the right values out of those pinks and blues and yellows.

We were very happy that William's work should receive this recognition—particularly as he had always set his face like a rock against the Royal Academy and all its works, and had twice refused the academic title. One of his most cherished possessions, in fact, is an envelope addressed to him at Burlington House and returned to the Post Office with the superscription "Not Known Here"! This he is always threatening to frame, as a certificate of his artistic integrity. We once, for amusement, worked out the number of pictures per minute which are passed before the judges' eyes before the annual hanging; it came to double figures and I forget what fraction. This, and the fact that any R.A. can claim the privilege of space for his works, irrespective of their merit, is surely enough to discourage any one naïve enough to go to the Royal Academy in search of the best in British art.

"You'll accept it, won't you?"—Something in his look made us doubtful.

"I don't know." William's eyes were hooded, his mouth twisted sideways in the grimace of concentration which has given him a permanent wrinkle in his upper lip. "Have to think it over—what good's a title to me?—*a bit more over that way*"—a stab of the paintbrush recalled me to my duty as sitter. "Adds a lot to one's expenses—don't *feel* like a knight——" and so forth and so on: gentle, vague, uninterested in the whole business.

I suggested that Edith Nicholson should be consulted, and, as we expected, her verdict was in favour of accepting the honour.

William and I then discussed the matter fully, and, in spite of obvious personal reasons which disinclined him from accept-ance, we finally agreed that he should take this tribute to his work. I presented him with a very fine fifteenth century armet, which had come into my possession some years before, as becom-ing to the knightly status, and William settled down to answer the queries of the College of Heralds, who wanted to know about his family crest—if such existed. William, who is vague about such matters, wrote to his half-brother, Edward, for information. Edward, at ninety-six, lived still in Newark, cheek by jowl with "the works" to which his life had been devoted. As no reply was immediately forthcoming, and he had another letter from the College, William wrote again.

"You must have patience, sir!" wrote the "big" brother to the "little" one. In a beautiful, clear handwriting, Edward told young William that all proper investigations were in hand, and he would be informed in due course. Properly reduced to his junior status, William went on with the Harewood portrait. By now it was getting on his nerves, and there were moments when the studio air was like gunpowder. Lord Harewood was the most charming of sitters, but William was not pleased with the background or the pose. Nor, as usual, could he get enough sittings; he was obliged to use a model for the robes—a method which does not appeal to him. It was terribly exhausting, working on that great canvas.

We still dined out almost every night; sometimes with friends, but William was generally too tired to welcome company. We had our regular table at the Apéritif, with occasional excursions to Quaglino's, the Hanover or the Café Royal. It was extravagant, but at the end of a long day in the studio, he needed the relaxation of change of scene. It was, unfortunately for our purses, only "a step" to the Apéritif—and we both liked good food and good wine.

After dinner we worked again—William by the light of his daylight lamp (later on he had a long batten fixed above the window and plugged with twenty or more daylight bulbs which enabled him to work even through the black mornings of winter), or sometimes friends came in. Most frequent and most welcome was E. V. Lucas, who would arrive at strange hours—sometimes after midnight—mellow from one of his many clubs.

"I love your painting, old boy—greatest painter in Europe—greatest *living* painter." E.V. took great pains to emphasise this. "But I hate your braces."

Strong men have been known to wince when William takes his coat off. Of an uproarious orange, in a woven silk stockinette, they are what is known as ostler's braces. He contends they are the only comfortable kind, but they are certainly a shock to the eye. To E.V., after dining at the Orleans, they were something more.

About this time, William painted several pictures for E.V.: a study of silver, which came to me after E.V. died, one of the windmills he loved, down in Surrey, and a little pochade of his cottage at Waldron, which he lent us for a holiday. E.V. was one of the real and intelligent admirers of William's work; another was Robert Nichols, who draped his long, slack limbs over one of the Napoleon chairs, and, with his head and his arms in continual motion, recited long passages from his unfinished *Don Juan.*

It is a pity the portrait of Robert, which William started on one of those night visits, was never finished; he is a natural subject for a painter. Last year, at Fen Ditton, he recited more of *Don Juan* with such fire and rightness of gesture and timing that it was impossible not to think how pallid any performance other than his will seem, when it is produced.

A member of one of the Dominion cabinets on a visit to London came and asked William to do "a quick sketch" of him. William's taste is not for quick sketches, but he liked his would-be sitter, and asked what time he had to spare. He was told, apologetically, only a few hours.

For once William rose to the challenge, and the sitting started after dinner. I ministered to them with relays of wine, coffee, tea and beer throughout the night; and when the curtains were drawn back, and there were the faint beginnings of dawn in the sky, there was a creditable head and shoulders on the easel. Of course, William was not satisfied; he never is, and was not likely to be with a portrait done under such conditions. He would probably have destroyed it, but the sitter and his wife, who had nobly shared the vigil, were pleased with it—probably as a *tour de force* in sitting!

It was nothing for William to paint up to three or four in the morning. It was then, often, that he worked for his own pleasure, as a relief from the Harewood portrait. I worked late too; it was the best time, the utterly quiet time, when we were immune from social invasions. For hours there would be no sound but the clatter of the typewriter and the rattle of William's brushes in his box. It had turned into a perfect working arrangement; we were both stimulated by each other's industry.

I often used to think that the people who saw William during the day, as the agreeable *flaneur*, always (apparently) ready to put down his palette and play darts, or show off his skill at bilboquet, or merely to sit and indulge in that seemingly endless flow of lighthearted conversation, could have no conception of the strenuous background that lay behind that air of leisure. He was invariably charming to people whom I regarded secretly, and in some cases making no concealment of my opinion, as time-wasters. I grew to understand that he got good out of them, that they relaxed him, and that after an hour's, or maybe two hours' dalliance, he went back to the easel with a renewed eye.

I have never seen any one work as William worked, when he was " on it." The fertility of his invention, the endless play of his imagination often made me feel dull and heavy. In a day he would paint a Still Life, design a menu card, throw off half a dozen "Blokes" and sketch out several suggestions for a book-plate—while talking to a dozen people and dashing out for "a breath of air" round the park in his little M.G. There was no end to his mental and physical energy. He would start off at 5 a.m. in top gear, with a small torrent of brilliant inspirations, not a few of which were connected with my writing—until I managed to convince him that at this rate I would shortly be removed to a sphere where writing is, presumably, of no value.

CHAPTER EIGHTEEN

The theatre again, and more portraits—Overture to an exhibition

I

WILLIAM was going to wear his father's court suit when he went to the palace; he looked excellent in it, as he does in anything which suggests the Regency. It was disappointing when the order went out for "morning dress," but in morning dress William set forth—to return with a faint halo of knighthood round his brow: which halo, however, was well on the slant by the evening. He had had shoals of telegrams and a great many people came in to offer their congratulations. In his usual simple fashion, William wondered what it was all about. Being a knight, as he pointed out, did not make him any better or worse a painter.

"Wot do I call 'im now? Sir Nicholson?" hoarsely inquired Sid, the one member of the household deeply impressed by the solemnity of the occasion. When I suggested that "Sir William" was the correct form of address, Sid demurred. "Seems a bit matey, don't it?" "For God's sake tell him to go on saying ' sir,'" said William, when I reported Sid's misgiving.

While all this was going on, the Langs materialised again. One afternoon, Mr. and Mrs. Matheson Lang came to talk about *Matador*. Lang and I were to collaborate on the dramatisation, and William, it was settled, was to do the sets. The terms proposed to William made me furious, although they only made him laugh. He pointed out that he was not doing the sets for Lang, but for me, and, beyond stipulating for a further sum to be paid when the play came to town, he allowed the proposition to pass. As things turned out, London was never to see *Matador*: partly because the Spanish war broke out, and the subject was considered "unsympathetic" for the British public, and partly because Lang may have misdoubted himself in the rôle of Don José. *Matador* was a great disappointment to him; he had visualised another *Blood and Sand*, himself in another dashing hero rôle, and he seemed unable to enter into the psychology of

182

El Bailarin, a psychology incomprehensible to him, as he had only a tourist's acquaintance with Spain. Ethel Griffies, who played Doña Mercédès, and André Morell as Pepe, ran away with the play from the first night—a grievous situation for any star.

Unlike most scene-designers, William was not content to make his sketches and hand them over to the painters. The sets were painted in Alick Johnstone's studios, directly under William's eye, and with his active co-operation. There were a few sensations —as when William pointed out that shadows made by Spanish sunlight on a rose-coloured façade are not purple, but burnt orange. The first set, of the façade of Don José's house, was a masterpiece of suggestive simplicity: a flakey granadino pink, broken only by the square doorway, the window with its reja and a little peephole with a broken shutter, which he had noted on a house in the Manigua.

The *chef d'œuvre*, of course, was the last Act, the bullring. On the first night, and on many subsequent occasions, there was a spontaneous burst of applause when the curtain rose on a stage empty of characters. It was exactly the combination of realism and imagination in which William, as a scene-designer, excels, and made a perfect setting for the best piece of production in the play. There was so much that needed to be shown—a glimpse of the arena, the distant *gradas* with the spectators, the *callejon*, the backs of the near-side *gradas* with the audience (we used to climb up and add our " *Olés*" to those of the supers when in search of a little diversion), and the entrance to the infirmary: and in some way he managed to keep it all clear, simple, self-explanatory and spacious—and glittering with light. My only reason for regretting that that production of *Matador* never came to town were Ethel Griffies's performance and William's sets.

We went down to Bournemouth, where Lang was playing a revival of *The Wandering Jew*, to talk about the play, and while there, heard the Abdication speech. The tired, hesitant, slightly cockney voice was very moving, and even William, who subscribed to the Abdication party (while agreeing with me that its handling of the situation was infamous), showed much emotion. The lack of comment and the silence in the crowded hotel lounge where we were listening were very marked; most people went quietly to their rooms. On the night we came back to town, crowds were sweeping past the end of Apple Tree Yard, driven from the palace by the mounted police. They were shouting "Down with Baldwin!"—and "We want the King!"

We produced *Matador* in Edinburgh; the cold was piercing and the snow started to fall heavily on the Sunday before we opened, but it takes more than a snowstorm to hold the Edinburians away from the theatre. A full house sat shivering, until the curtain went up on William's pink wall, off which the very heat of Spain itself came glowing, and you could positively hear the breath of gratitude and relief as frozen limbs relaxed and chilled lips broke into smiles at William's act of magic.

2

William always loved Brighton: its Regency flavour, its sweep of windblown promenade, its *mélange* of robustious vulgarity with Victorian decorum. We used to rush down in one or other of the cars, stay at one of the hotels which were a survival of the great Victorian tradition and combined comfort and quiet with a humorless pomposity which roused all the irreverence in William's nature—and wander round the Lanes in search of bilboquets, ship models, silk scarves, Georgian or Early Victorian costumes and pink lustre.

Like a good Bohemian, William loathes "smart" cocktail bars, roadhouses and modern "luxury" hotels; in such places he has an uneasy, a *depaysé* air—as a ghost of the old Café Royal might have if it found itself launched among a company of the Bright Young People of 1942. He has a paralysing (and quite unintentional) gift of making such places seem fifty times more vulgar by his mere fashion of sitting on a chromium chair. The polished counter of some little fisherman's pub, or the corner of a settle in a country inn are his natural elements, and, after my health made it necessary for us to seek a more salubrious air than that of Apple Tree, we soon acquired a good working knowledge of the little taverns of the waterfront.

One of William's simpler recreations was to walk along the promenade, spotting "types"—strange, withered, half-imbecile spinsters, port-wine-pickled colonels and occasional members of the racecourse gangs, with their brazen-haired "frails." He started to plan a book of Brighton types which would surely have rivalled the "Blokes" in popularity, but this never got farther than a few sketches.

Once we went out to Rottingdean—the degraded and desecrated

Rottingdean of to-day, which so depressed William that we never went there again; and often we wandered farther afield, to Arundel or Alfriston, where William painted and I read aloud, or listened to the endless fairy tale of the past—"once upon a time"—from which much of this book is compiled.

When our good friend Quaglino suggested finding us a flat in the same building as his own, William was too busy and I too tired to demur, although that soaring catacomb of "luxury" flat was not our own choice of a domicile. So my furniture was sent down from the north, and we entered into possession of a little white box perched up above the treetops, with a sparkling vision of the sea. It was flooded with sunshine from dawn to dusk, it had an admirable painting light, and at least it was less extravagant than our constant week-endings here and there, which our need of fresh air seemed to make necessary.

Lord Horder, at this time, had started to sit for his portrait. In fact, commissions were rushing in, faster than William could deal with them. At one time, if he had accepted all he was offered, he would have had about eleven portraits on the easels. The best that could be said for this demand on his time and energies was that it enabled him to exercise some choice. One of the portraits which he chose to do, and which gave him most pleasure, because he loves painting children, was that of the little Askwith girl whom Enid Bagnold made the heroine of her *National Velvet*. This is one of the most successful and interesting of William's child portraits, for he has contrived to make of it, not merely a portrait of the sitter, but a complete study of a certain phase of childhood, with all its reserve, its physical awkwardness and its sensitive awareness of its own limitations.

One of the things which amuse us is that portraits which please the sitters are often not appreciated by their wives. I do not know in what heroic posture the wives of great men would like their spouses to be immortalised ("wives of great men all remind us we must make them look sublime"), but one wife was certainly very disparaging about a portrait which most people regarded as a masterpiece of humour and humanity, and which, to do him justice, the sitter himself admired very much. Another so disliked William's vision of her husband, which perhaps was a little on the overtruthful side, that he took it back and painted her a small conversation piece—the first of its kind he had done since the breakfast-table study of Mr. and Mrs. Winston Churchill. William's good nature and readiness to see his sitter's point of view was an eye-opener to me, as I was inclined to think a sitter should take what he was given and be thankful for it.

William was seeing a good deal of the Churchills at this time. Mrs. Churchill had commissioned the portrait which William went down to Chartwell to paint. Considerable publicity was given to this portrait, at the time of the National Gallery Exhibition, in 1942, but William withdrew it at the last moment and would not have it shown, as he did not consider it "good enough." It is a light and pleasant sketch, very high in tone, but is hardly worthy to rank with the serious portraits.

Winston Churchill, to whose hobby of painting almost as much publicity has been given as to his hobby of bricklaying, was William's most ardent pupil, and William thought highly of his work. He liked the "bold and buccaneering way" in which Winston threw on his paint, his courage and attack were in line with his character, as was the quickness with which he seized upon William's teaching.

We went down to Chartwell together on the week-end that Winston Churchill heard that he was not included in the Chamberlain cabinet, and William spoke warmly afterwards of the fortitude and sweet nature with which he had accepted this crushing disappointment. We both remembered it in 1940, when we were celebrating my birthday at our favourite Hanover restaurant. The head waiter came to our table and spoke to William. "Winston Churchill's been made Prime Minister, sir." It seemed the most wonderful birthday present any one could have had. We were so excited that we walked from the Hanover right down Whitehall to the Admiralty, expecting there would be some kind of demonstration. But everything was dark, and, apart from a policeman and a stray cat or two, there were no signs of life outside the silent building. William agreed with me that the English are indeed incomprehensible; there must have been few that night who did not feel a recrudescence of confidence and a feeling of profound relief that the country was at last delivered from its long rule by old, venal men; and they made as much fuss about it as if "an owl had cried."

William could add much to the Churchilliana which already circulates among the Prime Minister's admirers; one of the pleasantest stories is that of Winston, fully dressed, with the inevitable cigar in his mouth, diving after dinner into the swimming-pool, to win a bet in favour of some charity for which a fête had been given in the grounds. William always loved the

Chartwell week-ends, when he painted black swans, or any other little subject that happened to attract him (the black swans were bought by Major John Churchill and used to hang in Lady Gwendoline's charming dining-room), played with the children and curbed or encouraged, as need arose, Winston's enthusiasm with the paintbrush. Those black swans; the cob won William's heart for ever by bringing a daffodil in his bill and presenting it to his mate, sitting on her nest.

3

Other pictures, not all connected with work, come back to the mind, as belonging to this period: the funeral of George V. seen from Hugh Walpole's balcony in Piccadilly; William, attired for some reason like the lilies of the field, complete with topper and black satin stock, procuring us a passage through the crowds by the masterful fashion in which he waved a card for somebody's reception. Hugh was not there—he had some position of magnificence in the Abbey. The endless, slow procession streamed along Piccadilly, its most poignant figure that of the new King, who, pale with fatigue, reeled, rather than walked after the coffin.

Then came the Abdication, and the following May a night when we walked the streets of the West End, which were empty of traffic, to see the illuminations of Coronation night. Bond Street was particularly beautiful, hung from end to end with long white banners, stencilled with golden crowns; the pale, translucent, Japanese effect of this decoration eclipsed all the gaudier trappings of the other streets and squares. The crowds were curiously quiet and orderly; New Year's Eve in Piccadilly Circus is much more rowdy than was Coronation night in the West End.

Lord Harewood had suggested that William should make a painting of the Garter service in the Royal Chapel at Windsor. To ensure a good view of the scene, William was put into an usher's robes, and, looking more solemn than any usher, stood down in the body of the Chapel while the Knights filed in. He made a beautiful sketch for which we went down on another occasion to gather detail, but for some reason the picture was never finished: perhaps because the subject was not of his own choosing. The historical record does not, in the main, appeal to him, and, with the Harewood portrait, he had worked, for the present, the heraldry out of his system. This was looking magnificent, and so it should, for it had tormented William more than any portrait he had embarked upon for years. He had actually started it three times, each time on a fresh canvas, before he solved the problem it presented. He was set on making of it something more than a "portrait of a nobleman in Garter robes," and the design of the figure, robes and banner which he at last developed is as beautiful and formal as a playing card. We all contributed our share to the Harewood portrait: Sid stood for hours for the legs and feet, and I slid my hand into a white kid glove and held the plumed hat for an afternoon, while William painted and repainted, despaired and rejoiced, as his vision seemed to be "coming," and then slid into oblivion again. There were days when he nearly painted the clock round, and others when the canvas was turned to the wall, and he could hardly bear to be in the studio. Sometimes, when it seemed to my eye to be almost perfect, he would say, "I shall never finish it."

It can hardly be sufficiently emphasised that, with the exception of a few of his smaller landscapes, none of William's work has ever come to him easily. The seeming lightsomeness—particularly noticeable in some of his later Still Life—covers an agony of effort which only the hand of genius can conceal. "I have to learn it all first." When "learnt," the final utterance is swift and sure—rather like a stammerer who, after long training, is at last delivered of a perfect sentence.

4

The studio is stacked with pictures ready for exhibition, and we have spent most of the morning addressing invitation-cards. William enters with his hat on. It needs but a glance to discover that there is trouble in the air.

The Leicester Gallery, it appears, has gone and redecorated its walls. The colour, says William, spells death to all his pictures. The exhibition, he says, cannot take place, as nothing will induce him to present his work against this unspeakable background. The exhibition, he amends, may conceivably take place if the whole of the Leicester Gallery is re-hung with some colour becoming to his canvasses.

Allowing a respectful pause for these statements to sink in, I—

or Robert Sielle, who has done the frames, and happens to be present—mildly inquire what colour he has in mind.

William draws a deep breath, and, with a gesture of impatience for our stupidity, utters the monosyllable *Red*.

We blench. Stealing a cautious glance, I wonder if this is the moment for a thermometer. Robert, bolder than I, asks what sort of red. In a few terse phrases William sketches out a red which flashes before our inner eyes at one moment vivid purple, at the next with a strong orange bias, and finally settles down into what a housepainter whom William was employing to repaint the dining-room cosily described as " purple-brown."

Robert (still manifesting a hideous courage) suggests it will take a good deal of red to cover the entire walls of the Leicester Gallery. William intimates, with curling lip, that it is a matter of indifference to him whether yards or miles are employed to cover up the hideous gaffe of the Gallery decorators. Robert timidly murmurs that he knows of an upholsterer . . . and the pair of them depart, leaving me to wonder whether I shouldn't, after all, have gone into action with the thermometer.

Towards lunch-time curiosity is too much for me; I go down to the Gallery. There is a vaguely hunted look about the personnel of the outer room and a breathless hush in the interior. The sight, as I enter the Hogarth Room, is remarkable.

There are two static figures—William's and Robert's—and two that seem to have solved the secret of perpetual motion. Of the latter, Oliver Brown is prowling up and down, occasionally tripping over a fold of red sateen which has unrolled itself from a bolt lying in the middle of the floor, and an unknown person— unknown to me by name, but evidently *un homme de bonne volonté*— is rushing up a stepladder with an armful of sateen, rushing down the stepladder, falling over the sateen, getting wound up in the sateen, sliding about on the sateen, stepping heavily on pictures which have got covered over by the sateen, and generally playing hell with the sateen, the stepladder, the pictures and himself. This interesting exhibition is viewed by William with a diabolical expression; he is a cross between Mephistopheles and Napoleon, having one of his worst attacks of dyspepsia on Elba. Slightly withdrawn is Robert, who looks as if he might blow up at any moment, and whose eye I hastily avoid; for it is more than obvious that this is no moment for laughter.

" Put it there ! " says William. The little man puts it there.

" Not there: *there*," snarls William. The little man attempts to commit suicide over the top of the stepladder and saves himself by sliding down on his stomach. Oliver Brown quickens up on the prowl, a sort of smothered honk comes from Robert, I have a coughing attack and William steps on one of his own pictures and breaks into a resounding oath.

Among growls of "Knock a nail in!" from William, snorts of "Impossible!—Ridiculous!" from Oliver Brown, and a series of most peculiar noises from Robert, who, I can see, is getting to the end of his tether, and ought to be got away while he is sound in wind and limb—I blink round at the walls and wonder what *really*, from William's point of view, is the matter with them. They are either an innocuous greeny-grey or an equally innocuous greyish-pink—the colour escapes me; but I am conscious of a slight feeling of sympathy for Oliver Brown who has to stand by and hear his decorative scheme damned as profoundly as a man of William's notorious moderation of expression allows him to damn it.

But I have also noticed a far more poignant matter: that the red which, under William's instructions, the exhausted slave is trying to throw over the walls is ruinous to the vermilion of the robes in the Horder portrait—the *pièce de résistance* of the exhibition.

William by now is green, Oliver Brown grey, the little workman striped with sweat and Robert puce. Red satin billows and bunches across the floor, and a little—a very little—of it has managed to cling to the walls. I nerve myself; after all, how can man die better than facing fearful odds?

"You know, William"—heavens, how loud my voice sounds—"I do think the plain walls are better—really—after all."

As sweetly as if no ripple has ever disturbed the surface of his usual tranquillity, William answers:

"I think you're quite right."

No explanation has ever been forthcoming, of William's unaccountable aversion to the new décor of the Leicester Gallery. It has not been redecorated since, and hanging days have gone by without a shadow of objection from the painter. It was "just one of those things"—and if it left us with about half a mile of red sateen on our hands, this was a trifle in comparison with the success of the exhibition itself. Almost everything was sold, and I was left regretting the disappearance of the records of our Spanish journey.

CHAPTER NINETEEN

Holidays: the Lido, Paris, Toulon, Rothéneuf, La Rochelle

I

AT LAST the Harewood portrait was finished! Even William admitted it—and, as any one familiar with his methods will agree, nothing is more difficult than driving him to the admission that a portrait is finished. Like all good artists, he is never satisfied, and he was still moaning that, given another six months, he "might" have done a masterpiece, when it was taken away.

For the better part of two years the great life-size had dominated the studio and formed a kind of sieve for all our communications. I mean, that every remark one made to William, every idea one might introduce tentatively for his approval, had to pass through the Harewood portrait before it penetrated. This created a very peculiar atmosphere indeed, and when it had departed the sense of space and blankness was almost equally disconcerting.

William went out and booked our reservations by air to Venice. We both prefer air to any other form of travel—I loving the speed, the sense of isolation, the convenience and comfort, while William loves the "patterns." Owing to a mistake on the part of the air line, we had to go by Amsterdam and Dusseldorf. We had very early breakfast in Apple Tree and went out into the exquisite early morning emptiness of Piccadilly to find a taxi. William was so light, so happy, so relaxed, it seemed as if he was already floating upon air.

There were not many patterns on the way to Amsterdam, for we were flying above cloud which curdled under us like meringue, with only occasional glimpses, down the thermal tunnels, of dark-green sea and toy boats trailing their white V's of foam. At Amsterdam we changed into a German plane—much inferior in space and accommodation to the Dutch one. Now there were patterns in plenty—the regimented patterns of the German landscape, slashed with the great Autobahns; and presently we were swooping down on Dusseldorf, with its Biergarten and fountains spouting out great volumes of water. The heat was tremendous, and they looked very tempting, but it appeared they were *verboten* to travellers by air. We were herded into a wooden shack to have our passports examined, then shot out on the blazing sunlight of the runways to wait for the little Italian plane which took us on the third stage of our journey.

Neat, elegant and well-appointed as the German plane had been the reverse, the little Italian took the air. The heat was stifling, and we thought it was some sort of a joke when the steward came round with blankets, which we politely refused, until we were made to understand that they were in some way obligatory. At the same time we were initiated into the use of some odd-looking rubber tubes whose nozzles we had noticed, looped up beside our seats. We realised that we must be going very high, if we were advised to take oxygen.

Quite suddenly, we were shivering. The cabin was invaded with a glacial cold, which made us gather the blankets about our shoulders. Around and beneath us were the snows, and, far below, flung on the whiteness like scattered jewels, lake after lake in every gradation of indigo, of blue, green, ochre or of pale, milky jade reflected the sky. Below the snowline, in hollows of the peaks, patches of emerald pasture caught our shadow as we flew over them. The glaciers swung below us, as we altered our course, with a wing tip that seemed almost to scrape the side of some peak that soared above us. William was quite white; his eyes, glittering, were recording every colour, every shape of the scene over which we were passing.

We had crossed the Alps, and reached Milan in time for lunch; it was dark when our luggage was loaded on to the motor-launch that took us out beyond the mist-shrouded islands to the musical-comedy wharf of the Excelsior.

We had arrived rather late for the Lido season, but had a fortnight of idling and sunbathing before the clouds swept down on the Dolomites and sirocco blotted out the horizon and turned the lagoon into a shallow cauldron where we continued to bathe despite the disapproval of the Italians, who openly regarded us as lunatics.

We wandered in the narrow streets of Venice by moonlight, in the wake of the Venetian cats, who seemed even more aloof, mystic and dangerous than their English prototypes, and, on days when the light was not too impossible, spent hours in St. Mark's and with the Tintorettos. *Susannah and the Elders* was William's favourite; he was bewitched by the luminosity of that pale, clear flesh, and declared he would never forget its perfect beauty.

LADY SPENCER.
By courtesy of the Countess Spencer.

The charm of visiting picture galleries in William's company is the bright irreverence with which he is capable of regarding world masterpieces. The pompous asininity, the carefully-coined phrase, the pontifical utterance of the self-appointed art critic are not for him, and it may be said with certainty that whatever future biographer of William Nicholson attempts to put into his mouth some windily-complicated generalisation on the art of painting is a liar—and an unimaginative one at that! He is a painter, and not a talker; a worker and not a theorist. He is not to be led by the nose by the opinions of others, and "fashion" in painting is to him a thing of vulgarity. He has a *flair* for the ephemeral, which preserves him from being betrayed into brief enthusiasms: he can smell affectation, or insincerity, in painting quicker than a cat can smell a mouse. This has led to his condemnation, by a few of the advance guard, as "out-of-date" — simply because he will not accept circus tricks as marks of genius.

I found very engaging William's theory (evolved one morning with Robert Nichols, who joined us in our *cabana* on the beach) of how the Old Masters invented some of their distinctly odd combinations of pose and drapery: of a group of them, having dined well, and having their palettes at hand, deliberately setting each other problems in foreshortening—"Now *you* lie down on the floor and tie your left leg round the back of your neck and *I'll* lie down on the scaffolding with my big toe in my mouth, and we'll draw each other"—or words to that effect. A pretty relief, after a morning spent in the shadow of greatness.

William, characteristically, just began to take an interest in the Lido when the weather became insupportable; it had previously been too "social" for him, and it is to be feared he endured it largely on my account. But when the hotel rapidly emptied itself, the dance band put away its instruments, the waiters started to drift like lost souls among the great, wide, polished spaces and the loggias piled themselves with derelict chairs, through and about which played a savage horde of wild kittens, he settled down and began to paint the *Fin de Saison* series which were sold almost before one had time to admire them, on our return to England. One of these, of the empty beach, the sea like aquamarine, and the long, five-o'clock shadows streaking away from the feet of the few lingerers, was typical of the delicate and care-free element which was a latter-day development in William's work. How far behind was the old, sombre, Pryde-ian influence, the dark, meerschaum yellows, blacks and reddish-browns, that

N

persisted far into his career as a painter. It would be interesting to know which painters of to-day have so completely sloughed their beginnings as William has his. "All my work to-day," he sometimes complains, "looks like ' early works.'" In so far as it has the freshness and delight of "new adventure" it is true; but only the superficial eye could overlook the background of experience which lies, nowadays, behind every stroke he puts on the canvas.

We had decided to take in the Paris Exposition on our way back from Venice. It was nearing its close, and, by daylight looked shabby and squalid, but after nightfall, with its illuminated fountains, was beautiful and romantic. We dined there most nights, at the Reine Pédauque, and the *addition* of one such dinner is preserved by William and has a poignancy of its own in 1942. We seem to have done ourselves shockingly well, for with foie gras, truite à la crème and quails we drank moselle and Beaujolais, and ended up with *fines* with our coffee.

By way of contrast, we ate also at students' restaurants on the *rive gauche*, and pursued a little *recherche du temps perdu* among the scenes familiar to William during his student days. We even visited Julian's, and found it exactly as he had described it to me—exactly as it must have been fifty years ago : with the deep frieze of palette scrapings and the broken iron stove in the middle of the room. But it was vacation time, and the *ateliers* had a lost, unnatural air of neatness and smelt of *eau de Javel* and turpentine. Term was due to begin, however, a day or two after our visit, and already *messieurs les étudiants* were sitting outside Les Deux Magots, clutching little cardboard attaché-cases that contained most of their worldly goods, and *engueule*-ing the passers-by at their leisure. William, with his pochade-box slung over his shoulder, his too-immaculate linen and too-prosperous mien, came in for all his share of the *engeulements*, but when he grinned and waved cheerfully back they recognised a kindred spirit, and somebody executed a very plausible fanfaronade on a hastily-produced cornet.

There was an exposition of Les Indépendents at the Petit Palais, which we were both anxious to see. It had turned bitterly cold, and, ploughing down the boulevard with our noses thrust into the collars of our coats, we caught the word EXPOSITION out of the corner of our eyes, and turned thankfully in out of the wind. We soon saw, however, that the art was of a type so *indépéndent* as to make Salvador Dali positively academical by contrast. I left William scowling at some very peculiar murals, and wandered away to a showcase in which were arranged in a row some neat tufts of fur. While trying to work out the inner meaning of these—which I decided must be some form of Abstract art—William came up, took my arm angrily and said, "Come on; this is utter nonsense." Just as we were turning away I caught sight of a label at the end of my tufts of fur, which I pointed out to William. *Stages of Venereal Disease in the Common Rabbit.*

A pair of live fowl in a cage completed our enlightenment. One of the birds, looking very pleased with itself, was a hen in process of being changed into a cock, while its companion, crestfallen and miserable, was a cock undergoing transformation into a hen. I think William was so relieved to find out that it was not all some nightmare form of new art that for the next half-hour or so he was unable to see the full humour of the situation; but when we left the *Exposition de Biologie* and went on into the Petit Palais, I only hope that people who saw us mopping our eyes and reeling with laughter in front of the Modiglianis did not ascribe our levity to any want of respect for the paintings.

2

There were more portraits on the easels by now. The great trouble was the light. When the huge and hideous block of Eagle House reared itself at the end of Apple Tree Yard, the value of the studio as a studio had dropped by nearly half (a point of view not shared by the landlord), although the builders had considerately faced the offices with white porcelain tiles, and the firm opposite which ran the garage had, with equal kindness, painted their façade white; so there was a kind of reflected light in the big room, which William loved too much to be driven out of it by such inconveniences. But there were winter days when it was necessary from morning to night to burn the huge and ruinous installation of daylight bulbs which he had had fixed on a long batten above the window.

It would have been reasonable, from every point of view, to spend the winters abroad, but although we often talked of it, it was always impossible, when it came to the point, so to arrange William's work that this should be practicable. Sitters could only come at certain hours, sittings hung over, and the psychological disturbance of leaving a portrait half-finished left William no peace of mind when "on holiday." It would have been possible, and certainly easy, for him to have worked on Still Life, but portraits are the painter's bread and butter, and we were still romping merrily along, spending about twice as much as we earned, and behaving very much as Nero did when Rome was burning. It is easy to see that now. Although neither of us is given to wishful thinking, it did not seem possible that the rumours which were already circulating in informed society could come to anything, or that any serious interruption could occur in our working lives.

William started the portrait of Lord Allendale in Apple Tree, and went up to Bretton Park to continue it; at the same time he was painting a pretty, blonde woman, a Mrs. Cherry, with the light of the window behind her, and two wire-haired terriers nestling in the folds of her dress of blush-pink satin, and somehow we struggled through the winter.

That was the year we went to Toulon, where we stayed at the little Hôtel de la Rade, which had been recommended to us by Richard Aldington. The harbour was full of ships of war, and little steam-launches were continually bringing the officers and men ashore; we much admired the verve with which the sailors, racing each other's pinnaces hell for leather for the quai, crashed the bows triumphantly into the stonework with total disregard for anything except winning their race. The lovely animation of a port, the rainbow of flowers that was the market place, enchanted William, and he was on the point of setting to work when the town was swamped by Easter tourists. The friend who was with us suggested our going out to Carqueiranne, where, in spite of the almost continuous mistral, we stayed several weeks. I think it was at Carqueiranne that the idea of war first assumed definite shape in our minds: sitting in our room after dinner, playing poker, with the guns of Les Porqué-rolles keeping up their heavy thunder. But we thrust it aside; in the morning the sun was shining, the tide running into the cove looked like rock crystal—William made an exquisite, spark-ling picture of it, which, to my sorrow, was sold immediately on our return to England—and the scent of the flower fields behind the little hotel was almost overpowering.

We went on to the country which William knows best, about Avignon; peaceful and fecund country that he loves to paint. Looking back, one wonders whether it was some subconscious

warning that led to our determination to spend as little as possible
of the coming year in England. "Let's go home and fill our
pockets and come back again to France," he said one night when
we were dining in a little inn overlooking the vineyards. We even
talked about renting a *mas* for six months or more : but here
William's enthusiasm was greater than mine. I read the local
papers; he didn't. What I read did not incline me warmly to the
idea of establishing domicile in the Midi at that moment of the
country's history. But I saw the reason for his enthusiasm;
France is, of all European countries, the country of the painter.
You have only to set up an easel to become a kind of aristocrat;
the artist is respected by every class. I was obliged to admit it was
otherwise in my own beloved Spain, where, said William, "a
painter was just something to chuck stones at!"

Whether we filled our pockets or not, we were back in
Rothéneuf the following spring. In fact, the greater part of 1938
and up to June, 1939, we lived in "the painter's country."

3

William always had "a thing" about La Rochelle, because of
the Callot engravings, and the great Callot map of the Siege
which hung on the wall at Apple Tree. So one day, when we
began to feel that we had exhausted the charms of Rothéneuf, and
wanted to escape for a little from the endless talk of *la guerre, la
guerre, la guerre* which was all that people spoke about when they
met at the pavement tables, or in the bar of the inn where we were
staying, we hired a car and set out for the Charente. We knew,
by then, that we could no more escape *la guerre* than we could
escape the judgment of God, but we also knew that by sitting
and talking about it we could do nothing but reduce our spiritual
resistance to this great cloud whose shadow was creeping daily
over more of our working horizon.

I remember a day when William was sitting at the window,
painting an odd little house on the opposite side of the *Place*:
one of those tragic little houses one comes on, scattered through
the French provinces, whose shutters are closed and its doors
bolted on all the contents, until some day when the inmate of a
maison d'aliènes shuffles off his mortal coil. Such houses are
impounded by the State until the death of the owner allows the
heirs to inherit; no one may enter them, they may not be let or

sold. Only the moth, the worm and the spider may have their way with them . . . what scenes there must be when at last the sunshine is allowed into those long-closed chambers.

It was perhaps the sadness of the subject and the intensity of William's concentration on it that broke down my resolution, when we were alone, never to mention the war.

" What shall we do if the war comes ?"

" *Work*," he answered.

But, looking at him, I wondered, for the first time, if even William could work, through the war that was coming.

The car was a very fine new one, but the driver was frightened of it. We told him to stop sounding the klaxon, but his nerves kept his finger trembling over the button, so that it kept on emitting two little croaks. If there was a car in the distance, his foot shook on the accelerator, and when he had to pass anything the tension came out through the back of his neck.

After Nantes the rain started thinly, and the cattle were being driven home off the Poictevin marshes. The sky lay right down low on the marshes and the sun looked like a flaming aeroplane that had torn a hole for itself in the sky. The mists were rising, and the backs of the cattle moved just above the mists, which they tore with their wide white horns. One started to see and hear all kinds of things that weren't there—soldiers plunging about in harness, cursing Henry dying in Chinon, and Creeping John and the Lionheart: there would be the same cattle and the same women in white coifs and the same endless spread of sour yellow sedge and hopeless sky, and the same wetness rising and condensing and coming down again in rain. And the adders were the sons of those that struck through a loose piece of mail and made a man's foot swell up so that he got lame, and there was no armourer to cut the harness off, so he got blood poisoning and sank down in the marsh and became mud and a blue flicker over a patch of grass. . . .

This was the mood in which we came to La Rochelle, where it stopped raining, and there was enough moonlight to see six-teenth-century façades, with balconies, or mouldings, or turrets; some of the houses have black and white timbered façades with slates nailed over the timbers to preserve them from the weather, and bitumen painted over the slate. It did not strike us then that these were ominous indications of climate.

The next day was Sunday, and there was a light brume that made everything a very pale grey. The fishing fleet was in, because they work the forty-hour week, like the shop people, and all the nets hung up to dry: pale blue, sapphire, faience and the transparent colour of shrimps before they are boiled. They looked like Tintoretto's painting of Sant' Orsolo and the ladies coming from the barge. The boats themselves had red decks and green and chrome yellow round the bulwarks.

The love of colour seemed to belong to the men, for all the women dressed in black, but the men had blue or red trousers, vests of every colour and emerald green or bright Reckitt's blue caps. There were a great many regional coifs worn by the elder women: broad ones of net and lace, with lappets and goffering, the high sugar cones of stiffened lace that we had seen in St. Malo, and round mobs of *broderie anglaise* puffed out with horsehair. After a look at the hard, handsome faces, high-coloured and shiny on the cheekbones, William turned to me with a grin. "Jane, this is a tough joint." I knew he was satisfied; he likes "tough joints."

Although we had intended to stay, at most, only forty-eight hours, we sent the car back to Rothéneuf; we bought prawns, cheese, grapes, white wine and *petit pains* and took them to the top of the tower of St. Nicolas, where the sun was blazing and there were thousands of flying ants, and William could get the strange perspectives of the quais and the boats and the fishwives collecting their boxes at the harbour steps.

I have written a great deal about all this, because in none of our wanderings had we come across an environment which made so deep, visible and unalterable an impression on William. His was the lovely experience of having dreamed about a place for years, and found reality more exciting than the dream. He often says he "can only paint when he wants to." I knew that, circumstances permitting, we were in for the biggest bout of landscape that had ever happened since I met William.

On the day we moved into the hotel which was to house us for the next five weeks, Chamberlain had the first of his conferences with Hitler, which made a great impression on the French, but every one seemed very nervous—although not so much so as a few days later, when the mobilisation began.

CHAPTER TWENTY

La Rochelle

I

From my diary:
WE WALKED round, after lunch, by the Hotel de Ville. There were crowds reading the *Rappel aux Armes*—mainly women: every one was very quiet; they stood about in little groups, hardly speaking. One of the fishermen told us that fifty camions had been requisitioned, and the men were leaving that night. Many of the women were pregnant; their faces were dull and quiet, for the wives of deep sea fishermen are used to concealing their emotions. No one made any fuss. Little boys and girls went round and round on bicycles, watching everything.

There was a crowd round a photographer's, and a car lined with white flowers. Presently the bride came out on her husband's arm, he in naval uniform, she a thin-faced little ginger-blonde with white satin ruched under her chin. A fat man gave it as his opinion that she was " *très bien—très, très bien,*" and three cheerful youths contributed reminiscences of the bridal night of a female cousin. Bride and bridegroom both looked calm and gratified.

At the Café des Colonnes, Madame burst into tears at the prospect of her husband's departure *pour la guerre*. The war has drawn much nearer—Hitler and Chamberlain having reached the point of exchanging pacific generalisations (worth how much?), and Czechoslovakia is arming hand over fist, while Prague ignores Hitler's ultimatum. It makes one feel sick, and as if one's insides had melted. William suggested we should ride out the storm in La Rochelle; I am willing, but worried about my manuscript in England.

The military have requisitioned the telephone and telegraph services; nevertheless, Ian rang up from Alençon and suggested he might join us. He says nothing now can prevent war.

In the restaurant there were hardly any diners, and the few who arrived came to hear the Führer's broadcast and were not interested in the food. A young saxaphonist from the casino came in; he was leaving for Toulouse. A few days ago he announced he was *fiancé*, and was invited to bring his *fiancée* to share the congratulations. To-night he created a furore by arriving with a blond young man of a little more than his own age, whom he gravely presented to the company as his *fiancé(e?)*. He waited long enough to translate the broadcast for the benefit of those who did not understand German, during which his companion became very hysterical, and they retired, no doubt to console each other. It was the speech of a lunatic, rather than of a sane man; high-pitched, ugly, rising into a shriek and cracking. Neither of us can understand how such a man should be allowed to be the leader of a nation.

2

From my diary:

We sat in the restaurant until after midnight. Outside it was raining and the cars parked round the base of the Duperré statue looked like cockroaches. There were hundreds of mosquitoes. Every one but ourselves had gone. Then the Ile de Ré steamer came in, with four tourists from Epping, who asked for oysters and soup and omelette. All the kitchen staff had gone home, so I went into the kitchen with Madame to help her to get the food.

William and Jean started doing aquarelles in coffee; Jean did one of the port and William did fish. One of the fish, said Jean, "*est évidement une hystérique*," and another was a *vieille fille* of the kind you meet in church porches. The English tourists regarded William and Jean with the amused condescension reserved by a certain class for artists, and inquired facetiously whether "Monsieur" was setting up as a rival to "my husband." I told them Jean was a sculptor, and they seemed taken aback that a restaurant-keeper should be an artist, and were less patronising.

After they had gone we sang French and English songs: *Temps de cérises*, and *Le blé d'or* and *The Girl I Left Behind Me*. Suzanne wanted the English songs "*un peu voyou*"; we tried to oblige, but our *voyou* songs turned out to be, in translation, so much less *spirituel* than the French ones that we were ashamed of them. Jean and Suzanne were very polite about it.

We discussed running a *café chantant* at the Grosse Horloge during the war: William's contribution was to be lightning caricatures, which Jean was certain would be the greatest success.

He has a reverence amounting to superstition for all the little *croquis* William makes on the menus, tablecloths and napkins, and, I think, would preserve every one of them if Suzanne's house-wifeliness did not defeat him. It is enchanting to listen to William and Jean "communicating": Jean being too lazy, and William too shy, ever to commit themselves in each other's language, but the most charming *bonhomie* and affection governs all their dealings.

A little before one o'clock, Suzanne said, "*Demain il y aura la guerre*," and brought a bottle of Roederer. Everything was deathly quiet, except for the music of the dance band next door. There were the reflections of the lighthouses in the *bassins* and the fishing-nets hung up like ghosts; and the cobbles were wet and round the lamp on the corner of the balcony you could see the rain shooting like white bullets, and the moths bumping into one another.

Eight hundred rochelais have already been mobilised, and this morning they called up another class of reserves. Our little *valet de chambre* left, carrying a pitiful little hamper, his red cheeks puddled with tears. "*J'ai arrangé les lits, madame, mais je suis obligé de partir à deux heures.*" Room not swept, ash-trays not emptied, new *valet*, a polite, scared-looking child of sixteen or so, as pale as though he too felt the war-wind on his downy adolescent cheeks.

We drank our champagne and left quietly; the whole town was asleep, the arcades deserted and the *Place* empty. It was about half-past one. As we stepped across the puddles, William said, "I don't know what will happen to work, Jane, if war comes."

I do not know either, for in these seemingly ideal surroundings, with a thousand subjects asking to be painted, with congenial company and all the simplicity of French living which William loves—no work is getting done. We are both too edgy, the future seems too blank, the prevalent unhappiness and anxiety affects us too deeply, to settle to creative work. It is the first time I have ever known William's sanctuary of work to fail him. He wanders round with a little Kodak, taking records of scenes he has not the heart to paint; a few rough drawings and a pastel of the port are the only fruits, so far, of these shadowed weeks. And Suzanne's langouste! The langouste is really a beautiful fellow; he is drawn in pastels as brilliant as the Sunfish which was bought by the Tate. He is to hang in the *salle à manger*—a lesson in aesthetics and dietetics for the customers. The best diversion we have now is discussing with Suzanne her plans and ambitions for the restaurant de la Grosse Horloge which she, without any previous experience, has had the temerity to buy, and aspires to manage herself—strange occupation for a lineal descendant of Henri Quatre! Jean is furious, and hates the whole idea, but she is obstinate as a mule and may even make a success of it . . . *si la guerre n'arrive pas?*

3

Then came the Munich meeting; the buffoonery of the Umbrella; the buffoonery of an old man's return to England prating "I bring you peace!"

Now they fêted us—*les anglais*—at the restaurant de la Grosse Horloge! There was a big meridional skipper of the fishing fleet—it was he, if I remember right, who gave the luncheon party which began at twelve noon and was still in full swing at four o'clock in the afternoon, when William and I, willing of spirit, but defeated in the flesh, staggered weakly back to the hotel—only to discover, when we returned for our dinner at eight, that the party had found its second wind! We were once more greeted with cries of welcome, swept into our chairs, absorbed into the heart of the company. I caught a look of despair from William, whose glass *le bon capitaine* was brimming with Châteauneuf du Pape; there was nothing for it but to abandon ourselves once again.

There was the skipper and his plump, agreeable little wife; the wealthy owner of most of the famous oyster beds and his elegant friend the lady who kept the marine store on the end of the harbour—who had started the afternoon so tailor-made and stylised that she might have been chiselled out of black jet and ivory, but who, by the evening came, had achieved the "sweet abandon in the dress" which the poet found so attractive, and with the thawing of her formality proved a very amusing person indeed; there was a bristle-faced colonel of the Maginot line, with whom William immediately got "on terms," assisted by the fact that the colonel knew three or four little English sentences on which he rang miraculous changes of inflection and meaning, which apparently gave the pair of them the very greatest satisfaction; there was a black-browed Chouan asparagus-grower from the Ile d'Oléron—they all toasted us and treated us as if we had some mysterious affinity with the man who had "saved" Europe from war at the eleventh hour.

That, I think, is how William sees France in retrospect: as a long table, surrounded by people of goodwill and good heart, beaming, friendly, hospitable, eager to honour the foreigners in their midst. No wonder the tragedy of France has bitten deep into him. But it is good to remember that he had ten whole months of this romantic France, this France, in a sense, of his own creation, before the disillusionment came in 1940.

We told everybody we were coming back "very soon," and accepted (in our innocence) the assurance of everybody that the winter climate of La Rochelle was mild and agreeable. Jean and Suzanne pledged themselves to find us an *appartement* where we could live our own lives of artists and not be dependent on hotel menus and régimes.

4

We had decided, when we returned in October, that we would spend at least six months in La Rochelle. Jean and Suzanne had kept their word; we found ourselves in possession of a delightful *appartement* on the port; William was enchanted to discover that he could identify the very spot—he declared, the very house—on the Callot map. All day long the sails went past under our windows, the dramas of the waterfront were ours just for the turn of a head. To make it even more homelike, we acquired Black.

Suzanne was responsible for Black. Having rashly mentioned in her hearing how much I wanted a cat, it was only to be expected that the door should open one day, and a tall, temperamental, round-eyed black kitten walk on tiptoe into the room.

The history of our cats would fill a volume by itself, but Black was, of them all, the most original, the fiercest, wildest, most loving and most humorous; he was a born clown of a cat. He not only joined in any game we cared to start with him—he invented games of his own, and, as William pointed out, Black's games, which he varied from day to day, were always the best. There was one game, however, to which he was obstinately faithful, and, if we did not begin it, he would stand by the door and scream with rage until we joined in.

The *appartement* was so arranged that the four rooms communicated with one another, and, having passed from kitchen to salon, from salon to dressing-room, from dressing-room to bedroom, you could complete the round tour by returning to the kitchen along a passage. It was Black's delight to be chased, and, in his turn, to chase, round this circle; but it was no simple chase, for every now and then he would cheat, would stop and crouch inside a doorway, then, when one reached it, he would leap up the door jamb, shoulder-high, and slide down again, gripping with his paws, before tearing on to the next doorway. This was his regular morning game, with which he coaxed or bullied us out of bed every morning; it was no use pretending to be asleep, or spreading out the newspaper to read; you cannot read with a very angry cat bouncing up and down on the foot of the bed, bawling to be played with.

At night, like many cats, he had mad steeplechases from room to room; but Black's steeplechases differed from the average in that they seemed always to have some savage purpose. He leapt like a stag, and with ruthless disregard for all but his own enjoyment. William, dozing on the divan after a day spent in working, would rouse with a yelp and an oath as Black took off from the tenderest portion of his anatomy for some incredible bound, and the current paragraph of *The Sun is My Undoing* broke up in confusion as Black tore across the keyboard of the typewriter. "Damn that cat!" said William, but he adored Black, for whom he had invented a game of his own.

He had brought out with him a beautiful irregular bowl of elmwood, nearly two feet across at its widest part, which he intended to use for a Still Life; this became Black's favourite toy. Climbing into it, he would lie on his side while William spun it. Round and round went Black in the bowl, prone with rapture, until William's energy gave out, when Black would gather himself up and stagger with a very uncertain movement to the chair or windowsill which he favoured for the moment, his eyes glassy and squinting with bliss.

He was the idol of the household; Léonie, the *bonne-à-tout-faire*, called him "*Mon fils*," and only occasionally forgot and addressed him as "*Mini*," which he detested; his resentment of the commonplace name was as obvious as it was ludicrous; he would get up and walk straight out of the room, when Léonie called him "*Mini*." Once he was lost, and La Rochelle was practically shaken to its foundations; our landlady brought her dog to try and sniff

Black out—Black who never stirred, tucked blissfully under the *couvrepied* and eiderdown on my bed.

Alas, when we left La Rochelle, the problem arose of how to dispose of Black, as our landlady could not keep him with her dog. We knew we could not take him back to England, but got Madame Garrigue's word to look after him, and try to find him a home while we were in St. Jean de Luz. Our feelings can be imagined when a wire arrived—"*Petit chat ne mange pas ne dort pas.*" At first we were for taking the next train back to La Rochelle; then William, his face agonised, pointed out that this was only to prolong the agony—that Black could not come home with us, and that, failing a good home, there was only one thing to be done. . . . We sent a telegram.

To try and put it out of our minds we went to Biarritz—a town we both loathe—and had a marvellous lunch, which neither of us tasted, as the tears were rolling quite openly down both our faces. We could talk and think of nothing but Black.

When we got back to our hotel there was another wire: "*Petit chat bien placé très content.*" We went back to Biarritz and had a marvellous dinner.

It was the first time we had succumbed to acquiring a cat abroad, and we swore it should never happen again; it meant too much heartache. The pity was, we both loved animals, and we could never keep any because of our frequent absences. There was a tortoiseshell kitten at Malaga which William lost his heart to, and some basket-makers in Sevilla had done their utmost to press upon us a furious, rust-coloured kitten which William christened El Moro on sight. Apart from our rabbit, Postlethwaite, whom William bought to amuse me when I was ill, we never had an animal of our own until we knew there would be no escape from England, perhaps for years.

Cats are enchanting models, and William made many drawings of Black, lying in his bowl, or rolling on his side to pat the gold-fish tank which, with its inmates, was another of his favourite toys. Other cats he has drawn are Winston Churchill's marmalade tom, of which he made a sheet of sketches which he gave to Mrs. Churchill, and our beautiful black neuter, Castlerosse, one of our two "Blitz babies," who accompanied us into our two years exile from London. From Frou-frou onwards, he has owned many cats, among them a splendid Russian smooth, but his favourite, after Black, is his "little black girl," Castlerosse's twin sister, whose sheer plebeian commonness is only equalled by her charm, and whose welcoming purr is guaranteed to penetrate stone walls. One always knows if "The Girl" is around, even if invisible, for the slightest movement on one's part is enough to call out that rich, metallic purr. She is as completely William's cat as Castlerosse is mine, and, although very pleasant to me, never mistakes her real ownership.

With Black and the goldfish, the *appartement* at once took on an air of domesticity, and my table, loaded with manuscript and books of reference, joined on to William's with his pastels and sketch books. It was one of the pleasantest places we ever worked in together, for the light was like crystal, and often, while I was labouring on the third book of *The Sun*, William was at the window, making drawings of the port, "learning it," in his usual fashion, before starting to paint. It was amusing, drawing from the window, for we were on the *cinquième*, which lent everything an odd perspective. In order that we might not be troubled with cooking, Suzanne sent us our meals from the restaurant.

Christmas came and went, in a downfall of snow, which totally demoralised the rochelais, who had not seen snow for forty years, and promptly took to their beds—as many as could afford it. Shops closed—there were no bread, milk or newspapers for four days. Just as the Italians thought us crazy for bathing during the sirocco, so the rochelais decided we were raving mad, when we put on our good English boots and tramped about in the deep snow, enjoying it very much. Instead of champagne for "elevenses," we had rum and hot milk—with a red hot iron dipped into it: a trick Madame Tremoulleau of the Colonnes had taught us. William clinched the matter of his insanity with the natives by sitting out-of-doors to paint the snow—but it may be added he did not sit for long. He finished from the window one of the most beautiful and coldest *paysages* I ever saw; for sheer biting cold, which comes off the surface of the canvas and hits you in the face, it is only equalled by his *Bretton Park Under Snow*, painted while he was staying with Lord Allendale, and now in the possession of Mrs. Hanbury Kelk. The contrast between the Yorkshire and the rochelaise snow is interesting: one all mauve, the other all green in its shadows.

(That visit to Bretton was productive of some good work; besides the portrait, on which he was officially engaged, William painted the Still Life of Begonias with Sealing Wax which was exhibited in 1942. He painted it in his bedroom, by the light of an ordinary oil lamp; it is one of the most brilliant of his many flower pictures.)

The port had taken hold of William, and all the rochelaise pictures, except one, are of the *quais*, the *bassins* or the shipping. G. B. Stern got one of the best, a beautiful green study of a cluster of little ships at anchor, and a swirl of water which looks like the eddy of another ship as it left the harbour.

One day, when the acacias along the Mall were just beginning to show faint crimson traces of bud, we went into a little park adjoining the Museum, through which a schoolteacher was conducting a little flock of pupils, to whom she was giving a botany lesson. William had already started to paint, and from where we were sitting the voices of the teacher and the children came clearly.

" *Premières manifestations du printemps*," declaimed the teacher, pointing to some little tufts of green that had started to appear on the winter-frozen shrubs.

" *Pre-mières man-i-fes-tations du prin-temps*," piped the children obediently.

"That's the title of my picture," said William, as he added the little row of children, in their pale frocks that looked like a border of spring flowers to the design on his canvas.

Not that La Rochelle was as innocent in all its aspects as this. Ignorant as we were, it did not take much observation to realise that it was, at that time, a hotbed of political intrigue. On most Sundays, and on some days in the week, a table was reserved in the restaurant for the politicians who came down to hold meetings and to harangue the rochelais. On sight, they were a set of thugs; we never saw among them a single person of education or showing even a modicum of breeding. Their manners barbarous and overbearing, they made the people sitting at the tables nearest to them uncomfortable with their sprawling attitudes and the vulgar loudness of their conversation. It sent a chill through one to realise that these were the people on whom the integrity of France depended, and it was largely on account of what I saw and heard at La Rochelle that I said on the outbreak of the war that France would be out of it in six months—a remark bitterly resented at the time by William, as francophile, in a different fashion, as Winston Churchill. One could feel, in the presence of those men, in their total disregard of the company in which they found themselves, in the coarseness of behaviour which

LORD AND LADY STRAFFORD.
By courtesy of the Earl of Strafford.

singled them out in a society not notable for its delicacy, the crumbling of the old cultural tradition of France.

Except for a small intellectual minority, there was no culture in La Rochelle. A visiting opera company billed *La Bohème* among its repertory of light operatic comedy for the week ; *La Bohème* was removed from the bill and some commonplace operetta substituted. There was no audience, even for Puccini, in La Rochelle. *La Kermesse Héroïque*, at the picture house, drew poor houses, and was soon withdrawn for a Hollywood sex drama. But for Jean and Suzanne, we should have wanted sadly for company ; but fortunately we were both working so hard that we had not much time to trouble about society.

Still, apart from intellectual limitations, the average rochelais *petit bourgeois* was a solid and decent person, and we sometimes wondered that they tolerated in their midst these unpleasant visitors. But they were cynical—and rightly—about politics; even Jean was cynical. " *Mais non, Weel-liamme!*" he demurred, one day when I had translated to him William's disgust at the game of politics, as it appeared to be played in France. " *Moi, je trouverais charmant d'être politicien!*" A platform, unlimited powers of oratory, an audience—what could be more delightful? Convictions?—" *Mais non, Marguerite, il ne faut pas avoir des ideés fixes ! Il ne faut pas prendre ces choses au sérieux. . . .*" Impossible to see Jean, with all his elegance of intellect and person, in that *galère*; equally impossible to avoid the reflection that his class, with their cool, disillusioned indifference, had contributed perhaps no less than the professional gangsters to the decadence of French morale.

5

In southern Spain there is a wind called *la tormenta* : one of those winds which, blowing off the desert, bring with them passions foreign to, or dormant in, the people over which they pass. *La tormenta* is always accompanied by a crime wave. It is hardly an exaggeration to say that a man can " get away with murder" if he can prove the *tormenta* was blowing when he committed it.

I do not know if a local version of the *tormenta* was blowing on the night which exhibited William to me in a totally new rôle

o

of belligerence which I had never previously associated with his character.

It started about ten o'clock, with the entrance of a drunken English skipper of a coal barge docking at La Pallice, who lurched up to our table and offered familiarities to Jean which we naturally resented. We resented it more because this dislikeable person insisted on proclaiming that he was "a hundred per cent English," and although we tried at first to ignore him, he made this impossible by leaning across us and bawling his assertions of nationality so loudly that we could not go on with our conversation. Finally William, white with anger, ordered him away from the table—to which every one's attention, by now, was drawn—on which he turned nasty and became abusive in the large, loose-mouthed, easy way of the lower decks. William stood up, and the skipper, a fellow as broad as an ox and at least twice William's weight, went for him.

I saw William pick up a bottle, had a momentary vision of our spending long, inconvenient hours in the courts for assault and battery, or whatever it may be called in French law, and, to my own surprise, found myself behind the skipper engaged in the curiously unfeminine act of throttling him by twisting his collar. Three or four men leapt up from a table and together succeeded in separating William—who by now had gone completely berserk and fought for possession of his bottle—from the skipper, who was thrust out of the restaurant, breathing fire and slaughter and promising reprisals. (We heard afterwards that he had been thrown out of three other restaurants before coming to the Grosse Horloge, so it was evidently just one of those shore leaves which had gone to his head.)

We had just settled down again, and Jean was patting William on the shoulder and telling him not to derange himself for these *canaille*, when a plate skimmed through the air. We blinked. It was followed by another, and turning round, we saw one of the waiters, whom we had always looked on as a quiet inoffensive fellow, crouching against the wall with a pile of plates in his arms which he was shying at the patrons with an aim fortunately not quite accurate as it was deadly. The few remaining customers were sitting at their tables, apparently paralysed, gaping at the plates as they flew through the air.

With some dim recollection of the soft answer turning away wrath, I got up and went towards the man, who cowered and shouted at me, saying something to the effect of, "Look here,

Charles, you can't do that"—and while speaking, was half-aware of a little stout man who got up from a table behind me and went to the lavatory. While Charles continued to shout and I to expostulate, the little man emerged in his shirt sleeves, took a short run, and made a beautiful tackle, which caught Charles round the knees from behind, bringing him and the plates to the floor with a crash. At the same moment, the *concierge* of the Clock Tower, evidently hearing the noise in the restaurant, and wishing to join in the fun, threw half a brick through the window.

By now William and I were practically hysterical. We sat at the table, mopping our eyes and whooping with laughter, while someone conveyed Charles, who had come to his senses, and looked very much as if he had just wakened out of a bad dream, into the back premises, and someone else swept up the broken china. Suzanne was as calm as though she had been running a waterfront restaurant for the whole of her life; she just stood there with a grin on her little white face, cursing everybody impartially; until suddenly she burst out laughing as well.

"*Alors—du champagne!*" she exclaimed, and hurried off to the cellar.

While the champagne was cooling, I remembered a letter I should have posted, and ran down to put it in the box just through the archway of the Grosse Horloge. (This history is getting like "And on the next step some fish were frying themselves in a pan.") The spectacle of two sailors engaged in a competition as to which could carve the other up more thoroughly with a jack-knife seemed just one of the courtesies of everyday life after the scenes in the restaurant that evening. In fact, it did not seem worth mentioning, when I got back to the table and lifted the glass of Roederer to my lips.

6

The next day was wet, and was a Sunday. The politicians arrived for lunch, trampling the mud from their boots all over Suzanne's clean floor.

When they had gone, and when Jean, Suzanne, William and I sat at our corner table, talking quietly, a little figure started to move, humbly and carefully, between the tables. First the chairs were stacked, then a pail and rubber were brought, and, on its knees, the small, shabby figure washed from plank to plank. As it came nearer it lifted its head. A square, pale, one-eyed face, thatched with rough black hair and a tuft of moustache, not unlike Chaplin's. He dropped his head and went on with his work, which brought him slowly nearer and nearer our corner. As we rose to be out of the way I saw, on the little finger of his right hand, a signet ring with a crest.

Jean told me his name. It was the Marquis de . . . there were several names, each prefixed by the aristocratic "de." I am glad I have forgotten his name.

CHAPTER TWENTY-ONE

Farewell to France—The War, 1939

I

THE BLAZING CALF with firecrackers spouting out of its horns was dragged round the Place and the air swirled with confetti. Right in the middle of the blitz on St. James's I thought of this; it looked very much the same, only the torchlight was burning houses, the confetti was black and people rushed at the firecrackers, as they fell from the skies, to extinguish them.

When a few warm days and a few buds brought us our "*premières manifestations du printemps,*" we made south, for St. Jean de Luz. We bathed, we became devotees of the ball game (the best *pelota* was the matches between the Pyreneean smugglers, whose immense shoulder muscles were developed by carrying contraband through the mountains), we idled in little bars—one in particular where the proprietor complimented our taste by bringing us the *real* Izarra, as different as the *real* Chartreuse from the liqueurs which now pass under their name, and, when the *fiesta* blew up, we danced and hurled confetti. . . . We had earned our holiday; William had left a pile of canvasses in the little *appartement* on the Cours Wilson, and I had finished the first and second books of *The Sun is My Undoing* and was well into the third.

At the end of a month we returned to collect the fruits of our labours, and found La Rochelle in the first fine careless rapture of its Air Raid Precautions. A dummy raid (with bags of flour to represent bombs) was a riot, the rochelais went into it with the same full-blooded zest they displayed on the night of the "ill wind." A man told off to act as a casualty put up such a performance that his yells were audible from the Place to the Port, and a dear old lady in a Vendéean coif was not to be persuaded they were mere histrionics, but, acting no doubt under the sensible French impression that no ill exists that is not amenable to a timely administration of lucre, insisted on pressing a couple of francs into the "victim's" palm. The ambulance, summoned to the *quai* to attend another "casualty," drove through the archway of the Grosse Horloge with such brio that it not only jammed itself, but caused a perfectly genuine and fatal casualty of its own. That evening, in the *Tout Va Bien* and the *Bar des Flots*, it was unanimously agreed that the death under the Grosse Horloge had put a pretty finishing touch on a very enjoyable day.

2

"We ought to see about getting a new car," said William, on our return to England. (We had sold both ours, the little M.G. and the Hillman, before going to France.) We were feeling "rich," the low cost of living in La Rochelle, as compared with our London expenditure, having left us with the illusion we were millionaires.

"Don't buy a new car," counselled, not only our friends, but the dealer from whom we had bought cars in the past. "Wait and see what happens."

There was something very grim about that "Wait and see," and about the tension which brooded over London during those months before the war. War was the shadow behind all our plans, and war made it difficult to settle to anything: although William exhibited his La Rochelle pictures, most successfully, at the Leicester Galleries, and I went so far—it is to be recognised now as a gesture of defiance—as to rent a large studio close to our flat in Hove. I was on the last lap of *The Sun is My Undoing*, and felt the need of an absolutely secluded and separate working place. William toyed with the idea of taking the studio next to mine, but went cautious at the last minute.

Once again the theatre was "after us." At the beginning of 1938, Derek Patmore and I had written a comedy called *French For Love*. This play was just the outcome of another of William's "little ideas," tossed out as lightly as one might puff a feather into the air. It was he who produced the anecdote about a worldly gentleman who refused to sanction his daughter's nuptials to a young man who had no experience of the other sex, and I suddenly "saw" the whole idea of a comedy and suggested it to Derek, being, just then, too busy, and, always, too lazy, to tackle a play by myself.

During our absence in La Rochelle, Derek succeeded in marketing this play, and had little time, on our return, to do more than "hand over" to me before he was wafted away to Roumania as special correspondent.

There was one set, which we wanted William to do, but he felt—and rightly—that the somewhat banal and "stagey" reproduction of the exterior of a villa on the Riviera, which was all we needed, was not the kind of thing to appeal to him. He had been offered a new portrait commission, and was anxious to get ahead with this before the war broke. Rehearsals were in progress when, in September, on one of those sunny Sunday mornings which were so pleasant, because we had the little flat to ourselves— we listened to the declaration of war.

I wonder what the declaration of war meant, on the whole, to the thousands of painters and writers who must have listened to it: apart, that is to say, from personal and private consider- ations. I think it is natural for the creative artist to think first of his work, and when William looked across at me and said "That knocks *us* out, Jane," I knew what he meant, and felt, for a while, a little sick.

For the painter war is formidable, unless he belongs to the school of artists that can capitalise it. Even if exhibitions con- tinue, are people going to buy landscape and still life during war-time? Even if they go to the exhibitions, are they going to have money to spend on what are usually classed as "luxuries," since there seems to be a curious sort of idea that, although it is necessary to feed the body, the spirit can look after itself? And even if, out of their conviction and their love of the beautiful, they continue to buy records of beauty which is only a memory— will landscape and still life pay the rent, and keep a roof over the painter's head?

It did not need much guessing that the rich, the portrait- commissioning class was going to be taxed, if not out of existence, out of their important function as patrons of the arts. There would be portraits—yes: but not in "the grand manner," to which William, as a portraitist, was accustomed. Portraits of brass hats, portraits of soldiers—people dashing in, during their few hours of leave, wanting "a record" on behalf of their families, of their townships, of some civic body which, in peace-time, they represented—a record which, from William's point of view, could as fitly, and more ably, have been provided by a photographer: caring nothing for the artist or for the work of art, for who troubles about such things in war-time? He knew, and I knew as well, that he could never rise to this type of demand—he whose work was governed so much by mood and environment.

There must have been a time—there was certainly a time—

when William could "toss off" a portrait: not that he did not hate doing it, did not hate it when it was done, and was not capable—with the duns hammering at the door—of slashing the whole thing up with a palette-knife. Such work, to him, was agony, and, happily for his peace of mind, very few examples are in existence. His conscience as artist is too tender to allow him, deliberately, to do bad work; he has none of the cynicism of the "fashionable" portrait-painter, who, despising the sitter's intelligence, uses his name and his prestige to foist the second-rate on a buyer—who "takes the cash and lets the credit go." William's credit has always been a great deal dearer to him than the cash. It was one of the small rewards of increasing prestige that he had, of latter years, been able to exercise some measure of choice in regard, not only to what he painted, but to where and when he painted it. Up to the outbreak of the war he had, mercifully, never lost the desire to paint at all: which was a blessing, as, unless he *wants* to do a thing, he simply *cannot* do it, no matter what the conditions.

Later on, Winston Churchill suggested that William should go North and paint battleships. But William did not want to paint battleships—and very wisely, since he does not know one end of a battleship from another; nor did he want to go up to Scotland and leave me in London, where, already, there was gossip about an "invasion." Nor, when the blitz came, although certain dramatic spectacles appealed to him, did he want to record it. "Why should I do what photography can do so much better?"

It was some time before I, whose reaction was anger, and determination to see all Germans in hell before I would stop working, could understand William's reaction to the war. It was his greater sensitiveness that felt more acutely than I, at first, the hopelessness of the human race which could sacrifice to barbarity all the qualities which raise us above the animals. He, whose few hatreds have a childish and harmless quality about them, who shrinks from dissension, whose instinct is to have a kind of smooth and silken quality in all domestic and social relationships, was stunned by the whirlwinds of hate suddenly liberated into his world. All beautiful things, for William, were discoloured by it; the daily scene had lost its purity, he saw it only through a dimness of unhappiness. Another, more personal, thought was in his mind; in the last war he had lost Tony. Kit, the promise of whose career as an architect was always bright in his father's mind, had now joined the Fleet Air Arm.

Still, he settled down bravely to paint the portraits of his landlords, Lord Strafford and Lady Strafford, in their library. Derek left for Roumania. Rehearsals went on, although our original management got "cold feet," backed out and unloaded us on to Richmond. A month later we were established in the Criterion, and William, I think, was in the stalls or at the back of the dress circle more frequently than I; he would bring me almost nightly reports and shrewd little criticisms. *French for Love* cheered him up, as, I think, it cheered up the people who went to see it.

On the first night we had had a party—the last of the many Apple Tree parties, except for a small one we gave for Derek when he came home on leave and we tried—optimistically—to get a successor to *French for Love* written. Apple Tree lent itself to hospitalities, and, looking back, I see like a scene in a fairytale, the shining floor, the candles flickering in their silver sconces, the beautiful shadow of the *Pandora* slanted across the sloping ceiling, the glowing stove, the men and women in evening dress— Alice Delysia, brilliant and elegant with all her French beaux she had brought on from the theatre about her, Athene Seyler's little daughter looking like a painting by Renoir—so many witty men and pretty women—and William at his beaming best, as he always was, as host; it was the last time that the war withdrew (in spite of the uniforms in our midst) so far that we hardly remembered it. There was a story that Apple Tree was haunted; it is a pleasant reflection, that there must be many gay, young ghosts, to-day, to drive out the older, unhappier ones.

3

Before the horror of war took hold of him, and, for a while, put a stop to his painting, William finished the Strafford portrait. To get its full flavour, one does well to compare it with the *Mr. and Mrs. Sidney Webb*, painted in 1929, for the London School of Economics; the two together—it was unfortunate that Lord Strafford, fearing a repetition of the raids, refused to lend his portrait for the National Gallery Exhibition in 1942—afford an almost Hogarthian commentary on the new and the old aristocracy.

The one, with its ugly modern fireplace of a suburban villa, its litter of documents, the earnest shapelessness of Lord Passfield's

P

trousers, his carpet-slippers, his wife's hand clawing absently towards an economical fire, epitomises low living and high thinking as thoroughly as the other epitomises high living and as little thinking as possible. One, from whose surface breathes luxury and privilege, ranks as a final essay on "the old order," now hardly more than a name, while simplicity to the point of austerity, self-sacrifice and the art of living for others have somehow found their way on to the Webb canvas. In these two conversation pieces, the painter has gone far beneath the surface of his subject, to produce a social essay as amusing as it is instructive.

The conversation piece at Wrotham is admirable, not only as a portrait of its *personnages*, but as a still life: the beautifully-painted desk in the centre, loaded with its bibelots—it seems too good to be true that the centrepiece is a statuette of Queen Victoria—the patches of sunlight on the carpet, the shelves filled with calf-bound volumes palely brilliant with their illumination of gold, the vase of madonna lilies and the knitting dropped on the floor, all build up towards the figures of the two old people: Lady Strafford changing one of the cards of her Patience, Lord Strafford dangling *The Times* from one drowsy hand. Nothing is of importance but the Patience, nothing in the newspaper is permitted to ruffle the traditional tranquillity of the scene. If a bomb fell on Wrotham (it did—very nearly), the Knave of Clubs must still lie smoothly on the Queen of Diamonds, and the butler will suffer if the evening paper is not there to his lordship's hand.

This, the last of his completed portraits up to the present (November, 1942), is William's sociological masterpiece, during the painting of which—he stayed for a considerable time down at Wrotham—he was writing me the most amusing of his long series of letters: full of little sketches and picturesque descriptions of the "high life" which, for William, has something of the fascination of a pantomime, and just as little relation to reality.

William is a born letter-writer; his writing is exactly like his conversation, full of "quips and cranks," of sly references, of "William-isms" and his own slightly cockeyed views on humanity. It is a pity samples cannot be reproduced here; but, apart from the fact that shorn of the rainbow-coloured script (he usually writes with coloured pencils, using them very prettily to indicate emotional shades in the text), the balloons, arrows and what-not that connect up the scattered lines of thought—we decided some years ago that a stranger, reading these letters, would come to the conclusion that the writer—and possibly the recipient also— was certifiable. Without a complete glossary of the "William" vocabulary (What, for instance, would the uninitiated make of "I've been lying under a cowslip, dear, sucking bees"?—by comparison with which "He had sold his message for a birth of potright" is crystal clear), together with copious footnotes to explain the obscurer passages, their meaning would be "wropt in mystery"; moreover there is the "William" spelling to be coped with, a system of phonetics which only becomes as clear as daylight when read aloud.

We had decided it would be wiser to give up the flat at Hove. At that time there was a surprising amount of certainty that there would be no raids on the West End of London; so Apple Tree, which had some of the characteristics of an old-fashioned carpet-bag, bulged its obliging little sides to receive the furnishing of the flat, the studio and of my cottage in the Lake District. We felt we would like to have "everything together," and one domicile was certainly less expensive to maintain than three, so chairs and tables were stacked ceiling-high in the stalls and looseboxes, and life narrowed down to "the village," as we regarded our little bit of St. James's and Jermyn Street. (It was so much of a village that on Sunday mornings William would go into Jermyn Street in his pyjamas and dressing-gown to buy the papers, and it never occurred to me to "tittivate" before running along to the dairy for our milk and bread.)

William was restless, out and about, settling to nothing. I was trying to "stick to it," but angrily, in a spirit of resentment and opposition, and it did not seem that any good could come out of work done under such conditions. I wonder if people remember the atmosphere of futility and unsettlement, during those weeks immediately before the blitz started: or how, with the falling of the first bombs, we all pulled ourselves together almost with a kind of relief, and started going about our work in as business-like a fashion as conditions would allow?

I was sure nobody would want a long period novel, at a time when actual events were so much more exciting than any fiction. William was sure that no one would want to buy work of his kind. We were both wrong. William was lunching at Chequers on that afternoon, Saturday, September 7th, when we had the first daylight raid on London.

It is hard to believe that there was anything extraordinary about our history during the blitz; it must have been the same as that of any other family living in the West End of London. We arranged our little scheme of living; our man Kershaw (who had replaced Sid and Sid's successor, and endeared himself to us, not only by his personal qualities, but by his devotion to the kittens) served dinner, in the middle of which the Alert invariably began: nothing would move William until he had had his coffee. Then, usually with the shrapnel pattering, William's Girl Kitten under his arm and my Boy Kitten under mine, we would all saunter down to the shelter which Kershaw had found for us, where we settled down to play Canfield or read until we crawled into our sleeping sacks for the night. The kittens developed strong anti-social qualities and their brawlings were nearly as disturbing as the H.E.s whose muffled vibration often shook us underground; we were obliged in the end to arrange a private shelter and allow them to settle their own differences in Apple Tree.

A night came when there was a muffled kind of thud and a sort of soft rustle. We were playing cards. William said: "Sit tight, dear. I think they've got us."

I played down two more cards before it dawned on me we ought perhaps to be doing something about it. Then Kershaw came in, rather white and very dusty.

"Don't be upset, madam—they've got the next door."

When we could scramble out, the square was crimson with flames, hung with red curtains blasted from the houses, and lashed with streams of water from the firemen's hose. That was the night they got St. James's Church, the Rectory and Albany. Kershaw and I rushed to see if the kittens were all right. Apple Tree Yard was choked with the apparatus of the fire brigade, and the house next to ours on the right was gutted. William and I went up to his bedroom and out through the skylight on to the roof, over which swung the ladders of the firemen, who were playing their hoses on the back of Lord Bristol's, which was by then a blazing shell. We sat there among the chimneypots, watching floor after floor crash in, and now and again the stars were visible, and then were blotted out by the volumes of blood-coloured smoke. We knew it was probable Apple Tree would catch fire, but it seemed useless to do anything about it; too late, then, to try and make selection from the things we would want to save. We sat there in a curious aloofness, accepting all we could not prevent, feeling nothing, I

MR. AND MRS. SIDNEY WEBB.

By courtesy of the London School of Economics and Political Science.

think, but a kind of desperate and shamed reverence for those
heroes of the night who continued their task regardless of our
presence, as they were regardless of the incendiaries which, for
some time after our emergence from our destroyed shelter,
continued to fall. We did not notice the dawn; how should we,
when the pall of smoke lay like a perpetual night over St. James's?

"Breakfast is ready, madam—Sir William."

". . . Don't be *silly*, Kershaw!"

Toast and marmalade, bacon and coffee, the kittens shouting
for their milk. . . . Was this the dream, or was it the waking up?
To this day we do not know how Kershaw performed his act of
magic, which brought to a close the nightmare of our night. At
four in the afternoon William decided that the time had come to
get out of London.

4

Of our two years' sojourn in Berkshire not much seems
important to this book, which we have tried to keep as a record
mainly of work and of working conditions. The effort to drag
up and down from town once or twice a week, to carry out two
portrait commissions, put too much of a strain on William, and
he abandoned them both for the time. The war was in his bones,
in his blood; it had deprived him of the peace of mind which, for
him, is an essential condition of creation. For the first time since
I had known him, he did not want to paint, and, if he had wanted
he had no suitable place in which to set up his easels. The charm
(to me) of Tudor cottages, their bane (to William) is the deep
overhanging thatch which blinds the little eyes set in their heavy
walls. For the first time the spirit was lacking to overcome these
and other difficulties, the work had lost its magic, the war was
an evil spell from which it seemed as though there was, for
William, no means of escape.

We did not realise, for some time, how much of this was
physical; seeking the stimulus of change of environment, we
spent a few months at Fen Ditton, and, on our return to Blewbury,
William vanished for three weeks into a nursing-home for a
mild operation, where, typically, he was the life and soul of the
party.

Never since the war began had he enjoyed himself as much as
he did in being ill. When he emerged from the nursing-home, the

enjoyment persisted; the next thing was the National Gallery Exhibition, which kept him on the run between town and country. In spite of the reluctance of many people to lend their pictures for exhibition in London, a very good representative collection was made and beautifully arranged, and, for the first time in his life, I persuaded William to attend his own private view; it was a thing one owed, he admitted, to the National Gallery.

New Year's Day, 1942; we walked through the crowded rooms, the record of fifty years of a painter's life. *Lottie Stafford of Paradise Row, Le Tricolor, Déjeuner de Marie, The Hundred Jugs, The Return of La Gioconde, City Dinner*: there were many that would be missed by students of William's work, but these famous ones—"*ces vrais Nicholsons*," as Jean would have called them— were there to delight the eye and warm the heart, among the host of smaller ones which, including the woodcuts and drawings in the farthest room, represented most of the aspects of William's work of the last half-century. Eleven thousand people, including Her Majesty the Queen, saw the exhibition, although there seemed, at that moment, almost to be "nobody in London"; it was bitterly cold, the wind swept the empty streets, screamed round Trafalgar Square, brought rain which turned to mud and solidified to ice. Still the public streamed into the National Gallery, where, in the rooms devoted to William's work, there seemed to be a continual blandness of sunlight. People came up from the country to see it; came, not once, but again and again. It was a bold experiment on the part of the Gallery, to show Jack Yeats's pictures at the same time as William's; the contrast between the rooms in which the Nicholsons and the Yeats were shown roused lively controversy between the supporters of two very opposite schools of thought. Loving the adventurous, and quick to recognise artistic sincerity as he is to detect pretensiousness, William was as enthusiastic about the Yeatses as he was about the more recent Burra show at the Redfern Gallery. In both these painters he found the living and ardent quality which seems lacking in a good deal of modern work. William has an admirable expression for some of the moderns who fail to convince him of their honesty. "Oh— him?" he will say, in his quiet little way that can be more blistering than a shower of invective. "Oh, he belongs to the ''Ark at me!' school."

On February 5th, William had his seventieth birthday, and golden telegrams rained on the thatch of Stocks. Very pleasant but rather absurd, from William's point of view, as he has never managed—excepting for a few dark months in 1940—either to look or to feel his age.

We had already discussed returning to London. Not to Apple Tree, that was definitely a thing of the past. He hankered after it, but the small practical streak which meanders uncertainly through the green pastures of William's romanticism warned him it could not be. The furniture had been stored, a few derelict oddments, unrecognisable through the dirt which silted in through broken windows and skylights, alone remained of that long tenancy. Through a friend we heard of a possible domicile.

It almost appeared as though the mere prospect of another removal was enough to start the creative stream flowing again. As our two-years' refuge began gently to disintegrate, as the feeling of transigeance crept into the air, William took promptly to his brush. Again it was Carqueiranne, a waiting car, a champing chauffeur, and William settling down to do "a little something" while his companions groaned their resignation; it was the Lido, and hotel servants glaring surlily at one oblivious of their efforts to strip the rooms for the *fin de saison;* it was Segovia, and a motor-bus snorting its impatience at William's tardy arrival with a still-wet canvas clasped in one resentful hand.

With roses drooping towards midsummer, the "torrents of spring" were at work in William's blood. He became suddenly and poignantly aware not only of the beauty of the countryside, but of the importance of recording it; bemoaning the "little time" that remained, the subjects he might have painted, the difficulties of getting, without a car, to the places he wanted to paint, he started to work like an angel.

G. B. Stern, our co-mate and sister in exile (it was by the happiest of chances that our flight had led us to the same village), reminds me of a contemporary Williamism which seems to deserve print. He and she were strolling home in the cool of the evening, under one of those translucent and ethereal skies which he has so often recorded in his landscapes.

"Oh, William—look at that sky!"

William looked up thoughtfully.

"The trouble is, I can't get any more of the colour I use to make it."

The downs were golden and brown and white with grain; the skies, evening after evening, melodramatic with colour. Apart from a few grousings at Nature, for not reproducing her effects, or for not holding them long enough—like an unsatisfactory sitter—William painted serenely. Having discovered that the one good painting light was at the kitchen-table, he painted still life with the cooking, household occupations and neighbourly intrusions of tradesfolk going on round, over and above him. The evil spell was over; the war could no longer stop the song of the bird.

A local artist lent him a little studio; he spent hours there, while I and my secretary reduced the accumulations of two years' wandering to more or less manageable proportions—I meanwhile tearing between rehearsals of a new play and doing my best to assemble at least the outlines of a new home.

Once again we were faced with the agony of parting with our cats, my Boy and William's Girl. These two, who had never seen a blade of grass before Kershaw brought them down to us in Blewbury, had become so completely bucolic—even to the extent, as William pointed out, of acquiring a slight Berkshire accent— that their return to the prison of a London flat was not to be thought of. The Girl, enchanted to be separated from her brother, for whom she had a truly fraternal loathing, went off purring at the top of her voice to kind friends at the other end of the village. The Boy, a natural globetrotter, a social success in all circumstances, took the middle seat of a first class carriage, tucked his paws under his chest with the utmost composure, and, in due course, became the idol of a household whose garden and apple-tree provided him with amenities not to be enjoyed if he had remained with his doting and desolate owners.

When at last we struck our tents, a bundle of new canvasses went into the van with the rest of our possessions; it seemed the best of omens for our "new adventure."

CHAPTER TWENTY-TWO

Epilogue

I

By THE fireplace stands a china cat, whose smile upsets William. "Can't I paint whiskers on it? . . . Look, if I paint out the corners of its mouth it won't smile. Ridiculous—a smiling cat!"

But I have a *penchant* for the china cat, which has a most elegant little painted hood of black lace and a tasteful design of rosebuds all over its pale blue body. I like the inquiring and intelligent gaze of its large green eyes, which William cannot bear. So he has found his own means of compromise: a large yellow paper butterfly, neatly cut out and gummed against the mantelpiece. The cat sits with its back to the room, its eyes glued to the butterfly—and William's feelings are spared.

On the mantelpiece is a beautiful white Staffordshire group of Adam and Eve, in front of which, originally, lay one of those flexible silver fish that sit up on their tails and obligingly disgorge comfits or pills or any little thing one cares to pop into them. Adam, however, has acquired the air of a successful fisherman, swinging a tunny fish from his right hand. The fish and the butterfly are William's contributions to the décor of our new home. There are others . . . the mantelpiece is, in fact, a battlefield of conflicting taste in ornamentation: William's French duck, my white jade kittens, William's porcelain horse, my Copenhagen rabbit, William's anthracite clinker, which stands up on two legs like some unpleasant little fetish, and a little bronze figurine that somebody brought me from Greece— thoughtfully as they may be arranged, invariably wander into "conversation pieces" before the end of the day: the duck kissing the rabbit, the little Greek boy pulling the horse's tail, or some more ludicrous combination.

"If you please, madam, am I to put these back in their places, or shall I leave them as they are?"

"Oh . . .! Leave them as they are!"

Here at last, after their long submersion in trunks and packing-cases, are the Hundred Jugs, the bilboquets, the Dightons and all the cherished objects which, miraculously, have survived the battle of London; almost every day some "new" thing turns up, and starts a train of thought so far-reaching that one recognises with despair how much is missing from a book like this.

Of course he should have written it himself—painting the words on to paper with that curious, brush-like movement of the pen which is so fascinating to watch—and then we should have had all those "William" turns of speech which those who know him will miss from these pages. He has a neat fancy in composition, of which, among many examples, the following "Epitaph, to embellish the Tomb of a Rotten Actor" comes back to memory:

> Turn, Worm! Turn Cannibal
> And dine on Comrade So-and-So,
> A-stewing in his juice.
>
> The Curtain falls at last,
> And Tragedy absurdly dies
> With the Early Worm who
> GOT THE BIRD!

"Tell us something about William Nicholson to-day," says someone who read part of this book before it went to the printer. The request makes me wonder if I have, after all, failed in my mission, for if the William of to-day is not present in this record of many yesterdays, something must be wrong.

Through the windows, slimed with their "blast-proof"—which, so far as we are concerned, is very far from *Blast*-proof, for it is really rather souring to have one's view of the outside world blurred in the name of A.R.P.—we have a murky glimpse of chimneypots, a more than ordinarily revolting Government building and the beginnings of a London fog.

"Oh, God, another filthy day!"

"Now then, Grumps.—' Why anybody chooses to live in England—'" chants William, in devastating imitation of my accents—"' There isn't any climate, only weather '—! All right, all right! Get your shoes on and come for a walk in the park."

"Well, for goodness' sake put on your overcoat!"

"I don't want an overcoat. You can't walk briskly in an overcoat—honestly, I'm much warmer without an overcoat than with one; it's much nicer to get warm with exercise."

Someone informs me he has been seen bounding on to a bus and bounding off it (it happened to be going in the wrong direction) when it was travelling at full speed. There's something wrong with this age equation; at this rate, when I am being pushed round in a bath-chair, William will be leaping on and off omnibuses, and will probably swing from the chandelier for my entertainment when I am bedridden.

It is only when I am asked for a picture of "to-day's" William that I realise that nearly all the pictures of him I have in my mind—apart from working ones—are in energetic motion: William taking the stairs three at a time, William launching his boomerang with that long run, ending in a windmill movement of his arms and whole body, of which Jack Churchill made an admirable cinematograph record, William—latterly—cycling, which in itself was a feat of acrobacy, as there was the pochade-box, with all its contents, to manage, and a sketch-book or block as well—war-time bicycles being, apparently, born without the carrier fitments which, in pre-war days, one took for granted.

A neat figure in olive-green steps briskly round to the Savile Club, plays a stylish game of snooker, comes back with a smile hung over its ears when the games have gone well, mumbling gloomily about advancing years when, as happens rarely, they have not. Once a month there is the Other Club, when the samite comes out, and William departs for what, for him, is the greatest pleasure of all: good company, good wine, good talk.

He is one of those who deplore the new style in table talk; after all, to one who remembers days when conversation was cultivated as an art, there is—there must be—something graceless about our modern fashion, when the loudest voice generally manages to create a monopoly, and the most indigestible subjects have a way of appearing with the fish, to culminate in acrimony with the coffee. Like a good Georgian—which he is at heart—he deplores the lack of lightness and sparkle, the intrusion of heavy topics, above all of serious argument, which interferes with appreciation of the *menu*—which, after all, is the *raison d'être* of dining. He cites Winston Churchill as an example of the perfect dinner conversationalist—not monopolising the talk, and playing skilfully between deep and shallow waters. And in these days, says William, when *menus* can no longer be taken seriously, there is all the more need of conversational dexterity to cover the culinary heroics of the housewife! He is forced, however, gloomily to admit that it is difficult to sparkle on beer.

Many people of William's age, I find, complain of loneliness;
having outlived many of their contemporaries, they incline
towards a rather bitter melancholy, finding fault with the present
and bemoaning a past which, one suspects, did not exist, except
in their imaginations. His love for youth and the ideas of youth
protect William from this fate for ever; for him the "best time"
is always the present; yesterday was grand, but to-day is even
better. To-morrow?—Well, wait until to-morrow comes. Not
many who have read the chapter preceding this one will accuse
William of an irresponsible egoism because he has managed, in
spite of storms of which no one is more sensitively aware than he,
to keep himself "captain of his soul."

This living in the present is an attribute of childhood. It
explains little Brigit Laver's delight when William taught her
to make *tiny* bunches of the *tiniest* flowers; it explains Priscilla's
theft of a ribbon from one of her mother's best nightgowns to
bind the bouquet she sent to William in the nursing-home, it
explains Ruth's hope that "she will marry someone just like Sir
William" when she grows up, and Gemma's starry-eyed content
when, on her first Christmas Day, she sat on William's knee.

I think one of the hardest things the war has done for him
has been to separate William from his younger grandchildren:
Ben's triplets, Simon, Rachel and Sarah down in Cornwall, and
Kit's lovely three in Hampshire. It seems a shame that Timothy
William should grow up without having cork mice made for him
by William, and dear fat Louisa without William to tell her how
beautiful she is, and Jane, "*une vraie Nicholson*," if ever there was
one, without the "magic" which no one but William knows how
to create. Some truth-loving soul may choose to point out that
when they were all in London, he did not see so very much of
them as all that; but when one set of grandchildren lives in
Hampstead, and another in Chelsea (not to mention the family
in Wiltshire) it is not so easy for a hard-working painter, whose
home is in St. James's, to see much of any.

If you wish to see William at his most vivid, see him in the
company of men younger than himself; he has an air of being
their contemporary, while, with men of his own age, I have seen
him, at times, almost as diffident as a youngster. He has a
masterly way of avoiding giving opinions, and an equally masterly
way of drawing them from other people. It is only fair to add
that when an opinion is wrung from him, he will reiterate it in
the face of all reason, all proof to the contrary; reiterate, not

argue, for argument bores him, and he is, possibly, the worst arguer in the world, chasing cross-currents and butterflies with the inconsequence of a kitten, until the brain of his opponent cracks under the effort of following him, and gives up, from sheer intellectual exhaustion.

William says, "Remind me to get some snuff for Mrs. A."

He says, "Remind me to get trail hooks for——" Never mind who. For our favourite poacher, if you must know, and Mrs. A. was our beloved "daily" down in the country, who said she "loved madam, but *adored* Sir William," with whom, each morning, as solemnly as though it were a rite, she took snuff— the very best Freyberg and Tryer. I don't know if Never Mind Who adored Sir William; he would not, perhaps, have expressed it that way; but when they got together they had the unmistakeable air of wearing the same Old School tie.

"But what," asks someone, disgusted with all this triviality— "what is the *real* William Nicholson like? What are the things that *matter* to him?"

One of the things that matters to him is not being plagued with foolish questions. The answer, if it is not visible in the letterpress, is to be found in the illustrations to this book; the answer is in his departure every morning to his studio and in his occupation during the whole of every day. The real William Nicholson is the painter, and the only thing that matters to him, when it comes to the last count, is his work.

2

William sits peacefully composing "Blokes" for Christmas cards. Every year he does "Blokes" for Christmas cards, and every year, round about January 31st, we find a bunch of William's cards which he has tucked under the papers on his table, because the effort of buying special envelopes and looking up addresses is too pedestrian for the creative mind. But it is great fun doing the cards, and, as William says:

"It is the thought that counts."

Christmas Day, 1942.

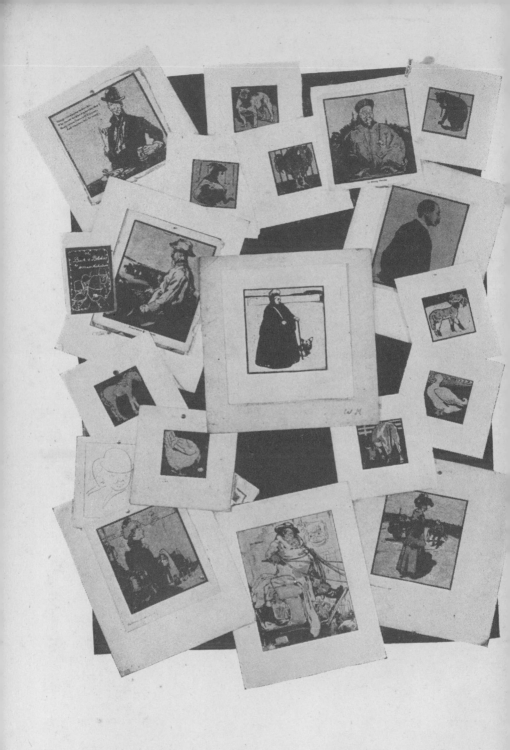